The Blood~Red Flag

By

Bruce T. Clark

authorHOUSE

1663 Liberty Drive, Suite 200
Bloomington, Indiana 47403
(800) 839-8640
www.authorhouse.com

First published by AuthorHouse 01/12/05

ISBN: 1-4208-1070-7 (sc)

Printed in the United States of America
Bloomington, Indiana

This book is printed on acid-free paper.

The Blood~Red Flag is at least 90% factual. The principal heroes, Daniel Austin and Ken Hawkins, are fictional, but all of the other major characters are real. The Miranda Mine is a famous part of the San Saba Valley's history; however, its re-discovery is out of sequence. It was found in the early 1900s, rather than in 1835. Every other event is historically accurate and in real time.

As I research and write my novels, I "spend" two or three years with fascinating people who lived in the long ago world of yesteryear, and I observe them in their worst moments as well as during their most exciting days. They begin as famous strangers, but as the months and years slip past, as I read the words they wrote, fathom the grand goals they professed, and come to understand the unshakable dedication they displayed, they become real, very dear friends who garner my devotion and respect. For that reason, I try to depict their strengths and weaknesses as well as their lives and deeds in the context of the historical events that involved them and the temper of the times that enveloped them, as honestly and as faithfully as possible.

Finally, I hope my grandchildren will read and be proud of my novels. Nothing "off-color" in word or deed will be found herein. The dialogue is squeaky clean and, although a number of characters are killed, be they friend or foe, they all die with dignity. My favorite authors never embarrassed themselves, their characters, or their readers. Neither do I.

Sincere thanks to many of my students, whose alert minds, perpetual curiosity, and occasionally uncanny insightfulness, challenge my resourcefulness. Thanks too for your intriguing suggestions and welcome computer research skills, especially Nada Rose McClelland, Addison Hart, and Nicole Wiest.

PROLOGUE
THE PREMONITION

SAN ANTONIO DE BEXAR
MEXICAN PROVINCE OF
COAHUILA-Y-TEJAS
JANUARY 1, 1834

It was Daniel Austin's twenty-second birthday that morning as the first dawn of a New Year leapt over the eastern horizon with a pent-up fury of a cornered lion, then scant moments later, crept timidly into his tiny Spartan room with a studied stealth of an alley cat.

He did not awaken from his restless slumber until the sun spilled its warmth across his face. Then he sat bolt upright on his hard pallet, all thoughts of sleep now gone. Suddenly he shivered as he was struck by an ominous premonition. His chest contracted in response to the icy hand that clutched his heart. Today might be the first day of his last year on earth.

Daniel heard a faint staccato sound of a flamenco guitar and realized La Fiesta del Dia de Año Nuevo was still underway. Discarding his threadbare blanket, Daniel walked to the bedchamber's solitary window. Scraping away a small portion of ice that had accumulated on the yellowed cracked glass, he looked at the peaceful sleepy village. Apparently, the revelers in the cantina two floors below were the only ones stirring on this crisp, frosty morning.

Peering off to his right, he could just make out the sluggish waters of the Rio Medina. The sight of the river made him think about his last birthday. He had spent the majority of that day at the Hoya Club with other members of the Georgetown College senior class. That evening, he and Roxanne had dined at the Lamplighter Inn, and then strolled along the shore of the Potomac River.

It had been an unusually warm evening in Washington, and the majestic riverbank had become a lover's lane. At least two dozen couples sauntered along wide cobblestone paths, enjoying the river's murmur, and the soft glow from the long row of gas lamps.

Many of the twosomes they passed cast unabashed looks of envy at them. He and Roxanne were a very attractive couple, that was for sure. They were both tall and athletically slender, with dark hair and eyes, and smooth classical facial features. Most of the passing men cast admiring glances at Roxanne, while their equally interested, but coy companions, appraised her handsome escort through shy eyes.

Alas, a year that began with so much promise had dissolved into chaos a few weeks later when Daniel had asked Roxanne's father for her hand in marriage. In a brief, very blunt meeting, Clement Mayfair had made it perfectly clear that the social strata he foresaw for his youngest daughter was much higher than any Daniel Austin might possibly reach. Only the timely arrival of his Uncle Stephen's letter had sustained him during those miserable days of sadness and humiliation, and helped him to regain a small measure of his self respect.

Now, as a new year began, here he was in the wilds of the Mexican province of Tejas, acting as a scribe for the leader of the American settlers. During the few months he had been in Tejas, he had learned to love the country and to admire its inhabitants. These Texicans had to carve out a hard living on this often-dangerous frontier. Perhaps that was what gave them their lust for life. Their Mexican neighbors, the Tejanos, were also admirable and industrious, devoted Catholics who seemed to be far more interested in the joy of today than in any profit tomorrow might bring. It was a different society, a different pace, a completely different world. After his disappointing final year in Washington, it was, however, a world Daniel Austin relished.

This morning, a big adventure would begin! Uncle

Stephen and he were embarking upon a perilous journey to Mexico City. His uncle had been granted an audience with Mexican President Antonio Miguel Lopez de Santa Anna. His Uncle Stephen would implore Santa Anna to restore the 1824 Constitution, reinstitute trial by jury, stop the unfair customs regulations that had been imposed on 20,000 Texican-American settlers, and return an individual status to the recently combined states of Tejas and Coahuila.

He and his uncle would be traveling in a heavily armed wagon train to Mexico City, the Mexican capital, which was more than 300 leagues to the south. The combined strength of the wagon train travelers and a squad of Mexican Lancers would protect them from the frontier dangers: scores of murderous banditos, as well as hordes of prowling Comanches and fierce Apaches.

He realized that far greater danger might await them when they reached Mexico City. General Santa Anna was famous for punishing people who displeased him by sentencing them to prison, or worse, by executing them. Daniel could almost feel bullets thudding into his chest from a firing squad, or imagined his body crumpling at the foot of a blood-spattered adobe wall. He shuddered as he turned away from the window. "Well," he thought, "I came to Texas to seek adventure. I have a hunch I may find far more excitement than I can begin to imagine, and perhaps more trouble than I'll be able to handle!"

x

ESTADO DE TEJAS

San Saba Valley

☆ Miranda Silver Mine

Celery Creek Canyon

San Antonio de Béxar

San Jacinto

ESTADO DE COAHUILA

Goliad

Galvez Island

ESTADO DE

Monclova

Rio Bravo

Rio Grande

Rio

Nueces

ESTADO DE NUEVO LEON

TAMAULIPAS

Saltillo

ESTADO DE SAN LUIS POTOSÍ

0   50   100   200 Miles

Scale

Mexico City
900 Mi.

Golfo de Mexico

San Luis Potosí

Tampico

PART ONE
DANIEL AUSTIN'S STORY

I

THE DEADLY STORM

MEXICAN PROVINCE OF
ESTADO TAMAULIPAS
JANUARY 15, 1834

By mid-morning, the bright sun had warmed the winter air to such a pleasant degree that the squad of soldiers who marched in the vanguard of the caravan were permitted to shuck their heavy woolen uniform jackets and stride along in thin cotton shirts and baggy white trousers.

This morning, the happiest travelers were the scampering children. Ahead of, as well as behind, and along both sides of the long line of slowly moving wagons, in pairs or in small groups, frisky teenaged boys, each one eager to prove that he was the swiftest runner, raced back and forth. Far out toward the distant horizon of the endless arid prairie the boys sped, until an overpowering sense of loneliness and impending danger became more important than the contest. Then, turning tail, they fled back toward the safety of the wagon train, whooping all the way. A dozen teenage girls, eyes shielded from the bright sun by gaily-colored, wide-brimmed poke bonnets, walked sedately beside their plodding oxen teams, and tried to look blithely unconcerned while they discreetly watched the races, and the boys, from the seclusion of their hood-shaded eyes.

In the two weeks they had been on the trail, Daniel Austin had made friends with many of the travelers, and had learned a good deal about Mexican customs and the difficult life in Santa Anna's military forces. Most of the infantrymen were poor conscripts, peons who had never owned a pair of shoes. Half of the forty-man infantry unit that accompanied the twenty-four wagons was barefoot. They all wore cheap, white cotton trousers and flimsy white shirts, each of which was dingy from continual wear and the prolonged absence of soap and water. The rest of the uniform consisted of a blue jacket with scarlet cuffs and piping, green epaulets, and a tall black leather hat adorned with a red plume and shiny brass shield. Wide, white ammunition bandoleers crisscrossed their chests, and bright red blanket rolls rested across their shoulders, fitting snugly against their necks.

The cavalry officers were a much different breed. By and large a handsome group, they wore uniforms with blue trousers decorated with wide red stripes running down the outer sides. Scarlet swallow-tailed coats were accented with dark green collars, lapels, and epaulets. Tan cowhide hats with rigid wooden plumes adorned their heads. The cavalrymen, known as Lancers, were extremely proud of their regiments, and fought ferociously at every opportunity to bring them ever-greater honor.

Santa Anna's army should have been as gaudy and resplendent as any military organization in recorded history, at least an equal of Napoleon's Grand Army or Alexander's Legions; but alas, it was not. High ranking officers often purloined funds that had been earmarked for purchases of uniforms and equipment. As a result, very few of the soldiers had complete uniforms. Even fewer had shoes. Some wore thin sandals. Most went barefooted in winter's cold as well as summer's heat. Hatless, shoeless men in thin cotton pants and ragged shirts, formed the core of the army. The foot soldiers Daniel had met in this caravan were no exception.

When Santa Anna's army was on the march, which it often was since uprisings were very common, the soldiers' families accompanied them to the edge of the battlefields, if one-sided suppressions can fairly be described as battles.

In addition to families were the traditional camp followers—cooks, laundresses, and harlots, as well as shady merchants with heavily loaded wagons, eager to trade cheap trinkets and shoddy goods for the soldiers' precious pesos. A great many children, orphaned by the cruel life peons were forced to live, trailed along in the untidy wake of a procession that stretched out for miles behind the vanguard.

Captain Alonzo Almonte, the dashing Lancer officer and elder son of Colonel Juan Almonte, one of Mexico's most celebrated soldiers, told Daniel that Santa Anna had not seen the tail end of a marching column for years. A dapper man who savored his luxuries, Santa Anna found the miserable conditions repugnant; but since soldiers were not supplied with food rations or most other necessities, the merchants and stragglers in this tail-end party served a vital purpose. If they had not foraged and commandeered food rations and supplies in the Sparta countryside through which they marched, Santa Anna's armies would have starved.

The soldiers who accompanied this wagon train were fortunate. Food was plentiful. As they marched along on this sunny day, they had not a care in the world. They were blithely unaware that this flat, treeless region, where no natural barriers were available to break a storm's fury, offered ideal conditions for weather phenomenons known as blue northers, great storms of unbelievable ferocity.

Being unprepared for a sudden storm, they were surprised when, without warning, a long line of dark, jagged clouds appeared across the distant northern horizon. Driven by gale-force winds, the dark clouds quickly surged forward. The temperature plummeted—first ten, then twenty, forty, then fifty degrees in a single hour. In an hour, a blinding blizzard was upon the caravan.

Without either heavy clothing or adequate shelter from the howling wind, the travelers became terribly cold. At first they huddled in their wagons, but the inactivity made them colder. Within minutes, most of them dismounted and began walking in an effort to retain some of their precious body heat.

The storm continued throughout the daylight hours as winds increased and the temperature continued to plummet. Even heavier snow began to fall. By dusk, ten inches of the icy death covered the ground, and people began to freeze.

"I'm going to wait for Monica and see if I can help her and her grandfather." Daniel shouted into Uncle Stephen's ear in order to be heard above the howling wind.

He carefully shielded his eyes with his hands and squinted through the driving snow for several long seconds before he saw Monica leading a pair of reluctant, half-frozen oxen that pulled her wagon. A second later, her shivering grandfather also emerged from the icy white cloud. He could scarcely believe the elderly man's appearance as he sat huddled on the wagon's high seat. His face was colorless except for the trembling lips the insidious cold had turned blue. He looked frail and desperate. Daniel realized that if he and Monica could not convince Guillermo Granados to quit the wagon seat and walk, the rest of his life could be measured in minutes.

The Austins had met the vivacious eighteen-year-old Monica and her grandfather at a fiesta de natal, held in honor of her uncle, Don Juan de Verdimente, the Vice-Governor of Coahuila y Tejas. Lipan Apaches had killed her parents when she was only five, and her grandfather had been Monica's guardian since then. They both had nearly perished in the cholera epidemic that swept across western America and northern Mexico two years earlier. Almost every family in both nations had lost members. Monica's cousin, Ursula Bowie and both of her young children had fallen victim to the horrible plague.

Stephen and Daniel had met the famous Jim Bowie at the fiesta and had been shocked by his cadaverous appearance. Bowie, a well-known adventurer, knife-fighter, and risk-taker, became the hero of American schoolboys after his famous duel with Norris Wright at Vidalia Sandbar. Newspaper accounts of the duel had Jim Bowie scorning bullet wounds and sword thrusts until he could close with his hated enemy and kill him.

Now, Jim Bowie had become a pathetic sight. The death of his beloved wife and children had driven him into the depths of despair. For the past two years he had tried to drown his sorrow with ever-greater quantities of tequila. He was known to the Mexicans as El Borrachero, the Drunkard. Peons snickered behind his back, ninos threw stones at him, and mongrels snapped at his rundown heels as he staggered from one cantina to the next. His only purpose in life seemed to be getting falling-down drunk. He pursued the relief of oblivion for as long as he could afford to buy tequila, or someone else would buy it for him. His many friends in Bexar knew that time alone would cure his deep lonely emptiness. It had healed the sorrow of many others. Eventually, it would do the same for Jim Bowie.

At this moment in time, however, Bowie's troubles were pale in comparison to those of the Austins and other wagon train travelers. Guillermo Granados was in the greatest peril. Daniel ran toward the front of the column and found Captain Almonte leading his horse through the driving snow.

"Captain, several of the elderly people are falling asleep on their wagon seats. If they continue to ride, they will surely freeze. If you use your influence, perhaps you can persuade them to walk?"

"Many of the old ones may be too weak" Almonte

told him. "Let us seek the counsel of your uncle."

Daniel and the captain waited beside the trail until Stephen Austin emerged from the swirling snow. He kept walking, but motioned for his nephew and the Lancer officer to join him. He had apparently come to the same conclusion as Daniel.

"Captain Almonte, we are allowing many of these people to commit suicide by riding in the wagons."

"I agree, Señor Austin, but they have become too cold and weak to walk."

"I've been walking, but I can no longer feel my feet. We have no other alternative but to stop, camp, and build a warm sanctuary for everyone," Stephen Austin concluded

"How can we manage that?" Captain Almonte asked him.

"There are two dozen wagons in this column. Almost all of the beds and sides of the wagons are made from old, tinder-dry wood that will burn like the fires of hell. We need to use half of the wagons for protection against the storm, and burn the rest."

"I don't understand!"

"We'll line up three of the wagons on each side of a large closed square, move them close together, then tip them over on their sides to form a wind break. Before we move the last wagon into place, we'll lead the horses and oxen inside the square and tether them to the wagons. Then we'll tip over that last wagon and build a big bonfire in the center of the enclosure. The wagons will become a high wall to shield the animals, as well as all of us, from the wind. Body heat from the closely packed animals will help to keep them warm, and provide additional heat for us as well. Then we gather in a circle around the fire. We'll have protection from the wind, and heat from the fire for as long as we can keep it lit. If we run out of wagons to burn, we'll burn furniture or other combustibles that may be in the wagons. Some people may lose more than others, but if we don't do this, we'll all lose our lives. If you agree, we'd better tell the others and get started right away."

Reluctantly, everyone, many with tears in their eyes, agreed to burn the wagons to save their lives. It took two agonizingly-cold hours to move the wagons into place. On all four sides, three wagons were linked together, end-to-end, and then tipped over. As the wagons were lowered onto their sides, the persistent wind caught the spokes of the weightless wheels and spun them madly around. The whirling sounds made Daniel think of the mythical Sirens who sighed and sang haunting songs in an effort to lure the ancient mariners to their deaths.

The encirclement was finally completed with the exception of the final wagon. Then outside of this inner wall, all of the remaining wagons were moved into position behind the ring of overturned ones to form another wall. Outer wagons were left upright in an effort to temporarily anchor the inner ones. These were the less sturdy wagons that would be broken up one by one to feed the flames.

Before the last opening was closed, the horses and oxen were herded into the enclosure and tethered around the perimeter. Finally, at the suggestion of Don Guillermo, four small but substantial fires were built, one on each side of the enclosure, instead of one huge fire in the center. As things turned out, his idea likely saved many of the people from freezing to death.

It was the most terrifying night any of the travelers had ever spent, but when the sun finally peeped over the horizon, everyone was still alive. Throughout the long dismal hours of darkness, they clung together in the center of their temporary fortress, surrounded by the wall of wagons, an inner living wall of animals, and sparse, barely adequate heat from each direction, thanks to the four separate fires.

Daniel had never been as grateful for anything as he was to see the morning sun. Daylight brought with it great tidings. The snow finally stopped, and a short time later, the violent, icy wind began losing force. By noon, the wind had all but disappeared, and

11

the warm sun was once more spreading its life-giving heat. By mid-afternoon, the temperature was well above freezing.

Captain Almonte examined every traveler who was experiencing pain, and concluded that few of them would suffer any permanent after effects. Two of the men and one elderly lady would probably lose some toes, but the fact that no one had perished was a miracle.

"You're alive," friends greeted each other that morning. "Thank God, we're all still alive!"

Happiness and prayerful joy replaced last night's terror and dread. But they still had two-hundred-fifty leagues to go, in half the number of wagons, before they reached Ciudad de Mejico, thirty more days on the trail if all went well. They had thirty days, Daniel thought, if they were not assaulted by more snow storms, raided by marauding Comanches, Apaches, or the bloodthirsty banditos that lurked in many hidden places, patiently but eagerly waiting to swoop down on unwary travelers.

The grateful blizzard survivors faced overcrowded wagons, and a lack of what little comfort that would have been provided by the soft mattresses and chairs that had been burned to keep them alive. But after enduring the perils of the frozen night, the rest of the journey seemed almost like a lark. Each of them took solace in the fact that he was a member of a large party, and protected by an armed force of soldiers. To risk such a journey without similar adequate protection would be foolhardy. Prickly cacti, steep arroyos, acrid dust, and lack of water could maim, break, choke, or soon dehydrate the unwary. On the lonely deadly plains, travelers who managed to survive the perils of nature would be forced to worry about attacks by prowling Indians and banditos. The strength of numbers was so obvious that only a very foolish or desperate man would dare to challenge alone the inhospitable terrain, the unpredictable severe weather, and the menace of stealthy, deadly human enemies.

II
PRISONERS

CIUDAD DE MEJICO
JUNE 30, 1834

Daniel Austin sat beside a heavily barred window in the dimmest area of the large room. He had to be careful. One of the patrolling guards might stop and peer through the window at any moment. He stared intently across the sunlit square toward an old, ivy-covered church. An hour ago, Monica Granados and her grandfather had strolled into the church to attend Mass.

It was the first time he had seen them since they all dined together at Hacienda Granados on the evening of the wagon train's arrival. The next day, Uncle Stephen had been granted an interview with Santa Anna. When that meeting ended, Stephen and Daniel had been arrested, and had languished in confinement for four months, forbidden to communicate with anyone.

Daniel had spent the past hour patiently prying the window up far enough to drop a note, tied to a chunk of stone, to Monica He was going to try to attract her attention without alerting their guards. Monica was a bright, plucky young lady. Daniel was certain she and Don Guillermo would help him to escape.

He had to escape. Uncle Stephen was too weak to attempt the perilous trek back to the Rio Grande, so Daniel would have to travel alone. He and Uncle Stephen had talked about the obvious risks: the long journey, the dangers along the way, and the very real probability he might be executed without delay or fanfare if he were recaptured. But Santa Anna's spiteful words and obvious intentions made escape imperative. Every Texican settler must be warned about Santa Anna.

In the last few weeks, on three occasions, Daniel had heard guards laughing and bragging about entire villages that had been put to the sword. He had also learned that more peons were being conscripted into the army. Even more telling, the prisons were being stripped of their inmates to serve in the army, a sure sign that Santa Anna was expecting more rebellions. Anyone living in Mexican territory had to make one of three choices: submit to Santa Anna's tyranny and live, rebel against him and die, or simply run away.

Daniel and Stephen Austin were sure that very few Texican/Americans who had settled in Texas would choose to submit or to run, but they needed enough time to prepare for Santa Anna's furious onslaught. They would not have time to prepare unless they were warned soon. The only person who could raise the alarm and give them that time was Daniel Austin.

Daniel thought back to the memorable meeting he had witnessed between his uncle and Santa Anna. Their conversation was burned into his memory.

"Why are you here?" Santa Anna had demanded of Stephen Austin.

"I came to seek justice."

"I embody justice."

"No, Presidente! The 1824 Constitution embodied justice because it guaranteed freedom and civil rights to everyone."

"The Constitution of 1824 is no longer feasible. I admit that I once agreed with its principles because I believed common people were capable of controlling their own destinies, but I now see how foolish that notion was. Freedom for the rabble is absolute folly. They are incapable of handling personal liberty. The 1824 Constitution was far too liberal, so I scuttled it. My only logical solution is a benevolent despotism. This nation must be saved from itself and I am the only one who can save it. I will institute a theocratic dictatorship. I will have a strong central government in which the provinces will share very little of the power. Of course, separate legislatures will be out of the question. The Catholic Church will rule supreme, and all of the old privileges, once enjoyed by priests

16

and military officers, will be restored."

"Do you really believe that will blind the people to your blatant despotism?" Stephen Austin countered.

"I have no desire to hide it. I openly declare it. I know what is best for Mexico and for her people. The people know that, and love me because of it."

"Surely, you jest, Presidente!"

"Not at all. Three times last year, in June, July, and in December, I resigned the Presidency and retired to my Xalapa estates. Each time, I was called back to serve and govern my people. They know I will care for them far better than they can care for themselves. No, Señor Austin, everyone who wants to live in any of Mexico's provinces will do what I want, when I want, exactly the way I want."

"Presidente, I can assure you that many people will refuse to live under your tyranny. I know my Texans will refuse. It won't take very long for them to see through unrelenting autocracy that lies close to the surface, just beneath sugarcoated assurances of benevolence. If I may remind you, in 1821, the recently established Mexican government commissioned my father, and in turn myself, to find industrious American farmers who were willing to settle on the northern plains of Tejas. That need was so great that the transplanted Americans were permitted to purchase 4,000 acres of land for thirty

American dollars. Deferred dollars, at that. For my service as the impresario, I received a land grant of 22,000 acres. Two of the conditions of ownership were for us to become Mexican citizens, and convert to Catholicism. We were welcomed into the Church, and treated like brothers by Tejanos—Mexicans who were born in Tejas. The number of American settlers, who call themselves Texicans, has risen to nearly 30,000, but you treat them like filibusters."

"Most of them are filibusters, Señor! Unwanted, traitorous people, in a land where they don't belong. They are here to seize what they can, giving nothing back in return. I want them out! Rebels who oppose my decree will be shot. I will not treat kindly Tejas rebels or any other rebels! Since you broached the topic, I will speak bluntly. The only useful purpose Tejas settlers have ever served is a protective screen against wild Indians who roam the plains of northern Tejas. Since your Texicans are nearly as wild as the marauding Apaches and Comanches, they are forced to fight; they make perfect buffers. The Texicans kill Indians. In return, Indians kill Texicans. But what does all of that matter, as long as they all stay far away from the rest of us?"

"I suspect you will face trouble from people much closer to you than Texans. Zacatecas residents will never buckle under to your threats anymore than my own people. I have been in touch with their leaders. They are all proud men, Presidente. Since they have now tasted liberty, they will not relinquish it without a fight."

"I have heard various rumors that the Zacatecas are raising a militia unit. The proud leaders of whom you speak must understand that if I am forced to put down an insurrection, militiamen won't be the only ones who die. Zacatecas has two thousand residents. If they persist in their folly, I promise you the only creatures left alive will be the dogs fighting over the bleached rebel bones among the charred remains of their once proud village."

When the meeting ended, Stephen and Daniel had been seized and confined in these rooms. Since they were located in the government building Santa Anna used for his office, their quarters were reasonably comfortable, but it was still a prison, a prison from which Daniel desperately needed to escape.

Uncle Stephen suddenly interrupted his reverie.

"Daniel, I see them!" He exclaimed

The Granados were standing beside the front door of the church, chatting with a priest who still wore his vestments.

Daniel waited patiently until his friends left the priest and began walking toward a waiting carriage.

He looked about to be certain that he was not being watched, then carefully adjusted the small mirror he and Uncle Stephen used for shaving. On his third attempt, he was able to focus a beam of sunlight on Monica's face. She turned away from the bright flash, but when it was repeated, she stared across the street, and was startled to see Daniel standing in the barred window.

Monica was just as quick-witted as Daniel suspected. After her first shock, she continued walking without a glance at him and waited for the next development.

Again, making sure that no guards were watching, Daniel dropped his stone-weighed note through the narrow window opening, and heard it fall softly into a flowerbed that separated the wall of the building from the sidewalk.

Equal to the task, Monica took Don Guillermo's elbow and casually steered him across the street. As they approached, Daniel heard her voice.

"I want to pick one of these lovely flowers. I hope no one will be angry with me, Grandfather."

Daniel saw her pick one of the flowers, then seize his note. She turned away and continued her walk to the carriage with the flower held gaily in her hand, while the rock and note nestled in the folds of her parasol. She had carried it off as though it had been rehearsed.

Daniel was more confident than ever that Monica would find the tool he needed to escape, as well as a way to get it into his hands. Most of all he hoped she would heed the warning in his note: BE CAREFUL!

Daniel fretted and paced about for the next four days while his uncle continually assured him that Monica, guided by her grandfather's wise counsel, was biding her time until it was safe to help them.

Finally, on July 4th, an ear-shattering thunderstorm roared out of the western skies and pelted the city with huge, opaque sheets of rain for hours. By nightfall, thick dark thunderheads had so completely obscured the new moon that it looked as if a giant hand had thrown a monstrous blanket over the entire world in an effort to keep every single ray of light from penetrating the cloying blackness.

The wind was so strong that occasional gusts would catch the falling rain at just the right angle and send violent jets of water rocketing through the tiny opening under the window. If they happened to be standing too close, they were stung by thousands of ice-laced droplets. Dan endured the discomfort because it seemed like a perfect moment for help to arrive. They had not seen a single guard since the storm began. No doubt they were comfortably safe and dry in their guardroom. The only people who might venture forth in this maelstrom would either be fools or Good Samaritans.

A moment later, Dan happened to be watching the window when a strong, hairy brown hand came through the opening, dropped a heavy metal object onto the floor and then withdrew.

May God bless Good Samaritans and good friends, Daniel prayed as he reached down and grasped his key to freedom.

The unusual tool that Daniel had requested was designed for wheelwrights who needed to lift heavy wagons in order to remove a wheel. The device was placed under the wagon, then a handle, attached to a metal-toothed cam, was cranked up and down. The rotating cam in turn extended a pair of steel rods that fitted one inside the other. Each time the handle was depressed, the rods, which protruded from the base of the tool, extended one additional inch. When the handle was raised, the current tooth disengaged and the next one slid up to the lifting position. The tool was only six inches long when it was compressed, but when the lift rods were extended, heavy objects could be raised nearly eighteen inches.

Daniel knew that he needed to work fast. He had learned that furious storms, such as the present one, often vanished as quickly as they appeared. As soon as this one ended, the guards would begin walking around the perimeter of the building once again. By then, he needed to be as far away as possible. Supper was due at any moment, but the guard who brought their meals never entered the room. He merely thrust their food through a narrow opening in the cell door that was wide enough to accommodate the large, flat tin trays. Nonetheless, Uncle Stephen, acting as a human shield, stood between Daniel and the door.

The window of their room was five feet high, by two and a half feet wide. Four iron bars, six inches apart, had been imbedded in the stone at the top and bottom. Daniel had fruitlessly tried to bend the thick bars a dozen times the day they were imprisoned. It was useless without the device he held in his hand.

He wedged the tool between the two center bars, near the midway point, then anchored it by pulling the handle enough to extend the inner rod. He tested the tool to make sure it was solidly seated, then began moving the handle slowly up and down. As the rod extended, Daniel could scarcely stifle his joy. The bars that had been built to withstand human hands could not withstand the relentless pressure of the slender steel lifting rods. Five minutes after he began, Daniel had moved the center bars so far apart that they touched the outer bars. Daniel had nearly eighteen inches of empty space to crawl through.

Several weeks earlier, he had discovered two dusty

old goatskin bags that originally had contained wine, under a pile of debris in a corner of the room. One of them was now half-filled with water from their earthen water jugs. The other contained a dozen small loaves of hard-crusted bread they had hoarded over the past few weeks. Both lay near at hand, bound together by a stout rawhide thong tied tightly around the top of each.

Since everything was in readiness, nothing would be gained by delay, and a great deal might be lost. Daniel gave his Uncle Stephen a good-bye hug, then quickly slipped through the opening to the ground below. He paused only long enough to grasp the goatskin bags his uncle handed down to him. Hanging them around his neck, he melted into the blue-black velvet of the watery night.

III
ESCAPE

An hour of rapid walking brought Daniel Austin to Mexico City's northern outskirts. The violent storm had driven all the inhabitants to places of shelter. He had seen neither man nor beast. He was grateful that he hadn't encountered one of the many packs of stray, mangy dogs that were rumored to prowl the city in search of food scraps. Daniel decided to continue walking until dawn or until the storm ended. He would stop then only if the crescent moon made an appearance in the aftermath of the storm.

The violent storm ended an hour before dawn. The clouds slowly began to dissipate, and a silvery sliver of the moon began to dodge in and out behind them. Daylight was not far off and Daniel knew he must soon find some sort of cover. He was certain that Santa Anna would send out squads of Lancers in pursuit as soon as his absence was detected.

Daniel walked for nearly an hour after dawn broke before he found a hideaway. As he reached the summit of a low hill and peered cautiously over the brow, he saw below him what appeared to be a deserted farm. Between Daniel and the farmyard lay a dozen or more uprooted trees. Since fresh dirt still clung to many of the roots, it was obvious that they had been blown down during the storm. He crouched behind one of them for a few minutes, watching the dilapidated cabin and sagging barn for any signs of activity or life. His patience was rewarded when he noticed that the cabin seemed to have a storage cellar with an outside door. He decided to investigate the cellar first. It might be dank and musty after a long period of abandonment, but it should keep him fairly dry, and would shield him from prowling Lancers or Dragoons.

Daniel concluded that the farm was deserted. He was on the verge of starting toward the cellar door when he was struck by a startling revelation. Lancer officers weren't fools. If someone as smart as his friend Captain Almonte was leading them, he would be positive Daniel would head north, probably walk as far as he could before dawn, and then seek a hideout where he could remain until dark.

He was still quite close to town. His pursuers had to realize that. They could concentrate their efforts on a small search area. They would simply calculate the maximum distance he could have walked during the night, then fan out along the outer perimeter of a quarter circle extending from northwest to northeast. Then, as they rode back toward the center of the circle, they would search barns, sheds, and other places of concealment, paying special attention to deserted dwellings. If he followed their predictable path, Daniel Austin would be a prisoner by noon and a dead man by sundown. This was his first day on the run. It would take him many weeks to reach Texas. Since he could not hope to outrun his pursuers, he would have to outwit them, not once, but time and time again, while they needed to outwit him only once.

He realized that hiding in either the cabin or the barn was a poor option. Perhaps he could hunker down in the tangle of fallen trees and trust to luck. No, Daniel decided, each man who appeared to be lucky simply knew how much to leave to chance. Common sense and patience were far better and much safer answers.

Hoping to find a hiding place in a rocky cairn or even a small depression under one of the uprooted trees, Daniel moved from one fallen giant to the next. Once again, good judgment and patience were rewarded. In the middle of the storm-caused tangle of trees, he discovered an ancient hemlock that probably had been felled by lightning many years earlier. During those scores of years, weather, insects, and rodents had rotted, nibbled, and gnawed at its center until it was just a hollow log. All that remained of the once mighty hemlock was its thin outer shell. Thick branches and still-green foliage on one of the trees that had fallen during the storm all but concealed the dark opening at one end. He might never have found it if a pair of frisky rabbits had not decided to leave their log shelter and venture forth at precisely the right moment.

"Thank you, rabbits," Daniel whispered quietly. "I'm going to borrow your burrow until dark, then you can have it back."

He was just able to wriggle through a small space between two large limbs that covered and concealed the opening. He pulled his sack of bread and water jug in after him, then carefully readjusted the smaller branches that had been dislodged by his passage. Now he could plainly see the cabin and barn through the leaves and still remain all but invisible inside his shadowy sanctuary.

The log haven was so cozy and secure that fatigue quickly overcame him. He fell asleep. The sun had moved well up into the cloudless sky before he was awakened by a sound of approaching hooves. Being careful not to betray his presence, Daniel peered out through leaves that were already beginning to turn brown, and saw a company of Lancers riding toward him. One horse and rider stopped less than twenty feet away. The officer-in-charge was so close that Daniel distinctly heard every word he exchanged with his subaltern.

"Lieutenant Gomez, have the men tether the horses here. If the fugitive came this way and left any signs of his passage, we'll never find them once the horses have moved into the farmyard. Search the cabin and barn. Pay close attention to the cellar under the barn. It's the most logical place for somebody to hide."

"If he came this way, Captain, he should be here. According to the map the Colonel gave us, these are the only deserted buildings in this area."

"I'm certain he would have come in this direction, but we may be ahead of him. He couldn't have come this far unless he escaped right after the guard delivered the evening meal, and he walked all night. If he is not here, we will spread out and work our way back toward the city. He may have tried to throw us off his trail by moving a mile or two off to one side or the other, but I'm sure he is heading north."

"If he kept going during the storm, he might have gotten lost. There were no stars to guide him in that black sky. Never fear, we will find the rogue."

"Of course!" He dropped his authoritative manner and smiled. "It was very considerate of the prisoner to escape during our first week in the service of El

Presidente. This is more exciting than garrison duty in Madrid, eh, Miguel? You should be grateful to me for convincing you to leave Spain and come with me to Mexico."

"Oh, I am, Pepe! Each day, for the rest of my life, I will recall and thank God for your intelligence and friendship. I will give Him even greater thanks when they recruit a new company of Lancers for me to command, and I am promoted. Then we can both be captains again. Meanwhile, you should thank me for insisting that we bring our own horses. Can you imagine having to ride one of those local plugs?"

The Lancers tied their horses' reins to convenient tree branches and proceeded toward the farm buildings, looking at the ground as they went. Daniel breathed a sigh of relief. If he had not had his wits about him, he would have blundered into the cellar.

His soft sigh must have been more audible than he imagined because Lieutenant Gomez's horse turned her head and stared intently toward the shadows that concealed him. She was a beautiful creature. As she pranced nervously at the end of her tether, her strong muscles rippled under a shiny hide which was solid, unrelieved ebony. She was as black as a coal at midnight. She and the Captain's palomino, with her silver mane and tail and four white stockings, were certainly untypical mounts. The enlisted Lancers all rode short, stocky mustangs that in all probability had been captured from one of the herds that roamed the plains. These big fillies made the smaller mustangs look puny. Both were tall rangy animals with deep chests, long slim legs, and smallish heads, indicating classic Arabian bloodlines somewhere in the past. They looked like a pair of swift sisters that could outrun everything else on the prairie. With one of them under me, Daniel mused, my troubles would be over.

He watched as the Lancers reached the cellar door. One of them reached down and carefully opened it; then two of the others descended narrow stairs that were revealed. At each step they probed the darkness ahead with the long, sharp lances that accounted for their name. Up and down, back and forth, went those lethal lances, cutting violent, enthusiastic but futile gashes in the air. Long after the pair had descended below ground level, he heard a medley of savage grunts and growls as the Lancers attacked the inoffensive darkness with undiminished gusto.

Daniel smiled, but quickly sobered. He could laugh now because he was reasonably safe. If his instincts had deserted him, he might at this very moment be impaled on one of those terrible lances.

The search of the cellar and tiny cabin ended very quickly, and the Lancers and both officers returned to their tethered horses. Before they were given the order to mount, the Captain spoke to them.

"Men, our search has only begun. Never fear, we will find the escaped prisoner. I think he may not have traveled this far. We will double back and look for him as we ride. A full goatskin of fine Spanish wine to the Lancer who spots him!"

The Lancers mounted, formed a column of two's with the Captain and Lieutenant in the front, and then rode out of the farmyard. As she past his hideaway, the black filly peered toward him. Daniel was sure that she couldn't see him, but he was just as sure that she sensed his presence in the shadowy log.

Since he was safe, at least for the present, Daniel decided to stay where he was until nightfall. He had three more loaves of stale, hard bread and enough water to last for a few days. Since the Lancers had strength and speed on their side, his weapons would have to be wits and stealth. Daylight was as much an enemy as darkness was an ally. He would travel only at night and hide during the day.

He remembered the ancient city of Teotihuacan, the place of the gods. The ruins lay about twenty-five miles north of Mexico City. On the trek south, the wagon train had camped there overnight, and his friend, Captain Alonzo Almonte, had taken him on a tour of the pyramids and shared their history. If he walked ten miles each night for the next two nights he would reach Teotihuacan. He could find hundreds of places of concealment. He could hide forever, or at least until his pursuers decided that he had eluded them. The only immediate problem Daniel foresaw was finding a hiding place by daylight tomorrow. He said a prayer, relaxed, and fell asleep once again.

The ordeal of captivity, last night's flight through the furious storm, and the strain of his situation had sapped a good deal more of his strength and vigor than Daniel had imagined. It was not until late afternoon that he emerged from his deep sleep of exhaustion and peered out through the leafy curtain. For the next ten minutes, he watched for any movement and listened carefully for any sound that might indicate an alien presence. Finally, deciding that it was safe to leave his sanctuary, he parted the wilting leaves and moved into the open.

Since he was still in a wooded area, he decided to continue his journey before nightfall and walk along the edge of the woods wherever possible. Whenever he reached an open space that was barren of trees, he would stop and scan the horizon for signs of activity. He would not quit the protective woods until he felt confident that he could cover the distance to the next copse of trees before a man on horseback had time to ride close enough to discover him. If he saw or heard anyone, he would tumble to the ground and remain motionless until the danger had passed. Daniel reasoned that it was a hundred times less likely for a rider to spot a still, prone figure than a walking man, particularly if he were silhouetted against the sky.

Daniel traveled until after midnight before he stopped beside a spring that bubbled out of the base of a rocky cliff. He gratefully filled both his goatskin bags with clear, fresh water, and put the remaining loaves of bread inside of his shirt. Near the spring, he discovered a row of berry-laden bushes. He stuffed sweet berries into his mouth with great relish until his hunger finally disappeared, then he stripped off his clothes and bathed as well as he could in the shallow catchment in the rocks. He dried his body with the cleanest part of his soiled shirt, and then scrubbed his clothing. When everything was as clean as possible, Daniel wrung the clothes out as well as he could, then dressed. Portions of the thin fabric were still damp, but would soon dry as he walked along.

During the evening, he passed a few small ranchos and an isolated hacienda. He gave each dwelling a wide berth so as not to alarm the inhabitants or the animals, lest they raise an alarm. Daniel's caution was rewarded. He'd encountered only one person who came along riding in an open buggy an hour before. Standing in the deep shadows of a thick clump of trees, Daniel had been close enough to hear the man clucking to his horse and to see a black bag beside him that usually denotes a doctor.

Daniel moved with all the stealth of a woodsrunner on his moccasin-clad feet. He walked into the wind whenever it was possible, so his scent would not be carried ahead of him to alert any animal to his approach. His father, Nathaniel Austin, had taught him to be a self-sufficient forest dweller before he had reached his tenth birthday.

His father, Nathaniel Austin, had been born near Boston in 1752. Fiercely patriotic to the Colonists' cause, he had been one of the youngest members of the Sons of Liberty. It was Lieutenant Austin's twenty-third birthday on the dusty morning that Captain Daniel Morgan and his company of Virginia militia arrived in Boston, "to make the British run!" The young officer was assigned to assist and to orientate Morgan and his men. That had been the beginning of a lifelong friendship. Nathaniel enlisted in the Virginia Company, served with Morgan's Riflemen in New England and New York, and marched with them again in 1779 when General John Sullivan devastated the land of the Iroquois. He had fought beside Morgan at the Battle of Cowpens in 1781 when the British Redcoats first realized that they had lost the war.

When it ended, Nathaniel Austin decided that the wild country along the Virginia/Carolina border had become home to him. Three years later, he met and fell in love with Daniel Morgan's lovely eighteen-year-old cousin, Julia. They built a sprawling cabin on a high slope of the Blue Ridge Mountains and raised a family of five boys and five girls. Nathaniel was nearly sixty when his son Daniel was born. Knowing that this would be his last child, the old woodsrunner tried to teach the youngster everything that it had taken him a lifetime to learn.

A very bright and eager student by the time Daniel reached his mid-teens, the darkly handsome, raw-boned young man could follow a game trail in dim moonlight and hit a moving target with an arrow as easily as he could with a bullet. He also mastered the rough-and-tumble style of fighting that was favored on the frontier, and could live off the land for long periods of time. His father proudly called him a woodsman. During the same years, his mother made certain he was well read and knowledgeable.

Unlike most families of their era, the Austins were blessed with many fine books. Shakespeare, Burns, Johnson, Marlow, Scott, and dozens of other favorite authors became as familiar to Daniel as the tracks of the deer, the boar, or the bear.

When Georgetown University accepted Daniel as

a student, Julia Austin's fondest dream came true. Her youngest son would be a scholar, not a wild man like his father.

The first weeks of his freshman year had been a harrowing experience for Daniel. His homespun suits and rough, brown cloth shirts were readymade objects of ridicule for his richly attired, urbane classmates. Many faculty members were also a bit scandalized that a refugee from the Carolina backwoods had insinuated himself into this hallowed institution of high learning. After all, Georgetown University had been designed to serve graduates of America's finest preparatory schools, America's elite of mind and of social position. It was no place for threadbare country bumpkins who had learned whatever they might or might not know by firelight in a rustic cabin on the edge of a dense primeval forest.

A single glance at this gangling youth made them aware that he belonged in the domain of wild animals, and even of wilder red Indians. His presence in their midst, in the very heart of such refined culture, was extremely disturbing.

As the green of late summer gradually changed to the vivid oranges, dark crimsons, and tawny golds of autumn, professors as well as the students began to suspect that they had underestimated this quiet young man from the frontier. By the time winter's icy winds had driven the bright colors into hiding for another year and the first snowfall of the season had covered the city with a shroud of dappled white, the last doubt had disappeared. Daniel Austin stood first on the academic list by a wide margin, and his skill in every type of game or contest left him without a peer.

"How can we hope to compete with him," many of the formerly smug young men asked themselves and each other. "His mind is like a sponge; he absorbs knowledge. And his body is as hard as a rock. He's smarter, stronger, faster, and more agile than any of us."

All of that was true, but unlike many other gifted young men, Daniel Austin wasn't a showoff. He was humble and helpful. He spent one or two evenings every week patiently drilling higher mathematics into one of his roommates, and willingly shared basic tricks of rough and tumble frontier wrestling with anyone who was interested. He nearly had to demonstrate his prowess in the art of self-defense during his very first night on campus, but used diplomacy instead.

The meals were served in a huge eating hall, large enough to accommodate the entire student body at one time. Long dining tables sat ten, four on each side and one on each end. Students, supplementing their tuition expenses by working in the kitchen, brought food to the tables. Since cooks carefully apportioned the meals, everyone received the same amount. The system had been imposed to make certain that no one stuffed himself while his neighbor went hungry. On each table, large pitchers of milk and cider were set out for everyone's convenience.

On that first evening, dinner consisted of meat loaf, mashed potatoes, green beans, and cherry pie. As soon as the plate of food was placed before the student who was seated directly across from Daniel, a large fellow sitting at the end of the table, reached out, neatly stabbed the slab of meat on his neighbor's plate with his fork and dropped it onto his own plate. Apparently still dissatisfied with a double helping, he then turned toward Daniel, his now empty fork poised in anticipation. Daniel intercepted the hand in midair, and quietly spoke.

"Don't do that!"

"Why not?

"Because I asked you not to."

"That's not a good enough reason."

"I'll give you another one. You're acting like a lout. Start behaving like a gentleman, and give the fellow's food back."

"No! And I'm going to take yours, too!"

Once again the menacing fork moved purposefully

toward the coveted meat loaf. Daniel reached out and encircled the bully's two middle fingers and forced those suddenly painful digits upward and backward toward the wrist. The bigger fellow struggled in vain for a moment and then gave up. Each movement brought new agony to his fingers, hand, and wrist. It was a special inducement to comply, a grip that policemen called a "come-along" because when pressure was properly applied, any miscreant was eager to come along wherever he was led and comply with any demand. That was now the case with the bully.

"Now," Daniel explained while still exerting pressure to keep the fellow's attention, "we can do one of three things. I can simply break your fingers. I can snap them off. Or you can return the meat loaf and stop this foolishness. Which will it be?"

"I'll stop! I'll stop!"

"Good decision. Put the food back, then I'll let you go."

The culprit quickly complied and was released. He sat staring intently at Daniel, shaking his aching fingers for several moments before he whined.

"You can't take a joke! I was only funning. I wouldn't have really kept the food. My name is Biff Butterworth, and I'm really not such a bad fellow. I just like having fun."

"The butt of your practical joke is my roommate, Michael O'Keefe, and I'm Dan Austin. I'm willing to put this episode behind us, as I'm sure Michael is. The only thing we ask of you is to consider the overall consequences before you do something."

Butterworth outwardly agreed, acting contrite and friendly for the rest of the meal, but Daniel detected a hard glint in his eyes that belied his words. Butterworth was a very confident individual. He was big and he was strong. He probably hadn't been bested very often in his life. Daniel knew that nobody liked to lose, but when you did, you either learned a valuable lesson or you harbored a lasting resentment. Butterworth seemed more like a resenter than a learner to Daniel. For now, he would accept the fellow at face value, but he would be on guard until he was certain that he could be trusted.

As that first year wore on, Biff Butterworth tried to best Daniel in every way he could, but not a single one of his efforts succeeded. By the time summer rolled around, and their first year ended, he realized that Daniel's friendship meant much more to him than winning contests against him. That discovery made Biff a better person.

Daniel finished his reflections and, hidden by the night, moved quickly along a dark path. Conjuring up the memory of that first college dinner had made him realize that he was hungry. Since he had been able to refill his goatskin water bags, thirst was not a problem, but he longed for some solid food. In the past twenty-four hours, he had subsisted on wild berries and small bites of hard bread. He needed more substantial food if he planned to continue his present pace. His stomach growled in agreement. He smiled in the darkness, remembering the meatloaf.

It was nearly daylight when he came upon a small sluggish creek. He walked along the bank for about a mile before he saw a small adobe hut in the midst of a dense grove of trees on a small hill that overlooked the creek. As dawn broke, Daniel crawled cautiously up the hill, then slowly stood and peered into the hut, being careful not to silhouette himself against the rising sun. It was deserted. He moved back into the squat trees that grew close to the wall and moved slowly to the back of the building. He was pleasantly surprised to discover that the view below was clear for more than a mile. No one could approach from that direction without being seen, and no one could travel along the creek on horseback without being heard. His prayers had been answered. He had found an ideal hideout. He continued toward the far side of the deserted dwelling and discovered an even more welcome site, a garden in which grew a fair number of green plants, as well as a supply of beans and squash, perhaps revitalized by the recent rain storm. On the outer fringes of the garden several rabbit runs were plainly visible.

Daniel found more than enough strong vines lying about to make four snares which he placed near the runs. Now, if God smiled on him, he would have fresh meat and vegetables for dinner. He dug up all the squash and beans he could find, washed them in the creek, rechecked his snares, gathered enough soft grass to make a comfortable bed, and contently fell asleep in the shade of a gnarled old oak tree.

He slept soundly until late in the afternoon. When he woke, Daniel instantly recalled where he was, and remained motionless until he was certain that no one had detected his hiding place while he slept. He moved his head just enough to look around the wide plain below him. Seeing nothing, he turned slowly and looked next toward the creek. Everything was quiet as a church on a weekday afternoon. Not until his scrutiny was completed did Daniel rise and stretch the kinks out of his muscles. Twelve hours of peaceful sleep had made him feel fit and refreshed once again. Now his only problem was a nagging hunger. He could eat a grizzly bear. Suddenly, he remembered his snares. He would settle for one rabbit. He uttered a prayer as he walked toward the other side of the dwelling where the garden lay.

His prayer was answered. A pair of large rabbits had been caught in two of the snares.

Daniel took the meaty rabbit carcasses down to the creek, along with an earthen pot he had discovered. He skinned and cleaned the rabbits and washed the old pot. Then he cut up the meat, several vegetables, and a cluster of wild herbs he had found growing in the garden and dumped everything into the pot half filled with water.

A short search around the small clearing produced enough tinder-dry wood to build a small, nearly smokeless fire. If there should be any smoke, it would be instantly whisked away by the strong wind that was blowing across the plain toward the creek.

Daniel built the small fire, surrounded it with broken adobe bricks, and set the pot and its contents over a small flame to heat. A long and patient hour later, he was enjoying a savory stew, and his hunger, as well as his longing for meat, were both satisfied.

Daniel dozed off once again, and awoke in the late evening. Again, he carefully surveyed the encircling perimeter before he moved. Pale moonlight filtering through the thick clouds gave the dim countryside an almost ethereal appearance. Rising, he walked down to the creek where he removed his clothes and spent several minutes in the cool refreshing water. When he returned to the adobe shack, he stripped the old jute sack from the bunk and filled it with vegetables he'd harvested from the garden. Then he took strong vines similar to those he had used for rabbit snares and fashioned a carrying harness for the sack and his two water bags. He could now drape the harness over either shoulder, or around his neck, whenever he wished, and keep both of his hands free.

IV
TEOTIHUACAN

CENTRAL MEXICO
JULY 7, 1834

Daniel walked for the next six hours. Stopping only for a ten-minute break each hour, he reached the southern outskirts of Teotihuacan a short time before dawn and paused next to the immense south wall of the Pyramid of the Sun. Almonte had said it was the third largest pyramid in the world. It was certainly much larger than the other pyramids that still stood in the ancient complex. Its sides were over seven hundred feet long and its summit rose two hundred feet into the sky.

The Sun Pyramid was not a single structure. It was actually several pyramids, stacked one atop another. Succeeding generations of inhabitants had labored for hundreds of years to bring the pyramid to its present size. Unlike the pictures of the Egyptian pyramids Daniel had seen, which appeared to be quite smooth, the Pyramid of the Sun had hundreds of steps. He also noticed that the entire pyramid had been built with stones that were small enough to be lifted into position by one man. Historians and other inquisitive investigators, still pondered the unsolved mystery of how great stones, each weighing several tons, had been moved from distant locations and then lifted into precise positions by the Egyptian pyramid constructors. Even more incredible were feats accomplished by the builders of the towering Moai statues on Rapa Nui, called Easter Island, by its discoverer, Captain James Cook. Captain Almonte said the pagan priests who served this temple pyramid had a labor force of enslaved servants who endlessly painted the stone surface with bright red paint. Perhaps it represented the blood that was annually shed by thousands of helpless people who were sacrificed to pagan devil gods. The Pyramid of the Sun was the focal point of the entire complex, as well as its highest building. At its peak, between 500 and 600 AD, Teotihuacan may have housed as many as 125,000 inhabitants in an ingeniously planned city that covered more than eight square miles.

In college, Daniel had read archeological studies that extolled Teotihuacan civilization which was a contemporary of ancient Rome, but had lasted five hundred years longer. In many ways, it was more advanced than many contemporary European cities.

Daniel decided to climb to the apex of the Pyramid where a small temple had been built. The ascent to the pyramid's dizzying summit took almost an hour.

Each step was more than a foot high and less than six inches wide. A great many of the ancient stones were all but obscured by long, green, slimy plant tendrils that seemed to invite disaster by reaching out and clinging to his boots. Daniel expended a great deal of energy and suffered some bruised and scraped fingers before he finally reached the summit.

He had risked the climb in an effort to discover signs of pursuit or any danger that might be lurking nearby, but now that he had arrived he decided that the panoramic view alone justified the climb. To the west he could see a lengthy plaza that once housed the marketplace. Northward, the Street of the Dead stretched toward the far end of the giant complex and opened into another large plaza at the back of which rose a mighty temple that Daniel remembered as the Pyramid of the Moon. He saw a tiny temple on its summit, much like the one next to which he now stood, but the distance was too great to see anything other than the temple's outline in the hazy sunlight of the early morning.

The tropical sun began its majestic climb, and each minute evermore of the ancient city became visible as the buildings and ruins emerged from the long, protective shadows being cast by the Pyramid of the Sun and other ancient buildings that were not in ruins.

Daniel wished he could have seen Teotihuacan in its days of bustling glory more than a millennium ago. In the spreading sunlight he saw a large temple on the western side of the plaza, its front wall adorned with a Plumed Serpent. He felt certain that this was the Toltec temple dedicated to Quetzalcoatl.

Eager to explore Teotihuacan with its fascinating buildings, houses, markets, ruins, and mysterious temple-pyramids, Daniel decided to descend. But he had gone only a few steps before caution made him pause. From his lofty perch he could look out over the city and the surrounding countryside in every direction except south. The summit temple below which he now stood, concealed the approach to the city along the path he himself had followed earlier. Retracing his steps, Daniel walked around the narrow catwalk that encircled the temple. It was nearly full daylight as he stood high on the pyramid's southern face, with a now unrestricted view of his back trail for many miles. After carefully scanning the arid, acrid plain for several minutes, he was relieved to discover that nothing large enough to raise a dust cloud was in motion.

Daniel carefully descended and entered the Street of the Dead, Teotihuacan's principal thoroughfare that once had been lined with impressive civic buildings and magnificent temples. Just beyond this ceremonial hub, with its previous incessant activity, stretching to the outer fringes of the city, clusters of private homes and densely crowded multi-family dwellings, lay along winding streets with inviting courtyards and carefully tended parks. Beyond the city limits, wandering paths and byways led to dozens of tiny villages filled with thatched huts that dotted the countryside. Each village was a nerve center for an ingeniously planned network of collective farms. As he remembered from his studies, each of the networks was strictly regulated by a local agricultural expert.

Daniel spent the next hour in the fascinating temple of Quetzalcoatl, then crossed the Street of the Dead and entered the plaza where the city's main marketplace had once stood. This was the heart of Teotihuacan social life, a place to meet friends, spend a pleasant hour munching on delicacies of the day, or to hear the latest news.

Teotihuacan lay in the very center of the obsidian glass industry. Each market day, he imagined dozens of ingenious cutlery designers were on hand to display hundreds of finely crafted knives, heavy-duty chopping tools and delicate, razor-sharp instruments. The city was also the gathering place for Central Mexico's pottery makers. He imagined potters' stalls were filled with huge water jugs, tiny table bowls, and every size in between, in every color, pattern, and design imaginable. Shoppers could also find various articles of clothing, feathered ornaments and headdresses, live birds and animals, and semi-precious jewels of every description.

In many ways, ancient Teotihuacan had been a shopper's paradise as well as a highly organized city. Daniel recalled reading descriptions of rigid restraint by religious and secular leaders who insisted upon, and zealously maintained total control of every citizen's heart, mind, body, and spirit.

Common people stood in awe of the priests and intellectual elitists who, since they were skillful astronomers, kept track of Teotihuacan's seasonal cycles as well as the seemingly endless chain of processions and other religious ceremonies. Continual public rituals were not the only expressions of adulation that were required. Fear of reprisal by a variety of bloodthirsty pagan gods compelled the residents to make religion the centerpiece of their private lives. Altars dedicated to the feathered serpent were erected in every dwelling, from the most indigent hovels to the richest mansions.

Now, standing in the center of the main plaza, Daniel closed his eyes and allowed his imagination to spin him back in time. It was 600 A.D. Here he was among Teotihuacan's busy merchants as they plied their wares. He could almost hear the bustling citizens as they scurried about the plaza on market day, eagerly selecting maize, squash, and beans. Of course, there were other markets in the city, but this was the one that the knowledgeable urbanites and a majority of the travelers favored.

The craftsmen and merchants lived in homes built in spacious courtyards around the perimeter of the marketplace. In many cases, the homes were factories as well as dwelling places. Captain Almonte described a squalor in Teotihuacan's lower classes in such a picturesque manner that Daniel could visualize the London tenements that Charles Dickens wrote about. Overcrowded tiny hutches built along alleys as narrow as rabbit runs where the few squalid open spots were littered with debris. But Daniel's history studies had convinced him that very few cities ever existed without harboring a slum area within their confines. Toltecs and Aztecs had been no different. Poverty and slums were fostered by urbanization. It had always been that way and it probably always would be.

On the other hand, most citizens of Teotihuacan seemed to live quite well. Unlike many other places in the ancient world, food was plentiful here. Telltale signs still remained that suggested the early forms of irrigation designed by local engineers which had been used to provide water for the crops that the hundred thousand people needed. Since such a vast amount of land had to be cultivated, Daniel assumed, they had probably drawn water from the swamps, lakes, and rivers, as well as storing all the rain that fell.

Daniel spent the balance of the day eagerly entering one fascinating site after another. Although most of the ancient murals had been erased by wind, weather, and time, a few faded ones remained. He discovered that the oldest murals usually depicted Quetzalcoatl, one of the other Toltec deities, or fierce warriors in feathered headdresses. But the later and still colorful murals depicted a gradual swing away from the warlike heroes to more peaceful and simple people who, Daniel assumed, were members of the merchant and trader classes. In some of the clearest murals, he detected people with slanted eyes and curious clothing who apparently were foreign visitors. He was once again grateful for Georgetown's history department policy that students should be conversant with all phases of ancient as well as more recent history. A knowledge of Mesoamerican civilizations made his day of exploration an exciting adventure.

Daniel remembered that Teotihuacan reached its apex of power and prestige about 600 A.D., then quickly declined. Some great catastrophe must have befallen the region since the population rapidly decreased and the once-proud city was little more than a series of disconnected villages scattered over a small area.

Around 700 A.D., Teotihuacan was abandoned and partially destroyed. As the centuries passed, many of the remaining buildings collapsed and dense vegetation began covering the pyramids and ruins. Now, more than a millennium later, Teotihuacan was still revered by many as a sacred place, but its glorious days of yesteryear had long since sunk into the quagmire of antiquity from which it would never rise again.

There were many interesting sites and artifacts to examine and ponder; so it was late afternoon before Daniel's empty stomach overrode his curious mind. By then he had reached the northern end of the great plaza in front of the Pyramid of the Moon. About halfway up the wall of the pyramid, he could plainly see a small dark opening that looked like an entrance to a grotto. At the base of the opening, there appeared to be a narrow ledge that resembled a balcony.

Daniel decided to climb up for a closer look. He had been right. The ledge, about six feet wide, fronted a six-foot high cave that led into the interior of the pyramid. Whether it had always existed or had been opened at a later date, he couldn't tell. Whatever the reason for their existence, the ledge and cave were welcome sights. He would be shielded while he slept, and high enough to see for miles in every direction except directly north. Of course, no one approaching from the north would be able to see him either. Since it was unlikely that anyone would approach on foot, he was certain to hear hoof beats before he saw anyone.

The peaceful stillness in the ancient city remained unbroken until an hour before the tropic sun dipped below the horizon. As he gazed down from his high perch toward the southwest, Daniel saw a thin wisp of dust curling skyward. The thin wisp became a thickening spiral as it moved steadily toward him.

The dust cloud was still a fair distance away when he heard the hooves of many horses. A short time later, a large band of horsemen entered the west side of the plaza. He recognized the two horses in the lead. One of them was a big palomino, the other was the black filly that he last had seen from the security of the hollow log. The palomino's rider was pulling a man with a bright red beard and hair along behind him on a rope. Obviously, the poor fellow was a prisoner. When he got closer, Daniel saw that his hands were tied behind his back.

Suddenly, the prisoner stumbled and tumbled to the ground but bounced upright again. If he hadn't been agile, he would have been dragged through the dust because his captor maintained the palomino's pace with no thought to the redhead's predicament. For the first time Daniel's attention left the prisoner and riveted on the riders. Something was wrong here. These men weren't Lancers. They looked more like a band of bearded brigands, but there was no mistaking the palomino and the black fillies.

Daniel tried to count the riders as the line of horsemen entered the plaza below him. He finally lost count due to the swirling dust but estimated that there were at least sixty riders. In addition to the riding horses, a third of the men led packhorses that bore large bundles on their backs.

When the leading riders reached the base of the temple wall directly beneath Daniel's perch, they dismounted, unsaddled their mounts, and settled into leisurely positions while the red-haired captive built a fire. Once the fire was properly laid, he hammered several iron rods into the ground that straddled the fire pit before he ignited it. These uprights would cradle the skewer on which chucks of meat would be roasted, as well as rods that would hold cooking pots. As the remaining riders entered the plaza, they broke into groups of eight or ten and began the same type of activities. It was dusk by the time all of the preparations were completed.

Half an hour later, shielded by the deep darkness

and the craggy wall, Daniel moved toward the front of the ledge and peered down into the plaza. Around each campfire, he saw men biting into huge chunks of half-cooked meat and tearing them apart with their teeth, or slicing it off close to their lips with sharp knives that glinted in the firelight. In addition to the slabs of sizzling meat, every man seemed to have at his elbow a wine cask or, at the very least, a bulging goatskin filled with wine.

Daniel continued to watch the revelers for the next four hours. Every hour the roar from below grew louder. The drinking intensified once the food was consumed. So did the shouting and the violence. At one fire, two men suddenly jumped up and began brandishing big, deadly looking knives. They warily circled each other for a few moments and then one of them leaped forward and buried his blade in the heart of his antagonist. When the unfortunate fellow toppled over and died, the spectators turned away in disgust. The fight had been much too short. Unless another one began, the evening's entertainment was over. The killer and his friends returned to their drinking without another thought for the dead man. He lay there like so much carrion until the red-haired prisoner dragged the poor fellow into the darkness.

Daniel watched the redhead as he came back into the light and returned to the main fire. As he walked along, he seemed to be the target for every brigand who could reach him with a punch or kick. Daniel wondered who he was and how long he had been a captive. One thing was sure, if he didn't soon escape he was sure to be maimed, or even killed, by his heartless tormentors.

It was long after midnight before the last outlaw fell into a drunken stupor and silence enveloped the camp. Daniel spent the next hour searching the camp's perimeter for any sign of guards and the sleeping figures for evidence of sleeplessness. He saw neither. The only sounds and movements came from the far end of the plaza where the horses had been tethered on a long picket line. Even when one of the animals stamped a hoof or snorted, and the sudden sound echoed around the plaza walls, the sleepers continued their undisturbed, wine-soaked slumber. They all seemed as lifeless as the dead man that the prisoner had dragged into the shadows.

Since it now seemed comparatively safe, Daniel descended the pyramid wall as quietly as he could and made his way around the edge of the plaza until he reached a place close to where he had seen one of the bandits tie the red-haired man to a thick stone pillar. He paused for a few moments and then continued on through the welcome darkness to a spot from which he could get to the prisoner and stay hidden from the camp by the pillar's shadow.

As he arrived at the back of the pillar, he reached around it with his arm, then clamped his hand firmly across the mouth of the prisoner and whispered.

"Don't move or shout! I'm going to cut you loose!"

"Are you a guardian angel, Laddie?" The query was made in a soft Scottish burr.

"No! Just a fugitive who wants to get out of here almost as much as you! All right, your hands and feet are free. Come around to this side of the pillar, then we'll move back into the darkness. Let's go!"

Staying in the pillar's shadow, they sidled into the darkness along the back wall of the plaza before Daniel spoke again.

"Let's gather up some weapons, food, and water, then sneak down to the far end of the plaza where the horses are picketed, and get out of here as quietly and quickly as we can."

"They're all tipsy. We could parade right through the middle of them behind a brass marching band and they would never hear a thing."

Daniel couldn't help smiling in the darkness. He certainly had to admire the fellow's grit.

"You're probably right, but since there's no band handy, let's sneak."

"I'm right behind you, Laddie."

They moved through the shadows along the wall of

the plaza with all the stealth they could muster. But it soon became apparent that the Scotsman's forecast was correct. A brass band probably would not have awakened the drunken brigands. When they arrived at the site of the first campfire, the former prisoner put his hand on Daniel's arm and whispered.

"We'll find everything we need here. This is Mendoza's campsite. He's the leader. He keeps all of the best things for himself and his brother. Just look at all of the fine chattels they have."

It didn't take them long to rummage through the big pile of weapons and equipment that lay near the Mendoza brothers. They each picked up a Kentucky long rifle, pairs of matching pistols, several powder horns, beaded hunting bags that contained bullet molds, lead, and greased patches, and a pair of long-bladed Green River butcher knives. Daniel stuffed as much food and water as possible into a large gunny sack, tucked the knife and pistols into his belt, cradled the rifle under his arm, and then reached for a serviceable looking saddle. The Scotsman stopped him and whispered.

"Look under those two fleece saddle blankets!"

Daniel threw the blankets aside and found a pair of silver-trimmed Mexican saddles that once had been the proud possessions of prosperous rancho owners.

"Let's take as much as the horses can carry," the

Scot advised. "I've enjoyed the local hospitality, but I've no desire to come back and shop here again."

They quietly staggered to the picket line under the load of new possessions. The selection of horses was simple. Daniel saddled the black filly for himself and the palomino for the Scotsman. They had both come away with a profit, but the biggest prizes were their lives. They led the horses quietly for the first half-mile before they mounted and rode north. Now they could fly like the wind, and no one could catch them.

V

SHIPWRECK

It was mid-morning before an unmistakable sound of meat sizzling, and the fragrance of boiling coffee stirred Daniel into wakefulness. The new friends had ridden hard all night, putting as much distance as possible between themselves and the banditos. It was an hour after dawn before they saw a thick grove of trees on the northern horizon. Tall trees meant plenty of fresh water, grass for the horses, and a few hours of much needed rest for the weary animals and their exhausted riders. Daniel estimated that they were at least ten leagues north of Teotihuacan. When given their heads, the two fillies, who were obviously blooded Arabians, settled into a ground-eating lope that defied successful pursuit by riders mounted on wiry mustangs that roamed the plains in wild herds.

The Arabian strain of horses, noted for smallish heads, deep chests, and sturdy legs, had been bred by Bedouin nomads for untold centuries for speed or endurance. Fierce and warlike, the Bedouins fought enemies, raided caravans, and pounced on any unwary traveler. Their way of life and their continued survival were made possible by their remarkable and unique horses, which they treasured as much as their freedom. In the vast Arabian Desert, man and horse were totally dependent on one another.

Daniel had been riding since he was old enough to stay on the back of an old plow horse who plodded slowly along at her own comfortable pace. In his twenty years he had ridden horses of every description, but none could compare with the big filly when it came to sheer power, endurance, speed, and eagerness to run. Her first dash across the prairie made Daniel feel as though he were astride a soaring raven rather than an earthbound creature, and at that moment the black filly became Raven.

Daniel rose, walked down to the bank of the stream, drank deeply of the cool water, splashed some on his face, and returned to the tiny fire over which his new friend had brewed the coffee and fried the meat. While they ate, they exchanged identities, something they had been unable to do as they galloped along.

"My name's Kenneth Hawkins, but my shipmates call me Hawk. I'm indebted to you for getting me out of the terrible mess I was in."

"I'm Daniel Austin, and it was a real pleasure."

Daniel turned and watched the hobbled fillies as they grazed contentedly about fifty feet down the slope. Neither of them seemed any worse for the long run through the night. Daniel gestured toward them as Hawk came to stand beside him.

"The first time I saw those fillies, they were being ridden by a couple of Lancer officers." Daniel told Hawk

"Mendoza and his gang of cutthroats bushwhacked the Lancer patrol yesterday morning without losing a single man. They slaughtered all twenty of the soldiers."

"How in the world were they able to do that?" Daniel asked incredulously.

"The night before the ambush, we had camped on the rim of a deep canyon. Diego Mendoza has raided Central Mexico for many years. He seems to know every arroyo, water hole, cave, and game trail from the seacoast to the mountains in the west. Just as we were breaking camp yesterday morning, one of the sentinels who was on watch a few miles to the south, rode in with word that a band of Lancers was approaching. To the Mendozas, those Lancers meant fresh horses, plenty of guns, and welcome supplies. Diego sent half his men, under the command of his brother, Jorge, to the opposite rim of the canyon, and strung the rest along the top of the near side. As soon as everyone was in position, Diego mounted his horse, and rode out toward the Lancers."

"With murder in his heart no doubt," Daniel said with a frown.

"From what I could piece together from the later conversations, he rode close enough to hit one of the soldiers with a rifle bullet, then he wheeled his horse around, and scurried back toward the canyon, with the Lancers a short distance behind. Of course, he led them directly into the ambush he'd skillfully planned. The entire patrol was wiped out in a matter of a few minutes. After they were all dead, the bandits climbed down into the canyon, stripped and looted the corpses, then loaded their booty on the Lancers' horses. As soon as the Mendozas saw the black and palomino fillies, they claimed them for themselves."

"I can't fault their ability to pick good horses."

"I can't fathom why those Lancers rode recklessly into a blind canyon that could easily be turned into a death trap. It's hard to believe experienced soldiers acted so foolishly."

"The two officers, a captain and his lieutenant, just came from Spain. It was their first month in Mexico. This was probably their first independent patrol. I guess, in their eagerness to capture the man who shot at them, they simply threw caution to the winds. In the process, they also threw their lives."

"How can you possibly know all that about them, Daniel?"

"It isn't nearly as mysterious as I make it sound. I overheard them talking while I was hiding inside a hollow log. They both seemed quite eager to make an impression on Santa Anna as soon as they could. A greater mystery is what a Scottish sailor is doing in the heart of Mexico, and how you happened to fall into the hands of those brigands in the first place?"

"Well, it's a long, strange story. Since we can tarry a while, and let the horses rest a wee bit, I'll start at the beginning. I was born in Aberdeen, a port city on the northeast coast of Scotland. I've loved the sea ever since I saw huge waves breaking over the rocks near our shanty. When I turned twelve, I ran away from home and joined a merchant ship as a cabin boy. For the last dozen years, I've been a seaman. I also taught myself to read. I study every book I can get my hands on. I also learned to reef, to make sail, and the coopers' art of making barrels. For the last five years, I've been a ship's cook."

"Now I know why the breakfast tasted so good," Daniel smiled.

Hawk grinned in return.

"Aboard ship, I found that I enjoy eating too much to leave the cooking to fools who don't know how to cook and are too lazy to learn. The only way to get a good meal each time is to do it yourself. So I learned to cook. Two years ago, I decided I'd seen enough

Atlantic crossings for awhile, so I signed aboard Isis. She's a big, five-masted trading barque, sailing out of Boston."

"I suppose she's one of Clement Mayfair's ships. Or do other people name their trading vessels after mythical gods and goddesses?"

"She's a Mayfair, sure enough. Her sister ship is Osiris. Is your interest in commerce, ships, or in Clement Mayfair?"

"Actually, none of them! I was once interested in his daughter, Roxanne. An ill-fated courtship that ended with the elegant Mr. Mayfair making me feel like an absolute fool."

"I saw the great man a few times. But, of course, I never met him, being, as I am, a simple seaman and cook. I know he's rich and successful, but he pays his crews right well. He's made most of his money in the triangle trade."

When Daniel looked puzzled, Hawk continued.

"Wool products, clothing, blankets and such, are loaded in Boston and sailed to a port in the south, like Charleston or Savannah, where the goods can readily be sold to eager local merchants. Cargoes of rice usually can be purchased in those ports at cheap prices. The rice is welcome at most Caribbean islands, where it can be traded for casks of rum. Jamaican rum is the best, but any kind of rum is worth a fortune to

New Englanders who need it to lift their spirits on bitter winter nights. For the better part of two years, I enjoyed good pay, easy duty, and tropic ports, fit to make a sailing man's mouth water. I hoped it would go on forever! But I didn't foresee the shipwreck!"

"Isis sank?" asked an incredulous Daniel.

"She sank right enough. Not all at once, but a wee bit at a time. We couldn't save her! We tried, but it was no use!"

"I hate to say this, because I want to hear all about the shipwreck, but I think we had better put some more distance between ourselves and those bad tempered fellows we left so suddenly last night. I have no desire to be one of their guests after the unpleasant way that they treated you!"

"A sobering thought! Let's saddle the horses and weigh anchor."

Earlier that morning, Daniel had shown Hawk how to hobble the horses by tying short lengths of soft rope around their front legs, just above the fetlocks. The hobbles allowed the fillies to graze, but discouraged them from wandering very far away.

As they walked slowly toward the horses, Daniel whistled and called softly to the black filly.

"Here, Raven. Come, Raven."

Raven didn't move, but she watched intently as he came toward her, pricking her ears forward at every whistle or word. He had every confidence that she would soon respond to his verbal commands or his whistle. There were several other tricks he needed to teach her, such as to stand still whenever her bridal reins touched the earth, often called ground hitching. She also needed to instantly lie down on command. In a firefight, where both of them would be targets, her unquestioning obedience could save their lives. She was obviously an alert animal. If she were as willing to learn as she was to run, her education process would go very quickly.

"So! You've named the black filly Raven. A fine name that suits her very well! See how she and her sister shine in the morning sun. The golden filly looks like a newly minted sovereign. How regal she is. Every inch a queen!"

"Sovereign would be a doubly good name for her."

"So it would." Hawk chuckled, "I'm glad I thought of it."

It was nearly dusk before they camped ten hours later on another hill from which they could see in all directions. The fillies had covered the distance in a long-striding, effortless lope that they had obviously been trained to maintain. Being careful not to extend them beyond their endurance, Daniel had called a halt every couple of hours and allowed the fillies to rest, drink, and graze for a few minutes before they continued.

Throughout the day the horses remained fresh and eager to run. It was comforting to know the fillies had such great strength and endurance. No doubt a time would come when both those attributes would be tested.

Their night camp was a pleasant wooded place, with a clear water spring seeping out from the base of a rocky cliff. After a long day, the horses as well as the men were ready to stop and enjoy a well-earned rest. While Hawk started a fire and began cooking, Daniel let the fillies drink their fill, then hobbled them and turned them loose to graze. By then supper was ready. As they ate, Hawk continued his story.

"On Isis's last voyage, the price of rice had hit rock bottom, so we crammed big, hundred-pound bags of rice, into every available inch of hold space before we left on the second leg of the triangle. From Carolina, we usually sailed southeast, along the Bahamas, to the eastern end of Cuba. From there, the southwest tact takes you to the Windward Passage and an easy sail to the Caribbean. Then it's a straight run to Jamaica."

"Which I've heard is a tropical paradise."

"Jamaica is a beautiful island! If you sail in from the north, you first sight the Blue Mountains, rising as if by magic out of the sea on the southern horizon.

Both major ports, Kingston and Montego Bay, are thriving trade centers. But on our last voyage, we took a different route because Captain Blake met a friend in Savannah that operated a sugar plantation in Cuba. Maybe he owed the scurvy fellow a favor, or perhaps he was just being accommodating. Whatever his reason, the captain agreed to transship the man to Havana."

"How far off your normal route did that take you?"

"Not far enough to make the detour matter much. Instead of sailing southwest through the Bahamas chain, it meant sailing southwest down the Florida Strait, and then a long tack over to Havana. The Havana leg was quick and smooth. When we left the Havana harbor, we had two ways to finish the voyage. We could sail east along the north coast of Cuba and enter the Windward Passage as usual, or skirt Cuba's western end, sail along the southern coast, past Isle of Pines and Caymans, and approach Jamaica from the west rather than northeast. Maybe to break the monotony, Captain Blake opted for the southern route. That proved to be his undoing, although the fates may have played the same role regardless of where we were."

"Now who's being mysterious?" Daniel laughed.

Hawk smiled and continued

"We'd just rounded Cape San Antonio at Cuba's western tip and entered the Yucatan Channel when a steady wind out of the northeast turned round 45 degrees to due east, and in the twinkling of an eye, grew to gale force intensity. Huge, towering thunderheads rushed in, covering the sky. The full moon that made the night nearly as bright as day, disappeared. The black night, and the hot, clammy air, made us feel as though we were inside the devil's gunnysack. Knowing that a fierce wind that had been gathering force across the whole breadth of the Atlantic Ocean would soon be upon us, bringing with it monstrously high and dangerous waves, the captain gave orders to shorten sail and to rig a sea anchor."

"I know about shortening sail," the fascinated Daniel interjected, "but what is a sea anchor, and what is its purpose?"

"When a ship is built, the first thing shipwrights do is lay down a keel. The keel runs down the center line of the vessel. The ship's support frames are connected to the keel. It's the foundation of the ship. The keel, extending far beneath the ship, also keeps it upright and stops any sliding to one side or another as the ship moves through the water. In normal seas, the keel, in concert with the sails, keeps the ship moving on course. The biggest danger is allowing a ship to broach. That means veering off course and turning broadside to the wind and waves. In those cases, the sails and the keel lose most of their effectiveness. To protect the ship from turning turtle, that means rolling over, the crew must keep the ship's prow turned into the wind and waves. That is the sea anchor's purpose. Objects such as anchors or anything big and heavy enough to provide a drag against the pressure of the sea, are fastened to a long, heavy cable, then secured to the bowsprit and lowered overboard. If a sea anchor works properly, and the pressure of the waves and wind is not too severe, a ship remains head-up into the wind in a seaworthy posture instead of exposing a vulnerable broadside toward the force of the elements. The wind and sea assault the bow of the ship, the narrowest and least vulnerable point, and allows the waves to slide past the ship's sides rather than striking her broadside."

"Seems like a perfectly logical course of action." Daniel grinned as he realized that he was being influenced by his new friend's precise, burr-softened English, speech patterns undoubtedly stemming from his years of shipboard studies and reading.

"Oh, it's logical enough, unless you encounter a rogue wave, and then the whole world goes crazy."

"A rogue wave?"

"A huge, towering wall of water that grows higher, wider and faster as it races across the long stretches of open ocean, gathering more speed and more water volume as it comes. I swear the wave that smashed *Isis* was twice as high as her masts, from the trough to the crest."

"I don't understand how a single wave can grow to such enormous height!"

"Well, let's suppose a big underwater earthquake occurs a few miles off the west coast of Africa, near the hump, just a wee bit south of the Sahara Desert. The tremor starts a chain reaction. First, a torrent of water is forced up to the surface where, given direction by the prevailing currents and driven faster and faster by strong desert winds, it has the entire width of the Atlantic to pick up speed and power. By mid-ocean, the force of the wave has built up enough pressure to drag along an enormous vacuum behind it, into which surrounding waters rush. More and more water means more and more power, a bigger and bigger vacuum, and evermore water."

Ken Hawkins stared into space for a moment and shuddered before he continued.

"That building cycle continues all the way across the ocean. The very first barrier the wave encounters would be the Leeward or the Windward Islands. But there's a fair distance between all those islands, so much so, that the growing rogue wave could easily pass between them. Now the wall of water is in the

Caribbean, gathering warm water as it comes, and is being funneled by South and Central America on the south, and the Greater Antilles on the north, along the length of the Caribbean. As the available space narrows, so does the wave, making it more powerful and higher. There is only one means of escape, the narrow Yucatan Channel, the meager distance between Cuba's Capo San Antonio, and the Yucatan Peninsula's northeastern tip, a distance of less than fifty leagues. Imagine a wave growing higher and more powerful as each hour goes by before it finally encounters an obstacle in its path, an obstacle on which it can unleash all of its fury, a helpless object that has wandered into the teeth of a disaster from which there seems no escape: Isis.

"It must give you a terribly helpless feeling!"

"I can't begin to describe it," Hawk assured him. "And then things got worse. The gale blew harder and harder for the next four hours. The waves built up until they were higher than any I had ever seen, even during winter storms in the Atlantic, over sixty feet from trough to crest. Isis rolled back and forth so hard we were shipping solid water over the rails! Crew members who were needed on deck rigged lifelines to keep from being swept overboard. But through it all, the sea anchors held the ship into the teeth of the wind. Even those men who had been expecting Isis to turn turtle began to gain confidence in her ability to weather the gale. Then, suddenly, all of our hopes were dashed."

Once again, Ken Hawkins stopped and shuddered as he relived the worst moments of the deadly storm.

Daniel sat patiently waiting for Hawk to continue.

"Since the very start of the storm, rank after rank of low-hanging clouds had been advancing on Isis, just like well-ordered soldiers marching into battle. Suddenly, a small opening appeared in that orderly array and lasted just long enough for a wee sliver of moonlight to creep down. The clouds quickly closed ranks and the light disappeared, but not before we saw a great mountain of black water coming directly toward us. It was nearly upon us! Too late to run, too late to do anything! Except pray! I remembered a passage from one of Walter Scott's novels when the hero 'looked death directly in the eye.' Now we were the focus of death's glare. Isis would be torn apart like a rag doll. Even if the ship survived, all of us would be hurled overboard and die in the raging sea. These were the final moments of my life! I had never known such terror! Out of a corner of my eye, I noticed that an inspection hatch that led down into the aft cargo hold was open. I dived through the hole a split second before the wave struck Isis. Since the sacks of rice had been piled as high as possible, I fell only a short distance before slamming into them. The breath was driven from my body, and I lost consciousness for a time. As I came to my senses, I had the sensation of being crushed by terrible water pressure. Moments later, the pressure disappeared as the water filtered down to the bottom of the hold. In the dim light, I saw water marks everywhere. Before it began to recede, the water had covered every inch of space the sacks didn't occupy. At first, it seemed to me as if the tightly packed sacks of rice, acting almost as a cofferdam, had kept the giant wave from flooding the hold. Since the volume of water had been limited, the bilge pumps might be able to pump out most of it, lightening Isis while crewmen sorted out the damage to the sails and rigging that the wave was sure to have caused topside. How lucky we were to have a cargo of rice, I thought! But never in my life had I ever been more mistaken."

"I think I can foresee your dilemma," Daniel said.

"When my head finally cleared a bit, I got to my feet, balanced as carefully as possible on the slippery sacks, heaving as they were in rhythm with the ship, and reached up toward the hatch. In the dim light, it seemed tantalizingly near! But the lip of the coaming was just beyond my outstretched fingertips. I tried to jump far enough to make up the difference, but it was useless, the sacks were too slick. The third time that my feet flew out from under me, I gave up and bellowed for help. Since there was so much chaos on deck, it took a long time before one of my mates heard my call, lowered a rope, and hauled me up.

"When I reached the deck, I couldn't believe my eyes! Even in the meager light, I could see Isis was a wreck. The wave had snapped off four of the masts. The jagged stumps bore mute testimony to the power of the wave. Three of our four lifeboats were gone. Washed overboard! The fourth boat swung uselessly back and forth on davits, her stove-in stern plainly visible. Splintered spars, ruined rigging, wreckage of all kinds littered the deck and trailed along the ship's side. The crew had faired no better. I saw dozens of injured men writhing in pain. Each man who was not groaning seemed to be dead. Many lay in grotesque positions, reshaped by the sea's awesome force. The few of us who had escaped the worst of nature's onslaught did whatever we could to make the others comfortable, but we could do very little."

"That helpless feeling again," Daniel said softly.

"The storm abated at dawn. The wind all but died, and the waves were no more than a gentle swell. As soon as it was light enough to see, we searched the ship for survivors or bodies. We found Mr. Collins, the First Mate, still tied to the base of the foremast.

His neck was broken. He was the only officer we found. The rest, including the captain, were gone, swept overboard. The Boatswain, Charlie Douglas, took a muster. Out of nearly sixty officers and crew, only eight of us were unhurt. A few men most likely would recover, but the rest were already dead, nearly dead, or simply missing. It was an awful discovery."

Ken Hawkins stopped talking, and Daniel realized how difficult it was for him to tell the terrible tale.

"Charlie Douglas found a sextant in the captain's cabin and plotted our position. 86 degrees, 33 minutes. W. Longitude, 23 degrees, 27 minutes, N. Latitude. Well out of the Yucatan Channel. Well into the Gulf of Mexico, and drifting west-southwest."

"I'm sorry, Hawk. I'm a little weak on sailing directions."

"The storm struck us quite near the southwestern tip of Cuba, and reasonably close to the northeastern shoulder of the Yucatan Peninsula. Now Isis had been carried away from those near-by landfalls and was drifting farther away every minute. Isis was 160 leagues southeast of New Orleans and 250 leagues northwest of Tampico, Mexico. If we continued our present drift, we'd eventually wind up somewhere along the coast of East Central Mexico. I checked our food stores and the undamaged water casks, and decided that the few crewmen still aboard had enough provisions to last for three or four months if need be. As you know, landmasses and hundreds of islands surround the Gulf of Mexico. Charlie and I were certain we'd run ashore somewhere long before our food and water ran out. Besides, we weren't too far from the normal sailing lanes. A ship might show up at any minute and rescue us.

"For the next three days, we drifted deeper into the Gulf, toward the Mexican shoreline. Charlie plotted our position at noon each day, and discovered that we were covering about forty leagues between reckonings. If everything continued, we were only four or five days away from land."

"Obviously, everything didn't continue."

"No. About an hour after the third noon reckoning, while I was cleaning up the galley, I was amazed to see a pair of furry gray shadows pop out from one of the storage bins and go scampering across the galley deck and into another hiding place. In all my years at sea, I had never seen a rat in the daylight before. They're always content to sulk about in the darkness between decks, and come out in search of food under the cover of the night. It was so strange that I alerted Charlie Douglas. He couldn't guess what could have driven them topside either. He'd been sounding the well and the bilges several times every day since the storm and the rogue wave, and he said the ship was drier than he had ever seen her. She was riding a bit deeper in the water than usual but everything seemed to be fine otherwise.

"At least the worst was over."

"So it seemed. Our good luck held for four more days. At noon on the seventh day, Charlie Douglas estimated that we were only about fifty miles off the Mexican coast. A sea bird landed on the remaining mast. Those birds seldom venture more than fifty or sixty miles from land. All the survivors were elated. By then, our number had dwindled to twelve. All of the others had died and had been buried at sea.

"I was in the galley cooking an evening meal when I heard shouts from the deck and rushed topside. A big seam had opened in the deck. As I watched, two more long seams popped open, and a torrent of rice rushed through the widening crack. We suddenly knew why Isis was dry, despite the fact that she was riding so low in the water. The rice was absorbing every drop of water that invaded the hold. Now the rice had expanded so much that the cargo hold could no longer contain the greatly increased volume. One glance at Charlie Douglas confirmed my worst fears. Isis was doomed! Water had saturated the cargo of rice and tripled the volume. It wasn't just expanding upward, it was pushing downward and outward. How long could the ship's frail timbers hold before they gave way. Not long! Isis' life could no longer be measured in years, months, weeks, or even in hours. Isis would slip beneath the waves in a matter of minutes."

"What could you do without lifeboats on a sinking ship?" Daniel queried.

"We gathered up everything that would float, bits of the masts, any spar we could loosen, biscuit tins, water casks, hatch covers, all the rope, netting, and rigging. Starting with a pair of undamaged hatch covers, we built two serviceable rafts big enough to carry us and our remaining provisions. We finished the job and got the wounded aboard less than two hours after we started, in the nick of time since Isis was ready to go under."

"So you all got away on the rafts?"

"Not all of us. Just as we were about to push off from the ship's side, I remembered that the sextant was still in the wheelhouse. I guess it was foolish to worry about navigating on a raft that would drift wherever the wind and the tides decided to take her. But the sea can be a lonely place when you've lost a ship, and a sextant would at least give us an illusion of plotting our own destiny. Despite Charlie's urging against it, I decided to rush back aboard, grab the sextant, and rush back to the rafts with all haste. I almost succeeded."

"Almost?"

"Isis was so low in the water that I didn't have to step up to the deck from the raft. I just stepped off of one and onto the other. I rushed into the wheelhouse, seized the sextant, and ran back on deck. Just as I did, Isis slipped beneath the waves and dove toward the bottom of the sea, carrying me with her."

"But you were back on deck! Couldn't you swim back to the rafts?"

When a ship goes down, particularly a vessel as big as Isis, she creates a great deal of suction, a lot more than any human being can withstand. No, Daniel, I said my prayers, and prepared to meet Our Lord because there was no way I could regain the surface without a miracle."

"But here you are! A miracle must have occurred!"

"I was dragged down a long way. All the light was gone, and the sea was very dark. The pressure was crushing my chest and ears. The pain was terrible. I was ready to die when an empty water cask that had been snarled up in some netting, tore the netting loose and started up toward the surface. If it had happened a moment later, it would have been too late. I would have been unconscious! But I still had the presence of mind to take hold of the netting, and ride along to the top, to air, to life! When I popped out into the sunlight, I saw the rafts only a short distance away.

But they might as well have been on the other side of the ocean, for there was no way for them to wait or to turn back, and there was no way for me to catch them. I followed in their wake for a long time before they finally disappeared. The rafts were going much faster than my water cask because the wind, as well as the tide, was pushing them along. Since I was so low in the water, the wind had no effect. The rafts went off toward the northeast while I continued drifting directly west, toward the nearest coast."

Hawk's brow furrowed and his teeth clenched as he relived his terrible ordeal.

"I don't need to tell you that those were the longest hours I ever spent, Daniel. I had no head covering, and the sun beat down unmercifully. By dusk, my hands were raw from salt water as well as from clinging to the rough netting. My shoulders and neck felt like a huge blister. Fatigue must have made me doze off because suddenly I heard a roar of breaking surf. I had never heard a more welcome sound in all my life! I held on to my life-saving water cask 'til it dragged me through the rocks along the beach and onto the sand. My whole body burned like the furies and my throat felt as dry as the Sahara, but I fell asleep thanking God, grateful to still be alive.

"The next morning, I hurt even more. When I was aroused by a violent kick in my ribs, I doubted that

I would live for much longer. I soon discovered that the savage-looking man who had kicked me was the leader of a gang of banditos named Diego Mendoza. As I lay on the sand looking up at him, I noticed his eyes. They were black, lifeless, and deadly, just like a shark's eyes. During my long months of captivity, I decided no shark had ever been as bloodthirsty or murderous as the Mendoza brothers. I'm going to try to erase the things they did from my memory if I can. They're much too terrible to remember."

VI
RESCUE

NORTHERN MEXICO
AUGUST 1, 1834

Daniel and Hawk had stopped for the night in a thick grove of cottonwood trees that grew along the gently sloping banks of a shady meandering stream. While Daniel cared for their horses, Hawk built a tiny fire and began preparing an evening meal. Daniel still hobbled the fillies at night although he was reasonably sure that Raven wouldn't wander very far away. If Raven stayed nearby, so would Sovereign.

Tonight, both men shared festive feelings for many reasons. Hawk's melancholy moods, a result of the vicious treatment and the humiliation he'd suffered during his captivity, were becoming less frequent. He laughed more and was cheerful much of the time. Another reason for happy feelings was the anticipation of the sight, sound, and most of all the taste, of the big antelope steaks that Hawk would soon have sizzling over the fire. Minutes earlier, as they were approaching the cottonwoods, they had surprised a small herd of antelope that were drinking from the stream. Risking the sound of a shot that might alert unseen enemies, Daniel shot one of the young bucks as he sped away. The shot made from Raven's pitching back at a bobbing target that Hawk saw as nothing but a fleeting shadow was remarkable. In response to compliments, Daniel characteristically reddened and suggested that luck had played a big part in his success. Hawk chuckled, but suppressed an urge to contradict his friend. He knew that luck had played no part in the skillful feat. A third reason for happy feelings was the result of Daniel's observation that the wagon train had camped in this same grove of trees during the first week of the journey to Mexico City.

A day's ride, two at the most, would bring them to the Rio Bravo. Twenty-five leagues beyond that lay the Rio Nueces, the southern boundary of Estado de Tejas. From there, it was only a twenty-league ride to San Antonio de Bexar. The flight from Santa Anna was almost over. The fight against Santa Anna was almost ready to begin.

The following day was a time of anticipation. They forded the Rio Bravo that evening at dusk and happily set up camp a short distance from the river in a dense stand of oak and walnut trees. Half an hour later, they sat comfortably on a fallen log, enjoying a rich, savory antelope stew flavored by a variety of native herbs that Hawk was so adept at ferreting out. When the meal ended, Hawk rolled into his blankets and quickly fell asleep. Each night they rotated the early and late shifts of guard duty. It was Daniel's night to watch and listen until midnight, then wake Hawk who would stand guard until dawn.

Tomorrow would be a special day, Daniel mused, as he sat in the welcome warmth of the still-smoldering campfire. It meant the last leg of their flight and the start of the mission Uncle Stephen had entrusted to him.

As the evening wore on, a great number of thick clouds moved in from the north and the once bright, star-studded sky was obscured. As midnight neared, the only light in the dim mid-summer sky came from a tiny silver crescent of new moon that now and then poked through the overcast. Just as Daniel rose to wake Hawk, a new string of storm clouds, driven by fierce gusts of wind, moved in and quickly painted the dull gray sky an ominous black. Salvos of stinging sleet began pelting down hard enough to produce bone-chilling misery for anyone who did not quickly find shelter.

Daniel draped one of the rain slickers they had taken from the Mendoza camp around his shoulders, shook Hawk awake, then ran toward the horses which stood in the shelter of a huge oak tree. Daniel was confident the storm's fury would soon end. It was too intense to last for very long.

Moments later Hawk, wrapped in his blankets and a hastily donned slicker, came and stood next to him.

"When did the nor'easter blow in?" he shivered.

"A few minutes ago."

"It's lucky we camped in these thick trees and on high ground. Even the horses are nervous."

The velocity of the howling hurricane continued to increase until its terrible intensity flattened most of the smaller trees, stripped huge branches off many of their sturdier neighbors, and then hurtled them to the ground with a disdain akin to that of a spiteful child casting down a broken toy.

As Daniel had predicted, an hour later the tail-end of the storm passed over them and sped toward the southwest. Minutes later, the same tiny sliver of silver moon reappeared and cast an eerie light over a soaked and subdued landscape. The endless sea of broken branches that littered the ground and the torrents of water that continued to fall from the trees bore mute but vivid witness to the storm's fury.

As the storm vanished and the stillness of night settled in, almost everything returned to normal. The sole exception was Raven, who was obviously upset. She danced nervously back and forth on her tether, snorted impatiently, and peered toward a dense stand of trees nearest the river.

As he watched Raven, Daniel recalled another time when she had behaved in a similar manner. He had been hiding in the old, hollow log. He was mortally certain that the filly couldn't have seen him, yet she sensed his presence. Raven's current actions convinced Daniel that danger was near and present. He nudged Hawk and whispered.

"I think Raven senses some uninvited visitors."

"Lancers, bandits, or Indians?" Hawk whispered.

"I'd say Indians driven into the trees by the storm. Lancers wouldn't wait in the fringe of the woods. Neither would bandits! They'd barge in, shooting as they came. That leaves Indians."

"What's our play?"

"Fortunately, there are enough large trees between us and them to give us plenty of cover. If we take it slow and easy, I think we can gather our weapons, saddle the horses, mount up, and get out of the north side of the woods before they know what we're up to. We'll have to leave everything else behind, but I'd rather keep my hair than the Mendozas' booty."

Daniel thought about how lucky they had been up to now. During the northward trek, after escaping from the banditos, they had been extremely fortunate. They had not sighted a single Lancer patrol along the way. They'd seen a number of Indians, but most of the bands were far away. One Comanche war party had come close before Daniel and Hawk became aware of them. But despite their legendary equestrian skills, they could only whoop, brandish primitive buffalo bows, and poke holes in the air with their menacing lances before the swift fillies hit full gallop, and left them farther behind with each lengthening stride. But their present situation was very different. These Indians were close, much too close! Before Daniel and Hawk could outrun them, they would have to outsmart them.

As quickly and as quietly as possible, Daniel and Hawk stuffed chunks of cooked antelope meat into their pockets, stuck a pair of pistols into the sashes they each wore around their waists, and cradled the long rifles in the crook of their arms. Weighed down as they were, it took a great deal of effort to pull their heavy saddles along with one hand, but somehow they managed. The fillies still sensed the danger and moved restlessly about until the men spoke reassuringly to them and then, as if by magic, they calmed down.

"As soon as those Indians lose sight of the horses, if they can see them from their hiding places, certainly when they hear the fillies start to run, they'll break cover and charge, hoping to stop us from getting through the trees and into the open. From here, there are two lanes leading toward the northern edge of the woods that are fairly free of trees."

As he spoke, Daniel pointed toward a pair of narrow trails.

"Can you see the two paths I'm pointing to?"

"Yes! They seem very narrow."

"They are. But they're our only chance. The horses can see far better than we can. What they can't see, they sense. Don't guide Sovereign. Trust her to avoid the trees on her own. You take the path on the left. I'll take the right. Once we get past the last fringe of the trees, we'll be safe. No Indian pony can catch these fillies once they hit full stride."

They saddled the horses and mounted.

"Ready, Hawk?"

Unwilling to risk a whisper, Hawk nodded.

"Okay, I have an idea. I'm going to give us a head start by scaring the fillies, and startling the Indians and their ponies. Hang on tight, Hawk, 'cause things are going to happen in a hurry."

Carolina woodsmen taught their children how to identify the tracks and calls of every forest animal as soon as they were old enough to understand. Quite often, they also learned to imitate the animals' calls. Daniel had become so skillful that occasionally his father had trouble deciding which call was real and which was false. It was this ability that Daniel now intended to use.

Hawk was startled a moment later when the call of a hunting cougar split the night's stillness. Before it could be repeated for a second time, both fillies were in full gallop, dodging trees their riders couldn't see, and bursting out of those trees into the clear before one Indian had time to calm his trembling mustang.

Daniel and Hawk could not contain their happiness. They both whooped and shouted in delight as their eager fillies thundered across the prairie.

"The hard part is over," Daniel shouted to Hawk as they rode knee to knee. "Now all we have to do is outrun them. That shouldn't be too hard!" he concluded optimistically.

They urged the fillies up to their fastest pace until they no longer heard the hoof beats of their pursuers before letting them settle into their favorite lope. At dawn, they stopped to rest the horses on a high ridge from which they could see their back trail for a long distance. Expecting to see nothing behind them, they were shocked to discover a large dust cloud rolling in from the horizon.

They led the fillies down to a place on the far slope where they could not be seen by their pursuers, and tethered them in a patch of lush, green grass. Then they crept back to the crest. Daniel waited until a dark passing cloud shielded him from the sun's reflection, then peered through the heavy brass telescope Hawk had taken from the Mendoza's camp. The magnified image that he beheld was disturbing.

A dozen or more Indians were galloping directly toward them. Each one of them was leading four or five mustangs behind him. Daniel handed the telescope to his companion.

"We're in big trouble, Hawk!"

Hawk squinted into the tube for a few moments.

"Why? I see a dozen Indians, and fifty or sixty horses, but as you often remark, no mustang alive can catch our fillies."

"No single mustang. But a whole string of them can!"

"Forgive my ignorance. Maybe I've been at sea too long. One mustang, or half a hundred mustangs, still can't run as fast as our horses, can they?"

"Not unless the mustangs are fresh! Our fillies are worn out!"

Seeing a look of doubt flash across Hawk's face, Daniel continued.

"Would you concede that a riderless horse can run faster and farther than one who's bearing the weight of a man?"

"Of course."

"Every one of those Indians is leading a string of

horses behind him. Their plan is crystal clear. They intend to follow us, switch to a fresh horse each time the one they're riding falters, leave the tired animal to be picked up by the trailing riders, and eventually run our tired horses into the ground. The question is not if they can overtake us, but rather, how long it will be before they overtake us!"

"I see! Do we stay here and make a fight of it?"

"No. Raven and Sovereign cover a lot of ground in that lope of theirs. If we rest them for a few minutes every hour, they won't start to flag for a long time. By then, we might find a place that we can defend. Better yet, we're not too far from the southernmost Texican settlements. The farther north we travel, the better our chances of finding a village or an outlying ranch. For now, running is good for us and bad for them."

Daniel touched Hawk's arm and began edging off the summit.

"Let's ride, amigo!"

Ride they did, as the fillies settled into a ground-eating lope. Except for short rests every couple of hours that lasted only long enough for a drink and a gobble of grass, they ran throughout the long night and for much of the next day. When they finally drew rein and dismounted late in the afternoon, the fillies had been in almost constant motion for the past twenty-four hours and were definitely showing signs of strain and fatigue.

"The horses need more than a few minutes rest this time, Hawk. The Indians, even with fresh mustangs, must be a long way behind us. I haven't seen a dust cloud in the sky for several hours. It's at least four hours until sunset. I propose that we stay put and let the fillies rest until dark, or until we see a dust cloud. I'd like to give them even more rest, but we can't let the Indians sneak up on us in the dark. Hopefully we'll find a place that we can defend before much longer."

"We've seen at least a dozen Indians following us, Daniel! There may be some more we haven't seen. How can the two of us hold off a score of men who, according to some of the things you've told me, are so good at warfare that they make a game out of it?"

"If they catch us in the open they can attack from all sides! We need to find a natural shelter of some sort, something that protects us from assaults on at least two sides and offers a substantial field of fire in front of us. Our rifles' long-range accuracy is so superior to trade muskets and arrows that we can stay under cover and pick them off one at a time."

Hawk rewarded Daniel's optimism with a smile. Daniel had purposefully made their chances sound far better than they were. Two protected sides and a defense perimeter might be workable if both defenders were skilled woodsmen, capable of anticipating attackers' moves, and deadly marksmen who could make every shot count. Hawk was none of those things. His life had been spent at sea. He'd never held a Kentucky long rifle before he escaped from the Mendozas. His ability was limited to the few lessons Daniel had given him. Hawk had never even fired a shot.

What they really needed to find, Hawk decided, was a fort surrounded by a stockade with protected parapets along its walls. He pictured mighty Fort McHenry standing defiantly on the shore of Chesapeake Bay as dozens of British rockets screamed overhead during the War of 1812. That's what they needed to ensure victory. Of course, they had no hope of finding such a fortress. Chances of escape were almost as remote, unless they found a hideaway the Indians couldn't attack in waves. They needed a miracle. Maybe God would give them one.

It was nearly sunset before they saw a dust cloud raised by their pursuers on the southern horizon. They had enjoyed four welcome hours of rest and inactivity. The fillies' fatigue had disappeared, and they were fresh and eager to run once again.

They rode north as the moonlit hours slipped past, until the rising sun announced a new day. And then, as if in answer to their prayers, a miracle suddenly appeared a short distance ahead of them.

In the midst of an otherwise open prairie, they saw a square, rocky mesa. Three of the sides were sheer cliffs that rose upward toward an absolutely flat top.

The front face of the mesa was, for the most part, as sheer and unscalable as the others, except for a natural, narrow staircase that led gradually upward across the entire width of the face. Daniel could see that there would be ample room to lead the horses up to the mesa's flat top before their pursuers arrived. The rocky passageway reminded Daniel of a sally port, the special entrance or exit of a fortress that was used only when it was under attack.

The mesa was a wondrous, welcome sight! Once on top the fillies would be out of sight from below and safe from harm. The rock-strewn, irregular front edge of the mesa's summit offered numerous sites from which concealed and completely safe riflemen could fire downward and pick off any attacker foolish enough to venture up the narrow unprotected path.

When they reached the foot of the rocky passageway, Daniel and Hawk knelt for a moment and said a thanksgiving prayer before beginning to climb. God had not only answered their prayers, He had given them a fortress even safer than Fort McHenry.

It took far longer than they had expected to lead

the fillies to the top of the mesa. Treacherous footing and the sloop's sharp incline made it very difficult for them. Scant moments after they gained the summit, four of their pursuers, each leading a string of mustangs, galloped into view.

"Maybe they won't realize that we're up here."

Hawk's words sounded like another prayer.

"There's some chance of that," Daniel acknowledged as he peered cautiously over the rim of the mesa, "but I'm afraid it's a very small chance."

Even the small chance vanished when their four pursuers, guided by the fillies' tracks, rode directly to the opening in the trees at the base of the mesa wall where the path began. The Indians did not long tarry. As soon as they were certain that the hoof prints led up the slope, they joined the rest of their party who, as they arrived in groups of three and four, stopped a short distance out on the prairie.

"What do you suppose they'll do now?' Hawk asked.

"Well, they have only two choices. They can ride away, or wait us out. While they're deciding, one of us can look for a source of water, while the other watches the Indians. Which would you prefer?"

"You're the woodsman. If there's water up here on the mesa, I'll bet you find it. What should I do if the Indians try to rush us?"

"I don't think they'll try anything as foolhardy as that. As you know, my father taught me a great deal about Indians, and I grew up with several Cherokee boys who are still good friends. First of all, I don't know which tribe these Indians are from, but I think I can tell you something about them. We have six things they want—our horses, our long rifles, and our scalps! None of which do them any good if they're dead, so they won't throw their lives away recklessly. The first thing they'll do is come up with a plan. If I were their war chief, I'd want to know three things. First, how close we'll let them come before we open fire; second, if we can shoot straight, and lastly, if we'll shoot to kill? To get to us, they need to find a way to storm up the face of the mesa along a steep narrow path, or wait us out. The configuration of the mesa doesn't allow them to climb up anywhere except along the path we found, so they have no third choice."

"If you were the war chief, what would you do?"

"I would have my warriors creep in as close as possible and find out if the white men are willing to kill. If not, I would send a dozen men up the path as soon as darkness falls."

"And if they know we'll shoot to kill?"

"They'll keep us penned up 'til we escape, or until they get tired of the game."

"If they force us to shoot, one of them will die."

"It's the price they're willing to pay for the horses, rifles, and scalps."

"I understand the rifles because they are so much better than either bows and arrows, or muskets. But why scalps and horses! They have so many horses already."

"Scalps are trophies of war, like the medals a soldier earns. They're also something to brag about when you tell the story of the "great race and battle." They want the horses for the same reason they want the rifles. Our fillies are much better than any of the horses they have."

"The Indians have never seen hide nor hair of the fillies! How do they know they are so good?"

"First of all, the fillies ran away from them. The Indians, swapping a tired mount for a fresh one each time a horse faltered, fell farther behind with every passing mile. Second, by now they've measured the fillies' stride."

"I don't understand."

"A horse's stride is the distance the animal covers each time its four feet hit the ground. If the left foot is the lead foot, you measure the total distance from the first left hoof print to the next, and that's the stride. The longer the stride, the bigger and faster the animal. To any Indian warrior, a good horse is a tool of war. My father used to say that after a white man abandoned a horse that was too worn-out to stand, an Indian would come along, get the horse up, ride him for another forty miles, and then eat him for supper."

"They sound like formidable foes."

"The Great Plains Indians are undoubtedly the best light cavalry in the world. The speed and endurance of our fillies is the only edge we have against them. I think our friends below will stay put for a while and decide on a plan. If they start moving in, fire a shot over their heads to alert me."

Daniel took a few steps toward the grazing fillies and whistled softly. At once, Raven stopped tugging at a bunch of grass and trotted toward him. Disdaining a saddle, Daniel sprang to Raven's back then guided her toward a nearby rock outcropping with the pressure of his knees and a handful of mane. He was hoping the mesa sat atop an artesian system where internal hydrostatic pressure would force water to the surface, past several layers of permeable rock. If such a system did exist, he would almost certainly find evidence of water seepage along the same level of the rocks that encircled the mesa's rim. He was almost certain that no water source, such as an open catchment, existed on the mesa. If it had, the horses would have found it by now.

Daniel rode slowly around the mesa's rim for over an hour. He dismounted several times to examine promising rock formations and moss clusters, but found no sign of moisture. Disappointed, he returned to Hawk.

"I'm afraid there are no springs up here, amigo."

"It's a good thing we refilled the goatskin water bags before we made camp last night."

"Yes! There's enough water to sustain us and the horses for a couple of days if we conserve. And then we'll have to rely on barrel cactus."

"Water from cactus plants?" Hawk queried.

"Although the pulp of a barrel cactus is bitter and acidic enough to make you violently ill if you eat it, it does contain a little moisture. If you lop off the top of a barrel cactus, you can usually cut out the pulp and wring it as you would a wet rag. When the plant is small, you can soak a dry cloth in the pulp, and suck the moisture out of that."

"It sounds awful!"

"Under normal circumstances, it is. Let's just hope those Indians give up and ride away before we get that thirsty!"

For the next several hours, Daniel and Hawk sat in a hidden rocky alcove where they could comfortably watch the Indians below without being seen.

Throughout a dwindling afternoon and early evening, the Indian warriors sat in a circle and apparently argued about the plan of action. Loud voices from the prairie were carried up to their high perch a dozen times. More than once one of the warriors jumped to his feet, stomped around for a while, then shook his fist at the mesa before resuming his seat. Daniel could not help smiling at their almost comical behavior.

An hour before sunset, a decision apparently was reached. The Indians broke the circle and began applying war paint to their faces and bodies. When they finished, they each chose a horse, and painted signs on the animal.

"Those are good-medicine signs they're painting on their animals," Daniel explained to Hawk. "They're going to test us, for sure! That big jumble of rocks near the base of the access trail doesn't leave enough room for more than two men to ride abreast. They'll all start together, but they'll have to string out before they reach the rocks. If we kill the first two ponies, they may realize that we could just as easily have killed the riders. If so, they either give up or come up with another plan. Since we're far higher than they are, remember to shoot lower than you normally would."

"I have an idea," Hawk said. "You do all the shooting! After you fire your first shot, I'll hand you my rifle and reload yours. It may discourage them if they think there are two sharpshooters facing them."

Daniel saw the wisdom in Hawk's idea and agreed.

Moments later, the Indians mounted their ponies and slowly advanced in a side-by-side double line until they reached a place just beyond musket range, where they stopped. Then, with a loud war whoop, the hideously painted warrior at one end of the line urged his pinto pony forward and charged straight toward the rocks. The man next to him followed, and then the next, and the next, until the Indians rode in a long, single file, each directly behind the Indian that rode ahead.

Daniel held his fire until the first warrior reached the outer fringe of the rocks before he put a bullet squarely between the eyes of the pinto pony. Since he was reaching for Hawk's rifle, Daniel failed to witness the painted rider as he sailed from his hapless pony and crash headfirst into a deadly cluster of jagged rocks.

Daniel's second shot struck the next pony, a tall bay, the same measured distance between the eyes as his pinto mate. The bay's rider was either more nimble, or more fortunate. Although he was thrown heavily to the ground, he was able to regain his feet and hobble painfully away from this place where instant death lurked. He was quickly boosted up onto the back of a war pony behind another warrior, an incredible display of strength and horsemanship, since he was fleeing from the deadly rocks at full speed when the remarkable feat was performed.

"A sad message delivered!" Hawk said softly, as he gazed down at the first warrior's crumpled body.

"Yes!" Daniel agreed. "Surely they know the shots that killed the ponies could have just as easily have slain their riders. They must also realize that many more of them will die if they try to climb the path. I hope they come back to get the dead warrior's body. I want to show them that justice is coupled with mercy. I won't fire unless they start moving toward the path. If I have to fire, my targets won't be horses."

The fleeing Indians stopped when they were safely beyond the accuracy range of a long rifle, then set up five teepees in a circle and built a large cooking fire in the center. Apparently, with no further thoughts of their fallen comrade who still lay among the jagged rocks at the foot of the high mesa wall or the white men who sat staring intently down at them from the rim, they unloaded from their pack horses several large slabs of meat which Daniel identified as buffalo. The Indians dragged the meat to various places around the fire.

Unmindful of the gritty sand that had accumulated

during the journey from horseback to fireside, each hungry warrior cut off a big chunk of raw red meat, usually with a rib bone or two protruding, then thrust it eagerly into the fire. Daniel peered through the brass telescope for a few seconds, then handed it to Hawk. As if by magic, the powerful instrument catapulted Hawk into the circle. He stared in fascination as each warrior held a hunk of meat in the fire long enough to singe the hair off, then extract and attack the meat with eager relish, gnawing, grinding, twisting, and tugging until a strip of the nearly raw buffalo flesh tore away from the bone. Each sat grinning in triumph as gobs of blood cascaded from his mouth and sluiced across his bare chest.

Despite the danger, Hawk couldn't suppress a grin.

"Meals aboard ship were never very elegant, but this is absolutely primitive."

"It is primitive," Daniel agreed. "Most of the tribes who dwelt along the Eastern seacoast from Georgia to New England, as well as those in New York and many other areas white men coveted, have been overrun by western expansion. Those tribes have been forced to forego their primitive, nomadic way of life and adopt the system we like to call civilization, just to survive. In some instances, like the Six Nations of the Iroquois, the assimilation process of blending the races into a reasonably workable society has worked well. In a few others, it is slowly beginning to take hold. In most cases, the process hasn't worked at all."

"Why should it?" Hawk queried. "I read a London Times article last year. It said that Indians that had lived in the same location for hundreds of years were told to leave and move west simply because a bunch of white settlers wanted their land. You can't expect them to be unceremoniously uprooted with nothing but a whimper! A story as old as mankind. Might makes right! If you don't look, talk, and act exactly as I do, I must be better than you. I've seen and fought that attitude on shipboard for ten years."

Daniel was pleased. Hawk's stern words identified him as a man with deep feelings about right and justice, as well as someone who could think and function in the face of danger.

"The primitive behavior and aggressive attitude you see down there around the fire guarantees that these warriors, and many others like them, won't go like lambs to the slaughter. Nomads never make willing farmers. I don't think the Indians of the Great Plains will either. I believe they'll fight for the way of life they have enjoyed for hundreds of years with the fury of a cornered wolf. 'Til we get out of this corner we're in, we'd better plan on doing the same thing."

The gentle south wind which had gathered great

quantities of heat on its daylong journey across the sun-scorched prairie was stymied by the towering cascade of shady rocks, and was forced to inch its way slowly upward along the jagged face of the cliff, toward its easiest means of escape, up and over the rim of the precipice. As the breeze climbed, it was chilled to such an extent by the shaded rocks that by the time it reached Daniel and Hawk, it felt cool and pleasant.

Daniel and Hawk built a huge fire near the rim of the mesa and roasted antelope meat over the blaze. The size of the fire had nothing to do with cooking meat or warmth, although it was actually much cooler atop the mesa than on the surrounding prairie.

The primary message the burning fire was meant to convey to the Indian warriors below was that the white men felt immune from danger. Undaunted by the array of painted savages, they were prepared to sit atop the mesa, enjoy their abundant food, and quench their thirst with a nearly endless water supply, until the foolish warriors finally saw the folly of their siege and rode away.

Daniel described the fire as disdain in face of danger. Hawk suggested that it was an ostentatious display of courage. It mattered not which it was, just as long as it worked.

Daniel and Hawk patiently watched the warriors

as they sat contentedly around their campfire until it was nearly dark. Then Daniel voiced his concern.

"They're letting the fire die instead of adding more fuel. I believe they intend to remove the body of the warrior in the rocks and then try to worm their way up the path. While there's still enough light left to see, let's move down the slope and take cover in a spot where we can see them if they try."

In case their vigil lasted throughout the night, they took one of the water bags and several chunks of dry meat in one saddlebag. Into the other saddlebag went the two pairs of dueling pistols they had taken from the Mendoza camp, together with an ample supply of pistol balls and powder horns. At close range, the short-barreled weapons might prove more effective than their long rifles. Fortunately, the pistols all shot the same size lead ball, an advantage in a gunfight, lest in the heat of battle the wrong size ball might be inserted in a pistol barrel. Daniel formulated a simple defense plan. Hawk would keep the rifles and the pistols loaded. He would not fire unless their hiding place was overrun. Otherwise, Daniel would do all the shooting.

They climbed down the slope, moving carefully from one shielding boulder to the next, until they reached a rocky niche, still high above the prairie, from which they could see all possible approaches to the base of the path. It was here that they settled down to their vigil.

"Since there are so many thick clouds in the sky, the moonlight will be dim much of the time," Daniel reminded Hawk. "It will make anyone who comes toward us difficult to see."

"Scan across your line of sight from one side to the other," Hawk suggested. "We detect movements from the powerful corners of our eyes that we might miss if we look straight ahead."

"I never knew that."

"It's an old sailor's trick."

Hawk smiled in the darkness. It wasn't often that he was able to teach his friend anything new about survival.

They scanned the area below them for the next two hours without success. Suddenly, Daniel touched Hawk's arm and whispered.

"Watch those clumps of sagebrush just to the right of the tall rocks near the base of the path."

Moments later, one of the clumps moved forward, followed by a second, then a third, and a fourth.

"There are four of them there, maybe more."

"I'd guess six or eight," Daniel agreed. "If they intend only to recover the body, I won't stop them. But if they set foot on the path, I'll fire. I hate to do it, but they must be stopped."

"Maybe wounding one of them would be enough."

"No! I can't risk it. This darkness makes precise accuracy difficult, and the Indians would most likely consider it a sign of weakness. My Cherokee friends taught me that in the Indian culture, there are certain times when only a death can tell the tale that must be told. I'm convinced that this is one of those inevitable times."

As Daniel finished speaking, the moon won its hide-and-seek game with the thick clouds and reappeared. In the dim light, they saw two warriors roll the body of their fallen comrade onto a blanket, then quickly drag it away. The next second, the moon ducked back into the clouds, but not before Daniel and Hawk saw a half dozen painted foes poised and ready to storm the path.

This path leading to the top of the mesa could be reached only by coming through the narrow cleft in the rock wall. It was so small and low that the horses brushed against the sides of the passageway and had to lower their heads in order to get through. Despite the dim light, the cleft was clearly visible from their hiding place because of a large phosphorescent rock a short distance away that bathed the opening in an eerie glow. Since the dead man lay some distance from the path, there was no chance anyone might stumble into the opening by accident. Daniel decided to center his rifle sights on the glowing rock. If the glow disappeared, he would fire because a man who could not dodge or hide, would be in the middle of the rocky doorway. At that short range, Daniel had no doubt that his shot would prove fatal to any intruder who was foolish enough to test his resolve.

A few minutes later, they heard several guttural words, then a grunt of exertion, probably as the dead man was hoisted up on someone's shoulder. Then silence.

"Maybe they've gone away," Hawk whispered. His soft words sounded like a prayer or a wish.

Whether prayer or wish, it mattered not, because at that very instant, the glow from the phosphorescent rock was blocked by the silhouette of a man's head and shoulders.

Daniel fired into the shadow.

The effect was immediate. The glow returned as the warrior fell backward, then quickly disappeared. As a second shadow quickly blocked the glow, Daniel fired a second shot from Hawk's rifle. Almost instantly, a third warrior tried to storm through the gap, but suffered a fate akin to his comrades by a shot from one of the dueling pistols.

Daniel continued his vigil with a pistol poised and ready while Hawk reloaded their weapons.

"Will the deaths of four of their friends be enough

to make them quit? Or will they be back?"

"I don't know," Daniel said honestly. "Violent death is not uncommon to the frontier, but these warriors must realize they can't get at us through that rift in the rock. I think they'll powwow for the rest of the night. They may try something else tomorrow, but I don't expect them to quit. They may decide to wait us out. The only thing that might make them leave is going home to brag about their successful warpath, all the ponies they stole, and the two frightened white men they chased up a mountain side."

The Indians did not attack the following day, nor for several more days. Most of the time they simply sat on the prairie and waited patiently. A few times each day, one of them would spring atop his horse and dash toward them, shaking a long lance or a short coup stick. As they watched the first wild dash, Hawk asked about the significance of the stick. Daniel explained that Indians held bravery in high esteem. The bravest act of all was to touch an armed and dangerous enemy with a short coup stick, and hence "count coup on an enemy." Each coup a warrior counted added a feather to his war bonnet. Once Daniel had seen a Cherokee warrior whose bonnet contained so many feathers that they bumped his heels as he walked.

"I'm for people earning feathers," smiled Hawk.

"To give the 'coup maker' more credibility, as well as to convince them we're alert and have plenty of powder and shot, I'll fire over any warrior who charges in close to us."

During the following week, this procedure became a ritual. A warrior would suddenly quit the campfire and race toward them, with his horse's tail flying out behind. On he would come, riding tall, shouting and shaking his lance or coup stick as he came, until the sound of Daniel's rifle ended the pell-mell charge. Then with a final shout and shake, he would casually turn and ride triumphantly back to his companions. How long this routine might have gone on is hard to say, but it was suddenly interrupted on the eighth day of the siege.

By then, the remaining water was so low that after Daniel had watered each filly by pouring enough to fill the crown of his hat, it was half gone. Hawk emptied the last few drops into the breakfast burgoo. Before nightfall, they would have to begin chopping down a few of the barrel cactus plants and extracting enough moisture to survive. It was not a procedure either of them relished. They had split one of the plants open a few days earlier in an effort to test the theory. The only similarity between cactus juice and water was the wetness. Cactus pulp was tough, bitter and nasty, but if you chewed enough of it for long enough, you could stay alive.

Perhaps the Indians were losing interest in the siege, or maybe they were growing tired of the coup game, because the first warrior did not quit his camp until mid-morning. But once his ride began, he thundered toward them, waving his lance and whooping in loud defiance. When Daniel's shot whistled past his ear, he drew back on the long rawhide thong that was tied around his pony's lower jaw. So abrupt was the tug that the animal fell back on its hunches and actually slid across the prairie for a short distance before skidding to a halt. Perhaps an unseen signal passed between the rider and his mount, for the next instant the mustang rose high on his hind legs, his fore legs beating a frantic tattoo in the air. So high did he rise, and so long hang suspended, that he resembled a marionette dancing at the end of a master puppeteer's string. Heartbeats later, the extraordinary display of balance ended with the pony momentarily tottering before his front hooves came crashing down. In an instant, he had turned away and was racing over the prairie, away from the dangerous mesa toward the welcome safety that only existed beyond the killing range of the white men's deadly rifles.

Not to be outdone, a few minutes later, a second warrior mounted and dashed forward. Long before he reached the imaginary line Daniel had established as his no trespassing zone, a volley of gunfire sounded beyond the northern flank of the mesa and a large group of well-mounted, well-armed, buckskin-clad frontiersmen galloped into view. The effect of their shots on the warrior who moments earlier had been so intent on counting coup was both apparent and immediate. He staggered under the impact of several bullets. His superior horsemanship and the fact that he was able to grasp a handful of the pony's mane as a means of retaining his balance were the only things that prevented a disastrous fall from his racing mount. It was apparent to Daniel and Hawk that the warrior had been seriously wounded. Nonetheless, he was able to wheel his horse and followed his companions. The remaining Indians, eager to escape the wrath of the fast approaching and proven-deadly frontiersmen, had each leaped astride a handy pony and scattered in several directions. Behind them they left dozens of horses and all of the booty they had collected during their recent raid.

Daniel and Hawk watched as two dozen riders in the rescue party hastened past the mesa and dashed after the fleeing warriors for a short distance before they reined in their horses and rode back to the mesa. As they approached, Daniel recognized the two horsemen in the vanguard. One was a grizzled frontier veteran named Ben Milam, who referred to himself as Old Ben. His uncle, Stephen Austin, and Ben Milam were old friends. Daniel had met him several times during the past year in Bexar. The second man was the famous scout and Indian fighter, Deaf Smith. Everyone called him "Deef."

The rest of the Texicans returned from their brief chase and dismounted near the base of the path. As soon as the horses settled down, Daniel leaned out over the mesa's rim and shouted down to Milam.

"Old Ben! It's Daniel Austin! You got here in the nick of time!"

"I don't know about that, Young Austin! It seemed like you were keeping the Comanche at bay without our help! C'mon down!"

Daniel and Hawk began collecting their things, stuffed the last of their cooked food and empty water skins into saddlebags, gathered up the camping equipment, rain gear, and personal items that could be rolled up in blankets and wrapped in waterproof slickers, secured the blanket rolls behind the saddles, and saddled the fillies.

The descent down and across the face of the mesa proved to be much more difficult than the upward journey had been. Both horses were skittish and reluctant to trust reoccurring areas of loose, slippery gravel. Daniel went first leading Raven. Each time one of her feet began to slide, she quickly lifted it and stood precariously balanced on three legs for a few seconds, then cautiously lowered the hoof and moved it about until she found a firm place to plant it. Only her confidence in Daniel, his soothing voice, and reassuring hand on her bridle allowed Raven to overcome her fear and to inch her trembling way slowly down the precarious path until she finally arrived on the welcome expanse of flat prairie. At her heels came Sovereign, who had simply followed along in Raven's footsteps. Daniel wondered if Hawk would ever realize how different leading the way had been for Raven and himself.

Ben Milam and Deaf Smith met them as soon as they emerged from the rocks at the foot of the path.

"Who's the stranger with you, Daniel?" Milam asked. "That sure ain't your Uncle!"

Daniel introduced Ken Hawkins to both men, then broke the news that Daniel had escaped from prison in order to deliver a warning to the Texicans.

"Santa Anna has imprisoned Uncle Stephen! Now he plans to bring an army up to Texas and punish us. He said we've forgotten our rightful place and need to be taught a hard lesson. Uncle Stephen sent me to warn all the Texicans. He's certain that Santa Anna is committed to quelling rebellions and unrest in the southern provinces. That will take at least a year, but the Mexican army will number more than ten thousand soldiers and they will be here by the early months of 1836."

"Thanks to your warning, Daniel, we'll have some time to get ready." Milam remarked. "Right now, we're on a big ride-around patrol to the outlying ranches to be sure everybody's okay. We have another dozen or so to look in on before we head back to Bexar. We'll be there by the end of next week. How about you two riding along with us until then? On the 15th, the Feast of the Assumption will bring most people into Bexar. Jim Bowie, General Sam, the de Veramendis, and Salazars for sure. Probably a good many more. You can deliver your uncle's message and we can hold a council of war."

"If General 'Big He Bear' Santa Anna is comin' hisself, the least we can do is fix up a real big frolic for him. Maybe we can't stop him from comin,' but we gotta be sure he's limpin' when he goes home!"

VII
THE FUTURE OF TEXAS

SAN ANTONIO DE BEXAR
AUGUST 15, 1834

At the conclusion of the Holy Mass to celebrate the Feast of the Assumption, the citizens of Bexar gathered in the main plaza for a fiesta. It was a day of great joy to celebrate the Assumption of the Blessed Mother, body and soul, into heaven, where she was crowned the beautiful Queen of Heaven.

Mountains of food were piled on long tables under a ramada of vividly colored wild flowers strung on green leafy branches and covered by awnings made from yellow-and-white-striped canvas. There were sweet drinks for ninos, bubbling wine for Señoritas, and aguardiente for caballeros. Every nino had a chance to attack a piñata with a long stick, and was rewarded by a cascade of dolces. Strolling bands played lively tunes to which people danced the jota, zorita, and fandango. The most agile dancers performed the jarabe.

In the late afternoon, minutes before the fast approaching siesta hour drove the crowd away from the plaza and back to their adobe haciendas,

Maria Lopez, Bexar's famous dancer, entertained her audience with la bomba, the most difficult and brilliant of all dances. She began by balancing a tumbler of water on her head then, as the music began, she danced around and around, one intricate step after another blending into a blur of fascinating motion and incredible grace. Below her daintily held skirts, her ruby-colored dancing shoes seemed to twinkle.

Then a gaily-costumed caballero stepped out of the crowd. He removed his neckerchief, tied the ends to form a loop, and tossed it into the ring. The dancer circled the loop three times before she finally thrust her foot forward, caught up the neckerchief on one flying toe, then flipped it into the air and caught it in her hand. All the while, not a step did she miss, nor a drop of water did she spill. Loops rained down on the ring from all sides, and time after time the talented girl repeated her artful demonstration of balance and skill. When the music finally ended, she bowed and left the plaza, accompanied by a salvo of thunderous applause. The entertainment over, the revelers were reminded that it was time for a siesta. They scattered to the various quarters of the village and would not be seen for the next couple of hours.

Daniel and Hawk, accompanied by Old Ben Milam and Deaf Smith, strolled the short distance that was required to reach the hacienda of Don Jose Antonio Navarro. Don Jose was the brother-in-law of the late vice-governor of Tejas, Juan Martin de Veramendi, brother of Don Juan's wife, Dona Josefa, and Ursula Bowie's uncle.

It had been Navarro who confirmed the dire news to Bowie about the tragic deaths of Ursula, her two children, and her parents, during a cholera epidemic that struck Monclova in September, 1833, and killed 571 people on the three days between September 5th and September 8th.

Their deaths ended exquisite happiness the Bowies had enjoyed since Padre Refugio de la Garza joined them in joyous wedlock on April 25, 1831. During those wonderful thirty months, Ursula brought forth a daughter, a lovely miniature of her mother, and a tiny son that Bowie never saw.

He had expected to return from a vital business trip to Louisiana by early June, in time for the birth of their second child, but he had been delayed several times by one difficulty after another. It was the end of September when he stopped at San Felipe for the night before beginning the final leg of his homeward journey. He had been in his room, preparing for bed, when a mozo arrived with a polite note from Señor Williams, the alcalde. The message requested Bowie to visit at his first convenience. It was from Williams that he received the news of his family's deaths.

Since that day, Bowie had not known a moment of peace. The burden of his family's sudden deaths was magnified by his feelings of guilt. If only he had not gone on the business trip to Louisiana, if only he had come home sooner, if only he hadn't sent them to Monclova, if only he had died with them! If only...If only... If only... The long dark days, and long, even darker nights became black weeks, then descended into unbearable months. The passage of time might have begun to heal the self-imposed trauma of an ordinary man, but Bowie was no ordinary man. The spectacular and greatly admired adventures that had created a somewhat notorious American hero would have been impossible for a common mortal. No, Bowie had always been bigger than life, brighter than life, disdainful of all the mundane activities that satisfied other men. The continuing grief was almost certainly one major by-product of that renown. His self-recrimination reached far beyond the depth and darkness to which an ordinary mortal could sink— an anomalous mental state that offered little hope of recovery.

During the two years that followed Ursula's death, Bowie became known as El borrachon, a coarse, but descriptive idiom, accurately translated as driveling drunkard. His nights were spent drinking tequila and trying to ignore the vicious vampires of agony that stomped and cavorted on his chest so mercilessly that he was forced to fight for air. As the terrible hours of night crept by, breathing became evermore difficult, until it was all but impossible. Long after dawn crept into the eastern sky, long after the final drop of tequila had been sucked from the last bottle, phantoms of darkness hammered rusty iron spikes through his throbbing temples and anchored them deeply within his feverish brain. His pickled mind and defeated spirit were no match for the hideous creatures that his imagination conjured up to torment him.

Bowie may well have perished in his private hell if Sam Houston had not sought him out in June 1835. Santa Anna would soon arrive, punishing, pillaging, and slaughtering as he came. Texas needed every patriot to repulse his vindictive onslaught. And there was no question about Bowie's patriotism, courage, or fighting ability. So Houston, another great man who had once wallowed in self-pity, came and saved Bowie from himself. No one else could have done it! Because he did, a glorious page in American history was written. But it was August 1834, not June 1835, and Bowie was still ten months away from salvation.

Jim Bowie was a notable absence at the Feast of the Assumption meeting; but many others who were destined to play key roles in the future of Texas were present.

Since Jim was absent, in his place sat his elder brother, Rezin. In some ways, the brothers were nearly opposites. Jim was taller, broader, brasher, far more robust and quicker to anger. Renowned knife fighter, tavern brawler, high stakes gambler, duelist, and the designer of a famous knife, Jim Bowie was not a man to be irritated or underestimated.

Rezin was both wise and slow to anger. His psyche boasted far more reason than rashness. He was not a knife fighter, brawler, or duelist, but he was an avid gambler. His willingness to take a risk had made him an equal partner with Jim and Don Juan Veramendi in a million-acre acquisition and sale of Texas land. Veramendi's influence had made land acquisitions possible; but it was Jim and Rezin who approached, convinced, and sold big slices of America's future to dozens of rich and eager speculators in the southern United States. It had been one such business trip that delayed Jim Bowie for so long.

Jim and Rezin always had been a good team. They had been born in Georgia and raised on Louisiana's backwater bayous. Both were honest, hard working men who were willing to bet everything they had on any investment that their good judgment indicated would yield a profit. Jim was by nature a plunger.

Rezin was reserved. Jim decided on impulse. Rezin studied every aspect before he made a commitment. Those differing viewpoints had served them well in every venture that preceded their current Texas land development project.

Their first gamble had involved buying the cotton harvests of the small farmers in the northern areas of Louisiana who lacked the means of marketing their crops. That required transporting cotton bales down the Mississippi River to the New Orleans' waterfront on flatboats, where the New Orleans Cotton Market provided a ready outlet for the hundreds of bales the Bowies accumulated. Each trip garnered a handsome profit. On their final sojourn, they met the infamous pirate, Jean Lafitte. A notorious, self-serving man, Lafitte's single redeeming moment came as Andrew Jackson's ally at the Battle of New Orleans, in 1815. Lafitte convinced the Bowie brothers that they could triple their cotton profits if they began selling slaves. So they quit their cotton business and plunged heart and cash into the slave trade.

Jean Lafitte bought slaves in Africa or Cuba, then shipped them to one of the countless isolated beaches along the Gulf Coast. There the Bowies, as well as many other slaver buyers, purchased groups of bewildered men, women, and children at pre-determined prices, as soon as they were brought ashore from the holds

Bruce T. Clark

of Lafitte's ships.

When the sale of the human cargo was complete, their new owners shackled them together in chained strings of a dozen, and the entire entourage headed northward along little known, seldom used swamp trails and bayou paths en route to suitable market places. Many slaves were sold to enthusiastic buyers at cotton plantations all along the line of march, as well as at formal slave auctions that were frequently conducted in plantation country villages and towns. Wherever these auction blocks happened to be, the outcome was identical. Forged official records were produced, which proved that every slave had been in America by 1808, (the last year slaves could legally be imported) or was a child of a slave who had been in residence at that time.

As these slave auctions proceeded, slave families ceased to exist. Human beings were bid on, sold, and delivered to new masters. Husbands and wives often were wrenched apart and forced to watch as their children were sold to the highest bidders. Owners claimed their new possessions, chained them, singly or in groups, and marched them away. Most would never meet again.

When the last slave disappeared, it was time for successful slavers to seek out local taverns, where they gathered to celebrate, and to spend the pieces of silver their marches of misery had produced.

After a few such slave trips, Jim and Rezin Bowie decided to terminate their misguided careers for two different reasons.

Their consciences simply would not permit them to profit from human misery; and second, they discovered to their sorrow that some Indian tribes living around the remote swamps and bayous were cannibals. On many a moonless night along the march to market, one or more of the slaves would be unshackled and led to freedom by a stealthy, helpful, red savior, to a hoped-for freedom that never came.

In 1824, the Bowie brothers quit the slave trade, pooled their profits, and set off to try their luck and skill in the bloody, bawdy, and booming town of Natchez, Mississippi.

Now it was ten years later, and Rezin Bowie was in Texas trying to salvage a land empire into which he had sunk his life savings. It seemed an impossible task since his most influential partner was dead, and his other partner, his beloved brother, was a drunkard. As if that weren't bad enough, Santa Anna, the dictator who disdained Americans, would soon cross the Rio Bravo, intent upon executing anyone who displeased him. Rezin sometimes wondered if it would be a noose or a bullet that would end his life.

As they entered Jose Navarro's long, well-shaded, cobble-stoned patio, Daniel observed Sam Houston standing at the opposite end. Born in 1793, Houston had been a soldier and a Congressman who fought in support of States' Rights prior to his 1827 election as the governor of Tennessee. Two years later, as he was nearing the end of his term, he wed beautiful, blond, Eliza Allen, a young woman half his age, the daughter of Nashville's Colonel John Allen. A dozen weeks after the marriage, Sam found Eliza weeping over a tear-stained love letter from one of her former suitors. Enraged, Sam sent the child-woman home to grow up, and resigned as governor. Assuming total responsibility for the failed marriage, Houston went off to Oklahoma, where he spent the next two years as a storekeeper and Cherokee spokesman.

Throughout those years of his self-imposed exile, Houston remained the close friend and protégé of President Jackson. It was not surprising when, at the President's behest, Houston arrived in Nacogdoches in 1833, took up temporary residence, and attended the Constitutional Convention held at Washington-on-the-Brazos. As soon as the convention ended, Houston returned once more to the Cherokee Nation. In early 1834, he returned to Texas, and had been a patriotic, outspoken advocate of Texas independence since that day.

Houston was engaged in conversation with three other men. The first, James Fannin, a man in his mid thirties, had left West Point after two unimpressive years to become a slave trader. He had arrived in Texas with his wife and two children a year before, and described himself to Steve Austin as the world's finest strategist, and foremost military leader. Daniel whispered to Hawk that Fannin was probably trying to sell Houston on his extraordinary qualifications.

Another man in the group was facing them as they entered. He nodded to them and smiled graciously. William Barrett "Buck" Travis was four years older than Daniel. The disorganized and somewhat moody South Carolina lawyer had fled to Texas after the death of a man who was reputed to be a lover of his unfaithful wife. Six months after Travis arrived, the wife appeared and attempted a reconciliation. When her advances were spurned, the wretched soul left Texas and disappeared. Buck Travis was as loyal a friend as he was a bitter enemy. Although given to occasional displays of a violent temper, Travis had proven to be courageous, dedicated to independence, and stoically dependable. As a reward for his efforts, Travis had been elevated to the rank of major and given command of the twenty-seven-man garrison in Bexar.

The third man, James Butler Bonham, was about a

year younger than Daniel. Despite his youth, he had become one of Travis' closest friends. Bonham was also a respected fighting man, someone you wanted near you whenever the going got tough.

Since other prominent citizens were still expected, Señor Navarro announced that the meeting would be delayed until they arrived. After accepting tart citrus thirst quenchers from the liveried mozos, Daniel and Hawk seated themselves on an old oak bench placed against one of the ancient adobe walls, all of which were draped with Spanish moss.

As he surveyed the guests, Hawk's attention was claimed by their attire. Mexican leaders, such as the Navarros, Granados, Mirandas, Garcias, Salazars, Mendozas, and Juan Seguin, the distinguished alcalde of Bexar looked cool and confident in traditional Mexican fiesta outfits that leaned heavily toward ornate fringes and gaudy trimmings.

Texican leaders, principally lawyers, were clad in stylish broadcloth outfits befitting their legal status. Most others wore buckskin, or simple trousers made from homespun, topped by bright calico shirts. Padre Garza, of course, wore his long white cotton robe. Wide-brimmed sombreros, designed to ward off the blinding effects of the nearly constant sunlight, were the only common item of apparel. Hawk shared his observation, and was surprised by Daniel's reply.

"Most of them have something more important in common. They're Catholics and they're Mexican citizens. As you know, Mexico won independence from Spain in 1821. The next year, Uncle Stephen was permitted to bring a large number of families to Texas. They're known as the 'Old 300.' In return for the right to settle in Texas, they agreed to convert to the Catholic faith, to obey Mexican laws, and to free their slaves. When the Mexican Constitution of 1824 was passed, it restated the rules, and provided equal protection under the law for those American settlers, called Texicans by the folks who liked them, and Americanoes by those who did not. Despite the new constitution, the Texicans were treated like second class invaders by some local residents and most local officials."

Daniel paused to sip his drink, and discovered a number of the other guests were listening closely.

"In 1826, Haden Edwards, one of the Texicans, fomented a minor revolution and then declared the Republic of Freedonia on land he had been granted. Since he was largely unsupported by Uncle Stephen and most of the other Texicans, his revolt ended bloodlessly a year later. Nonetheless, it served to alert the Mexican officials about an undercurrent of unrest here in Tejas. That unrest made them uneasy. Uncle Stephen tried to quell their concerns for the next three years, but had almost no success."

He paused for another sip of his drink and realized that his half circle of listeners now numbered almost everyone on the patio, including Sam Houston and the rest of his group.

"As you all remember, in 1830, Mexican officials forbade all further settlement by Americans. By last year, when Santa Anna assumed power, there were over 20,000 Texicans. Now Santa Anna has repealed the Constitution of 1824, negated trial by jury, made Spanish the only legal language for every document, and he has instituted trade and customs regulations that have brought commerce to a halt. For these reasons, Uncle Stephen requested a meeting with Santa Anna.

"At the meeting, Santa Anna expressed a concern he might lose the Estado de Tejas, which he wants to retain as a buffer zone against the Plains Indians. His only benefit, he says, to keeping some Americans in the area, is to blunt the Indian's lust for blood before they reach outlying Mexican villages. To accomplish his goal, he doesn't need 20,000 Americans. Therefore, he has created new laws. First, only legal Mexican citizens are welcome in Tejas. All others will be shot on sight if they are caught. Secondly, even legal citizens who break any Mexican law will be shot if caught. Thirdly, anyone who takes up arms against a lawful Mexican government will be shot on sight, without trial, without quarter. His message is crystal clear, gentlemen. 'Get out and don't come back.'"

Daniel paused and looked around the circle of hardened, determined faces, then continued.

"Uncle Stephen sent me with a message. He's sure Santa Anna will be too busy crushing local revolts to attack us right away. If the majority of Texicans pull stakes and run, he'll let the others stay; otherwise, he'll come north sometime around the end of next year. Santa Anna's principal targets will be the main Texican settlements at Goliad, Gonzales, San Felipe, and San Antonio. He'll strike down as many other people and places as he can along his line of march. He told us that after he razes all our 'rebel roosts,' he'll hunt down every last ringleader and put each of us to the sword."

"Almighty Santa Anna might not find that quite as easy as he imagines!" Buck Travis retorted angrily. "Texicans haven't cast everything we own into plow shares. We have a few swords left to fight with."

"Almighty Santa Anna might not find it as hard as you imagine, either," Houston scowled darkly as he delivered the stinging rebuke. For the first time, Hawk realized what most men at the meeting already knew. Houston and Travis were not friends.

"Santa Anna can put at least ten thousand seasoned

troops in the field. That's more than ten times the number of men we can muster," Houston spat out.

"Most of his soldiers are simple peons who barely know which end of a musket the rounds come out!" Buck countered.

"That's an invalid point," the lawyer in Houston protested, "for many reasons. As Daniel Austin just pointed out, the Mexican army will be busy putting down local rebellions for the next year. If they don't know which end of a tube the rounds come out of now, they sure as hell will know before then! Your second fallacy is this. Even if they can't fire a musket, they will charge forward on cue because they fear Santa Anna much more than they fear us. Finally, many of the officers in the Mexican army, particularly the Lancers and the Dragoons, are recent arrivals from Europe. They sure aren't poor peons! They're professional soldiers from England, France, and Spain. With a year to train and drill their men, they'll be able to produce light cavalry and assault units as good as those on the European Continent."

"You sayin' we can't whip a parcel of Mexicans?" a disbelieving Old Ben Milam queried.

It was Fannin who answered.

"What General Sam is saying, Old Ben, is that we have to outsmart them in order to win. We can't play the Marquis Louis de Montcalm to Santa Anna's

General James Wolfe on the Plains of Abraham. We must engage at a precise moment on a battlefield that favors us. Right, General Sam?"

Houston scowled once more. Fannin really loved to hear himself talk. Only a small handful of the men had ever heard of the Plains of Abraham, much less Wolfe or Montcalm, but Fannin knew something about tactics. Houston decided to say so.

"Fannin's right. We can't whip Santa Anna on battlefields that he chooses, but we can beat him if we fight him in places that favor us."

"Where might that be?" Travis demanded.

"Between the Rio Bravo and Red River. His army will have to ford dozens of creeks and rivers. There is bound to be hundreds of places where we can set up an ambush and pick off some of them. A small pack of Indian fighters like Old Ben and Deaf could pick them off, a few at a time, all the way across Texas. Cut, slash, and run, until they work their way into a big mousetrap. While that's going on, we can raise and train a fair sized army."

"We have a year to prepare, thanks to Daniel Austin and his warning," Juan Seguin observed, bobbing his head toward Daniel in silent salute, "but will one year be enough?"

"On the surface, it seems adequate, Señor Sequin," Houston replied, "but it's really very little time because of two things. First of all, when trouble comes over the horizon, men with families will have to protect them, something they can't do if they're miles away, getting ready to fight an approaching enemy. No Texican will be willing to leave his wife and kids at the mercy of unseen Indian enemies to intercept a bunch of approaching Mexicans. Men we recruit must be single, or older men with grown up families. There are some villages in Texas where all of the women and children can be forted up in one safe place. Half of those men can come to join us, and the rest can bide at home to protect the women and young'uns. I can guarantee one thing. Most men won't believe Santa Anna's really coming until he kills a few dozen Texicans."

"I wish we had lots more guns," Fannin said. "The Lancer officers you talked about aren't fools. They know it's pretty safe to figure one weapon per man. Once a man fires his rifle, he's virtually helpless 'til he can reload. If every Texican had a couple of extra rifles, he could keep shooting while his wife or kids reloaded for him. Each extra rifle would be almost as good as adding an extra man."

Alberto Salazar, a local merchant, asked a question that suggested he knew nothing about warfare.

"If Santa Anna's army is as powerful as you say, won't they simply crush everything in their path?"

"An army of ten thousand men doesn't march in a long line. At least two thousand of them are cavalry. Mexican Lancers are Santa Anna's eyes and ears, as well as his mobile attack force. As soon as his army crosses the Rio Bravo, Santa Anna will split his Lancers into squads no larger than a dozen men. In that way, his mounted patrols will be able to cover maximum amounts of territory in minimum amounts of time. Twelve man squads may range as far as a half-day ride from the main column. A dozen well-armed, well-mounted men are more than enough to subdue most ranchos and villages. If they run across anything too big to handle, the leader marks the spot on the map, skirts around it, and sends a rider back to the main column. Then a more powerful unit can be sent out to deal with the situation. Meanwhile, the original squad goes on to easier pickings."

Fannin paused and perused Salazar's face to be certain that he understood, and then continued.

"When you divide two thousand Lancers that way, you have two hundred independent strike units that can attack as many remote ranchos, settlements, and outposts as they can find. If every Texican had a few extra rifles, and the attackers expected them to have to reload after each shot, they could finish off a lot of the Lancers before they knew what hit them. It would almost be like having two or three times as

139

many fighting men to stand up to them. It would not only put more enemies out of commission, it would sap their morale to be hoodwinked by "dirt grubbin' nesters" that are supposedly no match for them. But, unfortunately, my whole idea is only a pipe dream. We have enough time to buy more weapons and to distribute them, but we simply don't have the funds to do it. War is a very expensive business."

Louis Rose, a man who had served as an artillery officer in Napoleon's Grand Army, spoke up.

"It occurs to me that very few of Santa Anna's foot soldiers have faced an enemy capable of defending themselves. What kind of weapons could they expect Mexican farmers or village dwellers to own? Sharp scythes? Rusty swords? At best, old muskets that don't fire half the time! The average man in that army must think he's invincible. Why shouldn't he? He has never tasted the bitter bile of fear or defeat. Before we can hope to defeat a force ten times the size of our own, we must instill that fear."

"Far easier said than done," Fannin interjected.

"Yes, but possible! The Emperor Napoleon used to say that most men who face cannon fire for the first time will run until they're too worn out to run any farther. If we just had a few cannons! If we could bombard the main column a few times from ambush, half of the trembling Mexican army would be ready to quit, despite Santa Anna."

Once again, Alberto Salazar voiced his skepticism.

"Forgive my ignorance, Señor Rose, but are not cannon much too heavy to be dragged around the countryside?"

"Some yes! Some no! The cannon I was thinking about is called a cohort. Perhaps you are unfamiliar with the word. A cohort was a group of between 300 to 600 men. Ten cohorts made up a Roman Legion. Napoleon named a small, portable cannon a cohort because he said the gun's surprise appearance, and the devastating effect of its double load of musket balls were worth as much as 500 men in the close quarters of a heated battle. Since we're only pipe dreaming, my dreams are about a gun that fires six pounds of grapeshot, and blows a hole in charging rank as wide as a boulevard in Paris."

"As long as we're dreaming, let's include several thousand European mercenaries." Houston frowned. "If we hire ten thousand, they can fight Santa Anna while we drink tequila at a pleasant cantina and await the battle reports. Everything Fannin and Rose said is true. More small arms, and a few portable cannon, make a lot of sense. For that matter, the mercenaries do too, but there's a big fly in the buttermilk. In all of Texas, there aren't enough riches to pay for our pipe dreams!"

Francisco Miranda, one of the youngest men at the meeting, cleared his throat and rose to his feet before he spoke.

"In the silver mine of my great grandfather are ten times the riches we need to pay for all our dreams!"

The dubious Salazar was the first to dispute him.

"Francisco, Lost Miranda Mine is the biggest pipe dream of all! Only a boy of your tender years could believe in such a foolish legend!"

Sudden silence descended on the patio as Texicans and Mexicans, young and old, leaders and followers, impetuous or placid, awaited Miranda's response. Despite his youth, Don Francisco had defended his honor in two previous duels. Salazar's provocative words certainly were grounds for a lethal challenge to be issued.

The young caballero stared silently at Salazar, but a sudden flush of dark crimson bore mute testimony to his outrage. It began in the open neck of his white silk shirt, crept slowly up his throat, invaded his cheeks, and finally darkened his entire face. Several expectant moments passed before he finally replied in a stony, measured tone.

"Miranda's Silver Mine is no legend, foolish or otherwise. My great, great grandfather found silver, and built a smelter to convert the ore into pure silver bars. While he was living among the Lipan Apaches,

Señor James Bowie actually saw some of those bars. You have insulted me, Señor Salazar, but I will take no offense, since wine very often replaces wit. I will, however, ask you not to try my patience any further on this subject."

Francisco's warning could not be mistaken for anything other than promised mayhem. Even the wine-dulled brain of Alberto Salazar comprehended the potential danger. The last thing he wanted to do was to incite further animosity, much less provoke a duel to the death, his own death. Nonetheless, it was excruciatingly painful to sit silently, and accept the young man's admonishment, delivered, as it was, in the presence of other Bexar leaders.

Padre Refugio Garza wisely broke the tension.

"Francisco is right about the mine and the smelter. Records were brought here to the Alamo from San Saba mission after a war party destroyed it in 1755. The lone survivor of that Apache massacre brought documents when he came to report the sad deaths of the other padres, as well as those of Señor Miranda and his workers at the silver mine. The padre who was in charge of the Alamo at that time recorded his testimony, which spoke of silver bars and Tomas Miranda's generosity. He said Don Tomas, who was a noted construction engineer for many years before he discovered the silver mine, credited his good fortune to Our Blessed Lord. So he annually made a generous gift to the church. I have not examined those old parchments for many years. I am almost afraid that the eighty-year-old, yellowed pages may have fallen apart by now. I remember one reference to an enigma about the mine. The San Saba padre inscribed a marginal note, saying Tomas Miranda had entrusted to him a copy of his will in which he bequeathed all of the silver in the smelter to the mission, and a cryptic letter containing clues to the silver mine's location. Unfortunately, the fire that destroyed the mission destroyed most of Miranda's papers as well. I fear the remaining scraps would be an insufficient source of data even for a most ardent researcher. There are seven stout chests filled with records from the San Saba mission in my smallest storeroom, but I have never had the time or curiosity to study them. In addition to the fact that most of the parchments are charred scraps, all of the official records are transcribed in Latin. I presume that data referring to the mine or the smelter is also in Latin. Correspondence from Señor Miranda would, of course, be in Spanish. It would require a very patient person, familiar with Latin, as well as Spanish, to discover references to Señor Miranda and his fortune of silver."

Padre Garza smiled and looked at Daniel Austin

before he continued.

"Most of us here today, for one reason or another, are not qualified to conduct such a search. But Our Blessed Lord, in His infinite wisdom, has sent us someone who is eminently qualified. Not only is he a recent graduate of one of America's finest Catholic colleges, Daniel Austin is also a Latin and Spanish scholar, an experienced and gifted researcher, and a young man with a well-organized and inquiring mind."

"As always, Padre, you are too generous," Daniel blushed, "but I have done lots of research in the past few years. I'll be glad to go through every scrap of paper that remains. In my studies at Georgetown, I discovered that one bit of data often leads to another, and another, until a seemingly impossible enigma is solved. Let us hope and pray that is the case with the Miranda Papers and the San Saba documents. With your permission, Padre, I will begin in the morning."

Padre Garza nodded as Sam Houston responded.

"Padre, that's wonderful news. If the silver mine can be located, we can purchase additional weapons for defense, and many other things, as well. Daniel, each one of our lives, as well as the future of Texas, may well depend on your success in finding that silver mine! All of our prayers go with you."

Daniel was excited about helping to find a silver

145

mine that could provide funds the Texicans could use to fight the war against Santa Anna. Early the following morning, Daniel met with Padre Garza, and saw the seven wooden chests for the first time. Examining thousands of tiny charred parchment scraps proved to be much more difficult than Daniel or Padre Garza had imagined. Almost all the sheets were fragmented. Others that appeared to be singed only along the edges, on closer scrutiny, had burned out patches. Obviously, red-hot coals had burned the flimsy material. Quite often they obliterated a key word or phrase that obscured the writer's meaning.

After one month of tedious work, although Daniel had peered through a magnifying glass for more than ten hours each day, four of the crates of records were still unopened, and nothing had been found that shed any light on the location of the mine.

On September 17th, soon after finishing an early breakfast, Daniel returned to the rectory where he was using one corner of the Padre's study as an office. He lifted an unopened chest of documents onto a scarred, old oak table that served as his desk, and pried off the lid. When he peered inside, his face darkened. Although contents of this chest seemed to have suffered much less fire damage than any of the others, for some reason, very few of the sheets were whole. Jagged fragments resembled the pieces of a jigsaw puzzle before they were assembled and sorted out.

Daniel carefully withdrew a few scraps to test the parchment's stability. Several of the ancient records from other boxes had disintegrated at his touch, but these seemed to be quite sturdy. He spread pieces he randomly selected on the table, and began trying to find two fragments that fit together, turning various pieces first one way and then another. He removed more scraps and added them to the puzzle.

He sat rearranging pieces for nearly an hour, then decided to ask Hawk to work on the intricate jigsaw shapes while he perused some of the other contents of this new crate. Just as he rose to summon Hawk, Daniel's eye caught a strange word that did not seem to belong in such a document. He continued to study the fragments, searching for a connection. Daniel's persistence was rewarded as three additional words, on three separate pieces of parchment, claimed his excited attention by adding to the mystery. The four words were: plata, entrada, lavera, guillotina (silver, entrance, skull, guillotine).

Daniel slowly picked up the pieces, and carefully examined each one. The tiny fragments came from a single document. He could plainly see handwriting on all three was that of Tomas Miranda. It was also obvious that the scraps came from a superior grade of parchment than that used by the San Saba padres.

Daniel walked to the open window that overlooked Padre Garza's garden, and called to the gardener.

"Jorge, please find Señor Hawkins. Ask him to join me here as soon as it is convenient, por favor. I believe you'll find him at the stable, caring for the horses."

The gardener nodded and loped away.

Daniel carefully emptied the remaining contents of the crate onto the table and spread them out in a way that would make it simpler to see fragments that seemed likely to fit together. He'd just begun when Hawk entered.

"Your smile tells me you've found something."

"I've found clues that indicate I'm in the right box, and four words that are somehow connected: silver, skull, entrance, and guillotine. Now we need to put enough of the scraps together to decipher this letter."

"You're sure it's a letter?"

"Pretty sure. It's Señor Miranda's handwriting on his special parchment, and two of those words have no reason to be in a mission report of any kind. I have a hunch "skull" and "guillotine" somehow are connected to "silver" and "entrance," and they all have something vital to do with Miranda's bequest to the San Saba mission. If they don't, I'd be mighty surprised! Let's go to work and try to solve more of this puzzle."

Hawk smiled as he sat down at the table. He had always enjoyed reading mystery stories. Now it seemed he was going to be in the middle of one.

Very carefully, they smoothed and laid out each piece of parchment the box contained, then moved them around, as Daniel had earlier, in an attempt to find scraps that fit together.

Since there were hundreds of tiny fragments of old cracked parchment that tended to splinter still more as they were handled, the process was tedious and exasperating. It was midnight before they fitted the last piece into place. Despite their care and patience, there were still a great many open places, the results of fire damage or age. However, they did manage to piece together some of the parchment and decipher more words around skull and guillotine. When they were translated into English, they said, "… th hidde e tra ce of th San S b m ne c n alm st be se n by loo ng thr gh one eye of th skull whi e the morn Sun sh n s thr gh the ot er. A adit li s di ctly beh d the g bl d of t e guillotine …

Daniel and Hawk studied the cryptic message, and finally decided that it said, "…the hidden entrance of the San Saba mine can almost be seen by looking through one eye of the skull while the morning sun shines through the other. An adit lies directly behind the g--- blade of the guillotine."

"Seems clear except for the phrase 'can almost be seen' and the g---." Daniel said. The g--- describes the guillotine's blade, but a g, with an unknown number of blank letters behind it, could be almost anything. But we do know the mine is somewhere around the San Saba River, and the adit, or entrance, can almost be seen, west of a thing Miranda calls 'the skull'."

"It would be nice to know more, but now we have a place to start. Unfortunately, the San Saba Valley has been in the heart of Lipan Apache country for a great many years. Before we go anywhere near the San Saba, we better recruit a force of experienced frontiersmen."

"A very large force," Hawk agreed eagerly.

"I think the best thing to do is to talk with Old Ben Milam and Deaf Smith, and let them recruit the men we need. What do you think, Hawk?"

"I agree! I just hope they recruit a whole lot of them," Hawk yawned. "Let's talk to Old Ben and Deaf, first thing in the morning."

VIII
ENIGMA

SAN SABA RIVER VALLEY
NOVEMBER 1834

"We must have explored at least a hundred of these high, narrow canyons that pockmark the sides of this San Saba River Valley," Daniel Austin sighed, as he and Hawk rode along the twisting gorge behind old Ben Milam, Deaf Smith, and twenty volunteers they had recruited. Each was a savvy frontiersman and Indian fighter.

Confident of success, the twenty-four men had left Bexar six weeks earlier, and traveled northwest until they finally reached the San Saba River. There they began following the river and poking through the maze of canyons that jutted off at right angles along both banks. As day after frustrating day slipped past, the jaunty nonchalance and happy grins that had marked the beginning of the trip began to disappear. They were replaced by haggard expressions of resignation and deep frowns.

No one could deny that the San Saba Valley was a beautiful place, but the countryside was just as rough and rugged as it was beautiful. The vast green valley was bordered on both sides by towering jagged cliffs that dominated the landscape for nearly forty miles.

The valley would certainly be an ideal subject for an oil painting, Daniel had concluded. Art lovers in quiet, musty museums would marvel at the variety of contrasting colors that ran in wide bands along the rocky walls, and a plethora of fauna that covered the gently sloping riverbanks. However, it was one thing to sit in an art gallery and admire the rugged terrain depicted in a painting, and quite another to traverse the treacherous area on horseback. At each step, a horse could step into a hidden hole, catch a hoof in one of the long, green, clinging plant tendrils that seemed to reach out to snare them, or slip on the endless loose black gravel that covered both riverbanks.

Riding straight through the valley would have been difficult enough, but they were not merely traveling through the San Saba Valley to reach a destination. They were seeking treasure. They needed to explore each gap in the high walls to determine if it might be the mouth of the side canyon that would led them to the site of Tomas Miranda's silver mine. That silver would be the means to purchase the needed weapons and ammunition for the Texicans to fight Santa Anna and his troops.

Both walls were pockmarked with honeycombs of

ragged openings that led away from the river. Each one seemed to be more perilous and impassable than the last. Most of the steep-sided gorges opened up for short distances, then ended abruptly, while others coursed through hazardous rockslides and gigantic boulders for miles. So far, they all had ended at an unscalable wall. None of the canyons had offered a glimpse of, or even clue about, a skull. All they had to show for six weeks of hard work and effort in the unforgiving countryside were saddle-weary riders on footsore horses. Raven was even beginning to show the first signs of fatigue.

They soon would be forced to admit defeat and turn back. Today was the first day of November. Harsh winter storms could not be far off. These canyons were already treacherous. It would be suicidal to meander around in them after the first snowfall.

If only we can find the Miranda Mine in the next few days, Daniel thought. It was a more desperate prayer than hope. If we find the mine soon, we can build a snug shelter to shield us from the cold weather, as well as protect us from attacks by the Indians. Once winter sets in, it will be less likely for an Indian hunter or war party to chance upon us. Of course, if they do, regardless of the weather conditions, there will be hell to pay. Either we've been incredibly lucky, he mused, or especially protected by God. We've seen hoof prints of many horses, but so far we've managed to avoid contact with the roving bands.

Daniel decided to talk over their next move with Hawk, Old Ben, and Deaf when they camped for the night. At best, he felt they had only one more week before they'd be forced to turn back. Past that, risks from weather and the Apaches would simply be too great. It was time for them to make a decision and stop trusting to luck.

That afternoon, they followed a narrow creek that flowed into the San Saba. It coursed through a rocky gorge for two miles before the riverbank fell sharply away, and ended at an unassailable, eighty-foot wall, which effectively sealed the end of the box canyon.

It was a remarkably pretty place. Having wandered over countless rich mineral deposits along its course, the waters of the creek appeared to be a pale celery green as they cascaded over the sheer cliff. Flowing waters glistened momentarily in the sunlight, then crashed down on the rock ledge. Engrossed in this natural splendor, Daniel was not as alert as he should have been when Raven slipped on a small patch of moss that concealed an unseen bit of loose shale. The filly quickly recovered and regained her footing, but in the process, Daniel lost his hold and nearly fell off. As he clung to the saddle horn in a nearly horizontal position, his gaze chanced to light on an unusual rock formation. In his single fleeting glance, it seemed to resemble a squat human head, with a long nose, and a pair of jagged eye sockets.

Sitting upright in the saddle, even in the fading light of late afternoon, Daniel could see a faint glow behind the rocky socket eyeholes.

Cautiously allowing Raven to pick her own way down the uncertain and slippery path to the canyon's floor, Daniel waited until they reached level ground before he called excitedly to Old Ben and Deaf who were leading the way.

"Hold on! I think I've stumbled onto the skull!"

Hardly containing his excitement, he cautiously rode up to them and pointed toward the skull's ledge. But a cluster of trees blocked the view.

"Ride back up the slope with me!"

Hawk joined them, and they carefully guided their horses up the path. Daniel's flushed face showed his excitement. Suddenly, they all saw the rock-formed "skull." It was visible from only one small section of the hillside. A few feet above or below the precise level, thick foliage concealed it from view.

Men with less wisdom or faith might have marked Raven's fortunate slip as a stroke of luck, but not so these men. Each one recognized it as a positive sign that God intended to help the Texicans. So sure were they of His divine intercession, that all four offered a silent prayer of thanksgiving.

It was nearly dusk. A hint of daylight was all that remained, but the last fiery-red sliver of sun refused to meekly submit to the darkness. The glowing sky was an additional sign to the four men that God was blessing their search. It hung tenuously on the brink of the horizon for several more precious moments before it finally surrendered, and dropped below the crest of a distant mountain.

In the shadowy darkness of the settling dusk, they returned to their companions below and shared their discovery with great excitement. As the men tried to concentrate on gathering wood for cooking fires, all twenty-four speculated about the skull and what it would reveal. As the first light of a new day peeked through the eye of the skull the next morning, what would they learn? No one slept! The anticipation was much too great.

Breakfast was prepared and consumed in the dark of early morning, long before dawn began to invade the eastern sky. The sun was just a faint glow when Daniel, Hawk, Old Ben, Deaf, and Francisco began picking their way over the razor-sharp rocks that led up to a narrow rock ledge a few feet below the skull. Francisco slipped on an outcropping, gashed his shin in the process, but in his excitement, hardly noticed the blood and pain.

When they reached the ledge, they scrambled up onto it and inched their way along until they reached a spot behind the base of the skull just as the sun burst into view. While Daniel and Hawk peered through one eyehole, Deaf, Old Ben, and Francisco squinted through the other. In the first second, Daniel thought he understood Miranda's reference to the g---- blade of the guillotine. The view from the skull centered on the waterfall as it tumbled over the high cliff and thundered down on the rocks below. In the sunlight, if one employed his imagination, the swift descent of the torrent and shimmering, silvery green color of the rushing water might remind an observer of a guillotine's blade.

"If we deciphered the clues correctly, the adit must lie behind the waterfall! Remember one clue said it could almost be seen from here. But how can entry be gained through such a torrent of water?" Daniel voiced the question others were pondering.

"I learned many things sailing around the world," Hawk reminded Daniel. "One of the most important is that some impossible things only seem impossible. We know that a key to Miranda's puzzle exists, now we must be smart enough to find it!"

Hopeful that the waterfall's glistening green hue was the g... blade of the guillotine to which Miranda referred, they carefully descended from the ledge, walked back to camp and shared their information with the others as soon as they arrived.

"There must be an opening behind the falls," Rezin Bowie concluded. "We need to check that possibility before we do anything else."

Most of the men agreed with Rezin's suggestion.

"That's a lot o' raw power in that waterfall, boys," Old Ben observed, "more'n enough to flatten anyone crazy enough to stand under it."

"True enough, Old Ben," Rezin agreed, "but I still think we must find a way to try."

Several ideas were suggested and discarded before they finally agreed to anchor a safety rope behind the falls. Although the eighty-foot high granite wall was over a hundred feet long at its base, the falls covered only about one-fourth of that width. If the wall was divided into four equal parts, the falling water would have covered the inner quarter of the southeastern half.

A man could freely walk near the base of the wall along the northwestern half until he got close to the falls. The granite ledge would be slippery due to spray from the cascading water, but by exercising caution, a careful man could traverse the ledge.

The northwestern-most quarter of the wall was far rougher and more broken than the southeastern half, but still navigable. The only difficulty in traversing the entire distance would be the quarter of the wall covered by the murderous weight of tons of falling water.

Matt Clancy and four others rode a short distance down the creek, found a shallow place to ford, and then rode back up along the far bank. Matt tethered his horse and very carefully and very slowly made his way over the spray-covered section of the ledge, to the edge of the falling torrent. There he uncoiled a strong rope that he carried, one end of which was weighted with a slender stone. He began twirling the weighed end around and around overhead. On every revolution he allowed more rope to slip through his fingers, thus lengthening the arc. Finally, confident that he had enough momentum, he hurled the rope across the face of the waterfall to Hawk, who was waiting expectantly on the far. Matt's heave was so accurate that the stone passed perilously close to Hawk's head. Undaunted, he reached up, grabbed the rope, and wrapped it securely round his forearm.

The rope was then pulled taut, snug up against the cliff face behind the falls, and anchored at each end by four men. Then Hawk, belayed by a harness around his waist that was hooked to the rope, braved a stinging spray, and began examining the first part of wall just inside the fall's outer edge. Drenched and shivering after mere seconds in the icy water, he discovered that there was a narrow space, just large enough to form a small air pocket between the waterfall and wall. This meant a man would be able to breathe while he made his way along the ledge behind the waterfall, and searched for some type of opening.

Obviously, the smaller the man, the less pressure the water would be able to exert. The smallest man by far was the diminutive Peewee Potts. Famed as an excellent horseman, his short stature belied the upper body strength he had developed as a blacksmith. In the gauntlet of the waterfall, it would take all of his strength, as well as that of the four men on each end of the rope, to hold him against the awesome force.

Potts, excited by the adventure and his important role, bundled up in a rain slicker and a tight hat with a chinstrap, then he looped the safety rope through his body harness and tightened it around his chest. Once he was out of sight under the falls, the rope would be kept taut, and only payed out a tiny bit at a time in order to hold him firmly against the wall.

Peewee's trip beneath the waterfall was easier than anyone could have imagined. The wall behind the waterfall curved slightly inward. Each step Peewee took gave him a little more space to walk and to breathe. The rest of the party could scarcely believe his pace as the rope was payed out on one side and gathered in on the other. Peewee soon emerged on the far side of the falls, at which point the men let out a cry of joy! The moment Daniel saw the frown on Matt Clancy's face, he knew Peewee's report was not good. The bad news was confirmed minutes later when the dejected Peewee and the others returned to camp.

"No good, Daniel! I felt my way along the whole wall. The falling water has made it smooth. It seems to be really solid. There are some cracks, but nothing like an opening. I'm awful sorry!"

"It's not your fault, Peewee. You did a good job, a lot better than any of the rest of us could have done."

"One more thing," Peewee continued. I was kind of shaky as I got out of the torrent. I kept my balance by leaning on a part of the wall just beyond the falls. It felt as smooth as the wall under the falls. I wonder why?"

"Maybe the falls used to be wider than it is now. If so, the water would have smoothed that part of the wall, too," Daniel suggested.

"That makes good sense! I bet you're right."

Understandably deflated, the men returned to camp where they cooked a meal and warmed themselves around a big fire.

"I thought we really had the answer," Rezin Bowie told Daniel and the others. "Now, I'm stumped."

"Ever since we saw those falls last night," Daniel responded, "I've been pondering Señor Miranda's phraseology. He said 'an adit lies directly behind the g--- blade of the guillotine.' When we looked at the waterfall, we agreed that the 'g' might mean green, glistening, or something similar. But that 'g' isn't as puzzling as the two lines " directly behind the blade of the guillotine," and "can almost see the adit through the eye of the skull." We saw the falls, but nothing else. We assumed that the waterfall was Miranda's guillotine blade, and that the high wall had to be the thing directly behind it. But we see the waterfall! We don't almost see it! We do see it!"

Daniel sat quietly thinking for a full minute, while the others waited in anticipation for him to speak.

"What if the falls are the reason we can't see the adit? What if the falls are the reason we can almost see it! Then the waterfall wouldn't be a guillotine's blade, but only the veil that hides the real blade from view? If so, the blade must be part of an apparently solid wall that drops down like a guillotine blade, and exposes the adit after the falls are redirected."

Daniel's four listeners all looked incredulous.

"After the falls are redirected? How could that be done? What leads you to such a conclusion?" Rezin asked with amazement.

"To begin, I don't think Miranda would describe

the waterfall as a guillotine blade. Many parallels, offering far better descriptions, come to mind. And why did he stipulate the g--- blade of the guillotine?"

Rezin and the others nodded.

"I see your logic, but what does it mean?"

"A green, glassy, or gleaming waterfall dropping into place makes far less sense than a granite blade dropping into place. A granite blade that drops down and seals off access to the mine, then is raised again to restart the cycle? A cycle similar to the guillotine blade that is held aloof until it is needed, slams down with instant finality, and then has to be raised again each time it's reused."

"Go on, Daniel!" Rezin urged.

"Padre Garza described Miranda as a professional engineer who designed and built buildings, bridges, and aqueducts for many years before he discovered his silver mine. Padre said Miranda was intelligent and self-sufficient, with knowledge, experience, and ability, sufficient to design a smelter, and manpower enough to build it. I'm convinced he used that same ingenuity and engineering ability to design a hidden adit to the mine. Some type of sliding portal that drops down, then raises again like a guillotine blade. In addition to knowledge and manpower, Miranda required two other things."

"Power to operate the system!" Hawk jumped in.

"Correct! And the waterfall answered that need. Miranda also needed a way to regulate the power. I expect to find a control device, as well as a means of diverting the creek's path on top of the cliff."

Rezin Bowie's incredulous expression emphasized his words of doubt.

"The whole thing sounds pretty far-fetched to me!"

"I agree," Daniel admitted, "but there's a very easy way to find out for sure."

"By examining the top of the cliff, I'll bet!" Hawk frowned.

Daniel smiled at his friend.

"As usual, you've hit the nail on the head!"

"Forgive me if I overstate the obvious, but scaling that cliff's flat wall will be no easy matter."

"Assuming that I'm correct," Daniel continued, "and Miranda's system is controlled from the top of the cliff, I think we can eliminate the need to scale the wall. There must be a way to the top which we haven't yet discovered. If we discover one, we can pretty much scrap my theory."

"Since the front face of the wall is uniformly flat," Francisco Miranda jumped in, "it is obvious that no simple route to the top of the cliff exists."

"If one does exist," Daniel reasoned, "it has to be concealed around a corner of the front wall, on one of the side walls."

"A couple of you men stay here in the campsite! Daniel, I think we should start poking about, starting with the closest side wall?" Rezin suggested.

"Let's go!"

The men mounted and rode down to the corner of the southeast wall. There they dismounted and began forcing their way through thick timber and tangled underbrush that obscured the base of the wall. They hacked a path for nearly a mile, but found no breaks in the wall that offered a means of ascent to the summit. This wall appeared to be every bit as high, flat, and unassailable as the front wall.

They turned and retraced their steps over the path they had cleared. When they reached their horses, the men rode along the front wall, crossed the ford, and rode to the corner of the northwestern wall. Once more, an impenetrable stand of timber growing tight against the mesa's flank, stymied their ability to see more than a short distance. The visible portion of this wall appeared to be as smooth and impossible to climb as the front and the southeastern walls.

Convinced that they were on a wild goose chase, a majority of the men were ready to admit defeat and turn back by the time they had hacked a hundred yard path along the base of the wall. They finally reached an overgrown thicket of bramble bushes, and that proved to be the final straw for most of the men. After a strenuous day of cutting and digging, the general grumbling offered amble evidence of the men's resignation to defeat.

"Let's quit for today, Daniel." Rezin suggested. "We can hit it again in the morning."

Daniel nodded, and turned back with the others. Only Old Ben remained. He squinted at a grove of pine trees that skirted the edge of the brambles for several long seconds, and then called out to them.

"Stop! I see something!"

Old Ben walked along the edge of the brambles for a short distance, and suddenly disappeared through a tiny, all-but-concealed opening in the pine trees. He soon reappeared, and beckoned to them to come.

"This is the dangest thing I've ever seen," Old Ben announced as they reached him. "I noticed a few of these pine trees are growing bent over. On hills, it ain't surprisin', but these bent ones are all in pairs. And they're bending away from each other, just like small pines do when they grow along a narrow path. People walking along the path everyday push against them. Sooner or later, the trees get bent over a ways. Course, big pines don't bend! This path's been here for quite a spell, ever since these big pine trees was little fellas. Just follow me along."

The dozen men, led by Daniel, Hawk, Francisco, and

Deaf, eagerly followed Old Ben along an overgrown path as it curved through the pine trees in an arching semicircle. As they finally emerged from the trees, they found themselves standing at the base of a steep rock chimney. Long ago, perhaps as the result of an earthquake, a fissure had split the wall from top to bottom, and tumbled chunks of sheared-off rock into the breech. The result was a natural stairway leading to the summit of the cliff.

"You have found a way to the top of the cliff!" Daniel exclaimed. "I can't believe it! You have found it!"

"A stairway to the top!" Francisco yelled. "My great-grandfather was truly a very clever man!"

The men were so elated that they began jumping about, shaking hands, and hooting like wild Indians. Hawk, smiled broadly and cheered loudest, yelling "Hoorah! "Hoorah!" He made no effort to conceal his pride in Daniel's investigative powers.

After the whooping and dancing had run its course, Rezin Bowie put their feelings into excited words.

"Daniel, you have strange and mystical powers, or you're the best doggone puzzle solver I ever knew! My hat's off to you! I've no doubt we'll find the key to Miranda's mine, just as you said! Now boys, in addition to Daniel's brain, I believe we had a lot of divine help. Join me in kneeling and saying a prayer of thanksgiving."

All the men feel silent and dropped to their knees as Resin offered a grateful prayer of appreciation. Thanks to God's intercession and Francisco's great grandfather's brilliance, their efforts would be rewarded with enough silver to help the Texicans defeat Santa Anna's army.

IX
RESOLUTION

CELERY CREEK CANYON
NOVEMBER 1834

When the prayers ended, Daniel led the party up the natural staircase. Miranda's ingenuity was far more amazing than even Daniel imagined. Reaching the top of the cliff, they walked a short distance up the creek, and discovered the water coursing through a short, very narrow, rocky gully with high banks. Down the center of this gully ran a ridge, or spine, as high as both banks. At the upper end they discovered a large metal trough with strange protrusions jutting out from each side. Situated as it was at the mouth of the gully, it was obvious that the trough had been placed there to guide the water to either side of the central spine. The creek was now being diverted into the southeastern half of the gully. That side was the waterway. The northwestern half was a wadi. At the far end of this dry wadi, a waterwheel, similar to the ones Daniel had seen turning the great grindstones at grain mills, stood idly by. Beneath the waterwheel, they could see a large rusty winch with several loops of heavy cable still wrapped around its sturdy drum.

169

Hawk, after his many years at sea, recognized the simplicity of the system immediately.

"The big, funny looking things on the sides of the water trough are shaped like the rudders of a ship. Water pressure against the rudders swing the ship, or this trough, in the opposite direction. As you can see, the rudder that's in the water is forcing the trough to this side. When this one's raised, and the other one's lowered, the trough will swing over to the side with the wheel. It's as incredibly clever as it is simple!"

"My great-grandfather was a genius! Let's try it," Francisco Miranda suggested.

"I wouldn't suggest that just yet," Hawk cautioned.

"Why?" Several of the eager men chorused.

"In addition to the creek being diverted over to the other channel, and exposing the wall now covered by the waterfall, notice that the winch cable runs into the top of a metal pipe that disappears down through the rock." Hawk observed. "Miranda workers drilled down through the cap rock, then inserted a pipe, so they could lower a control cable down into the mine. After all of these years, the creek will still divert, but if we try to activate eighty-year-old cable, weakened by rust and the lack of use, it might snap. If it does we're back to scratch. Worse than that! We'll know that we threw away our only chance."

"What do you propose, Hawk?" Daniel asked.

"We need to oil the winch parts and the cable."

"We don't have any oil," Rezin reminded him.

"No, but we have plenty of bacon and other food that we can cook down for their grease."

"Good idea, Hawk. Some of you men go back to the camp and gather up everything that will produce grease. We'll have a fire ready to render it by the time you return."

Six men ran to the rock chimney, and began the scramble down. They ran back along the bent pine-tree path, unmindful of the sharp nettles that tore at their clothing and the exposed parts of their bodies, then mounted their horses and raced back to camp.

They gathered all the fat-laden rations they could find, remounted and rushed back. This time they eased their way along the piney path with a bit more caution; then made up for the delay by scurrying up the rocky chimney with such haste that they were breathless when they reached the top. By now a big fire was blazing, and they cooked everything until they had several cups of grease, which were emptied into a small iron kettle. A few men, hungry from a long day of searching and climbing, actually tried to eat some of the charred and flinty food.

As soon as the substance had cooled, Hawk began lubricating the winch's moving parts and coating the cable by pouring the remaining oil into the thin pipe that protected it.

Daniel watched as Hawk scrubbed and lubricated the winch parts. He was amazed how quickly the red rusty color began disappearing as parts were restored to the iron-gray shade he had always associated with strong metal.

"That's quite a transformation, Hawk!"

"I learned some tricks fighting the effects of salt water."

"How about the cable? Do you think it'll hold?"

"Miranda thought of everything! Did you notice the small metal cap at the end of the feeder pipe? It's snug. I doubt that very much moisture or debris has worked its way down the pipe despite the years. I'm just being extra careful by greasing the whole cable. I know everyone is anxious, Daniel, and no one will sleep tonight, but I think we had better wait until morning before we set things in motion. This needs to be done slowly and carefully."

"I concur, Hawk. No point in taking chances. I'm sure the others will agree, but they'll all be churning up inside by then."

"Tell 'em to relax, Dan. Morning's only a lifetime away!"

Years afterward, the men who waited on top of the cliff, as well as those who descended to the ground below, called it the longest night they'd ever known.

The next morning, as soon as it was light enough, Hawk checked the winch and cable. After carefully examining each part, he concluded that nothing more could be done to safeguard the equipment. Some of the men were waiting below. It was do-or-die time. He signaled Francisco and his helpers who waited near the trough, then watched anxiously as they slowly raised the trough's rudder paddle that was in the water, anchored it in place, and then carefully lowered the opposite one into the water. As soon as water pressure pushed against it, the trough swung obediently over to the other side of the gully, and guided the water into its new spillway.

The next instant, water reached the waterwheel, which began spinning and providing power for the winch. In turn, the winch began extracting the cable from the pipe that had protected it for eighty years.

The men waiting at the base of the falls had an even more unique experience. One second the water was gushing over the precipice and down the face of the cliff, the next second it abruptly halted. Sounds of the old cataract were still echoing when several feet northwest of the old falls, a new torrent of water suddenly burst over the summit and cascaded down to the shelf below. The great southeastern waterfall that had endured for eighty years died, and another, northwestern one was born.

Then another totally incredible thing happened as the men looked on. A rectangular section of wall that the old waterfall had concealed suddenly opened and slid slowly backwards. The huge slab continued to recede for a short distance, then the upper end began tilting forward and down while the lower end moved backward and up. The ingenious transit continued until the heavy slab settled into a gently slanted position. The granite blade that had sealed Miranda's mine from intrusion now became the front half of a sturdy ramp that descended into the bowels of the earth.

Recognizing Daniel as the principal catalyst in the discovery, the men on the ground who witnessed the opening of the wall did not attempt to descend the ramp. Instead, they patiently waited for Daniel, Hawk, Rezin, Francisco, the others joined them. Despite hopes that his solution to Miranda's enigma had been correct, Daniel was overjoyed by the near miraculous sight that greeted him.

"It's fantastic!" he exclaimed to Hawk.

"Your ability to decipher the key is more fantastic. None of us can believe you figured it out!"

"I'm sure some of you could have done the same." Daniel replied modestly. "If something must be, but isn't, then in order for it to be, it must be something else."

"That explanation is more cryptic than the Miranda puzzle! When I figure it out, I'll let you know! Here come Deaf and Old Ben with pine torches. Let's see where the ramp leads us."

In the sputtering light of the torches, Deaf and Old Ben led Daniel, Hawk, Rezin, Francisco and a dozen others down the ramp into the darkness below. As Daniel stepped off the ramp, he found himself in a narrow, oddly-shaped, subterranean chamber, the low ceiling of which was crisscrossed by thick, heavy timbers. Obviously, the miners responsible for the excavation had been following a meandering vein of silver. The first thing Daniel noticed were big machines that he rightly assumed were used to facilitate silver mining operations. Wherever the light reached there seemed to be another unusual looking piece of equipment. Moving to the opposite side of the cavern they observed the dark mouth of a tunnel. As they walked closer, they saw a set of narrow gauge rails leading into the opening. Perched on these tracks was a string of small, high-sided ore cars used to transport the silver ore out of the mine.

Before plunging into the tunnel, they decided to explore the rest of the entrance area. At the far end of the chamber they found a collection of machinery, furnaces, crucibles, ladles, and bar molds. Will Riley and Ben Berry, experienced mining engineers from

175

Bexar's copper mines, said the equipment was used for smeltering. They also found more than a hundred clay oil lamps. Near the lamps, they found casks of olive oil, sealed in wax to retard evaporation. Hawk lifted one of the containers and shook it.

"It's nearly full, after all these years."

"I can't say I'm surprised," Daniel smiled. "Señor Miranda seems to have thought of everything."

They opened a cask and started filling the lamps. Francisco Miranda lit one, and began poking into dark corners of the entrance area that daylight could not penetrate. He made an interesting discovery.

"Pegs have been driven into the walls. They're a little higher than my head, a short distance apart, and run all the way around the chamber. I think they're lamp holders. Watch this."

He reached up and hung a lamp on one of the pegs to confirm his theory.

"Good work, Cisco!'" Daniel called to him. "Now, as we explore the tunnel, we can hang lamps on the pegs as we go. It'll be as bright as day."

"A couple of us could pile some of the lamps in an ore cart, then start hanging lamps along the tunnel." Cisco suggested.

"Good idea," Hawk agreed. "I'll give you a hand."

They loaded the cart and set off down the tunnel, accompanied by a series of ear-splitting squeaks.

"For the love of heaven, stop!" Rezin thundered over the unearthly racket. "If we don't grease those wheels and shafts, we'll all go deaf."

Hawk quickly recruited some helpers and showed them how to lubricate all the dry wheel bearings and axles. By the time Daniel and his team finished filling all the lamps, Hawk and his men had applied lamp oil to all six carts. They loaded two more of them, and started down the tunnel. Within a short distance, as the oil penetrated the old rusty parts, the carts began rolling smoothly and far more quietly.

They followed the meandering tunnel's course for almost half a mile before Will Riley, the most experienced mining engineer, called a halt in order to study the ancient timbers that supported the roof and the walls of the mine.

"The shoring is incredible," Riley announced. "I've never seen anything this safe and secure. How about you, Ben?"

"Safe, secure, and extremely clever," Ben Berry agreed. "Miranda copied his system from the bees!"

"What's so unusual about it?" Rezin Bowie asked.

"A mine is nothing but a hole in the ground. Like any other hole, it will cave in if it's not supported. To prevent cave-ins, as miners follow metal veins through the earth, they install heavy timbers to shore up the walls and roof. This tunnel is very different. It's being supported by a series of hexagonal boxes instead of regular, straight shoring timbers."

"It's almost like a honeycomb," Daniel observed.

"Exactly!" Riley agreed. "Honeycombs have great strength because of the hexagonal shape. These six-sided boxes can support more weight than straight shoring timbers because the more pressure applied to any one of the sides, the stronger the whole structure becomes."

Riley's words were greeted by blank stares, so he continued.

"If extra force is exerted at one point, this unique pattern of support timbers distributes all the pressure evenly, and adjusts and compensates for additional loads. Quite simply, the roof supports the walls, and the walls support the roof. Short of an earthquake, miners working inside these hexagonal honeycomb boxes are as safe as a toad in God's pocket. It's absolutely ingenious!"

None of the others could have begun to explain how such a phenomenon was possible, but everyone trusted Will Riley because he made it all sound so simple. They felt completely safe as they continued their journey along the tunnel.

They followed the gradually descending tunnel for more than two miles, according to estimates by Will Riley and Ben Berry, before they finally reached the end of the mine. Will Riley judged that the tunnel's gentle but continuous slope had brought them to a point at least five hundred feet beneath the earth's surface. Ben Berry studied the end wall for several minutes, then extracted several chunks of rock from various places with a miner's pick before he turned to Will Riley.

"It's cerargyrite. Heavily concentrated horn silver. Extremely rich ore, and easily amalgamated."

"Right," Riley grinned, "and the whole tunnel is as dry as a bone. No need to sump. I thought we might get a good deal of seepage since the mine's directly beneath the creek. Apparently the creek bed is solid enough to forestall that problem, and any moisture that gets in is siphoned away by various runoffs in the rocks. If you're all set, let's see if everything we need to extract the ore is somewhere in the smelter area."

The procession tramped happily back up the length of the now well-lighted tunnel. The men felt the need after all this excitement to eat a hearty meal, since the last few meals were either omitted or eaten hastily.

Riley and Berry inventoried the supplies in the smelter. Less than an hour later, they concluded that an ample supply of every necessity was available.

When they rejoined the others around the cooking fire, Daniel could contain his curiosity no longer.

"Will and Ben, since you are both knowledgeable

about mining, can you educate the rest of us?"

"As you may know," Riley began, "almost all of the silver that's produced is a by-product of other ores, primarily lead and copper. But small quantities can also be found in gold and zinc. As a by-product, only a tiny amount of silver may be found in every ton of mined matter, but because of silver's great value, even a low-yield operation can be profitable. The balance of the silver comes from hi-grade ores, such as argentite and cerargyrite. Cerargyrite is often called horn silver. It can be extracted by an easy amalgamation process."

"It really is a simple procedure," Ben Berry told them. "Raw cerargyrite is treated with mercury at room temperature. This reduces horn silver to silver ore that dissolves in mercury to form an amalgam. Then the mercury is distilled from the amalgam by heating it, and that leaves the silver."

"Are you saying cerargyrite is quite often found by accident," Daniel asked.

"Yes," Riley nodded. "Miranda's Mine is basically a silver bearing lead mine. Until they struck the vein of cerargyrite, his miners were smelting low grade silver out of lead ore. I think we should concentrate on the horn silver for as long as the vein lasts. It produces a far higher yield, and amalgamation is a much easier process."

"You and Ben are the experts. We'll do whatever you think best, Will, if that's okay with you, Cisco. After all, it is your great-grandfather's mine," Daniel reminded Francisco and all of the others.

"This silver is here to help us defeat Santa Anna! It was God's will that we discovered it," declared Francisco. Rezin, Old Ben, Deaf and Hawk nodded to indicate their agreement.

"Matt Clancy worked with me for more than two years before he struck out on his own," Will told them. "Matt knows all about this kind of operation. So with Ben, Matt, and me, we have three shift leaders. There are twenty-four of us, and there's only room at the end of the tunnel for four or five men at a time. Let's divide the group into three, eight-man squads. Five men at the tunnel end can rotate, four on, one off, twice each hour. Two of the others can run the ore carts up and down the shaft, keeping them in motion, while the eighth man keeps tab on the amalgamation procedure. That way we'll be operating twenty-four hours a day. Is that agreeable with you, Daniel?"

"Sounds like a good plan, Will!"

"Okay! I'll post a roster of the three teams, and we'll rotate the jobs of the men on the teams. Once winter sets in, there won't be much difference twixt night and day down here. But if the teams want to rotate their hours once a month, we can do that too. I'm sure you'll all agree that it's one thing to be stuck in a dead-end mine during the winter, when the Indians are snug and warm in their lodges, but it's quite another to be trapped in a cave by a war party after the first thaw. So, I suggest we work hard all winter, collect all the silver in portable bars, and head back to Bexar as soon as the weather allows travel."

"That is a good plan, Will," Daniel acknowledged. "Now the horses are our only other problem. There's plenty of grass for them in this canyon for as long as they can reach it, but this canyon is like a funnel. When snow flies, it may pile up in drifts that make it impossible for the animals to paw their way down to the grass. I think that after you draw up the roster, while your team sets things up at tunnel end, the rest of us better forage along both banks of the San Saba and bring in enough silage to get the horses through the winter. There's room to store it at one end of the entrance hall. There's also plenty of space to tether the horses if we have a blizzard. It'll take us a couple of days to collect and transport the silage, but we'll rest a lot easier when we know we're well prepared."

"Let's put the rosters together. The sooner we get started, the better," Will Riley agreed.

They spent considerable time composing rosters in an effort to equalize required skills among the three teams. Daniel, Hawk and Rezin became part of

Matt Clancy's team three, with Old Ben Milam, Deaf Smith, Peewee Potts, and Francisco Miranda.

For the rest of that day, and for the next two days, teams two and three rode back and forth between the mine and San Saba, from dawn until pitch darkness made travel too hazardous. By dusk of the third day, everyone agreed that the horses would survive, even if the winter were long and cold.

The three mining experts spent the next two weeks teaching the twenty-one novices what they needed to know in order to operate a mine efficiently. By the end of the second week, every man was able to accomplish all the basic tasks, so a rotation of jobs was established that broke the daily monotony to some extent. But as the days went by, confinement in close quarters was difficult to accept for men who had always been at home in wide-open spaces. On several occasions, harsh words were exchanged, and a dozen fistfights were averted only because cooler heads prevailed.

On Christmas Eve, despite a heavy snow that was falling, and the many towering, wind-blown drifts, Old Ben and Deaf set out to hunt game. They spent the morning breaking trail for the pair of packhorses that they hoped would be needed to haul back fresh meat. In late afternoon, their efforts were rewarded when they discovered a herd of elk bedded down in a secluded forest glade. In the biting cold, it took all of their patience and skill to field dress two big bull elk, roll them onto pinebough sleds, and tie towropes from the elk's antlers to the horses' packsaddles. In the nearly impassable conditions, it was late evening before they finally returned to the mine, having coaxed two foot-sore, reluctant horses to pull their heavy loads back down the length of the long, snowy valley. In the throes of mid-winter's biting cold, it had been wishful thinking to believe that hunters, even hunters as skilled as Deaf and Old Ben, would succeed. So when they returned with the elk, it was Christmas Eve, the Fourth of July, and everybody's birthday, all rolled up into one. Willing hands made quick work of the elk, which were soon skinned and butchered. Twenty-four men slept happily that night in anticipation. Old Ben and Deaf had found no Indian sign, so Christmas dinner would be a holiday feast. Everyone looked forward to stuffing himself with elk steaks and ribs.

A very merry Christmas was at hand.

More snow fell that night, but as dawn broke, the storm clouds disappeared and rich blue sky stretched out toward the horizon. Since it was a holiday, no work was scheduled, other than necessary cooking. Most men planned to sleep late, but their appetites overcame their fatigue. Designated cooks spitted the elk meat as soon as they had enough light to see, and began roasting it over big fires outside the entrance. Quite soon, sizzling sounds and tantalizing aromas wafted into the sleeping area and claimed everyone's attention. Instead of getting extra sleep, men spent the balance of the day swapping stories. The most interesting tale by far was Rezin Bowie's account of a famous fight at Vidalia Sandbar.

X
THE VIDALIA SANDBAR

THE MIRANDA MINE
CHRISTMAS DAY, 1834

"At the end of 1824," Rezin began his tale, "Jim and I decided to check out some opportunities we'd heard about in Natchez, Mississippi. As you know, Natchez lies at the end of the Natchez Trace, a wagon road that leads south from Nashville. Being a freight wagon depot, as well as a Mississippi River port, it seemed likely that Natchez would be an ideal place for folks to join a wagon train, and to restock their supplies before moving farther west. Expansion fever sure was in the air that winter. Any fool could see it coming, and coming fast!

"You know, we Americans are a funny breed. In foreign countries, when a boy reaches manhood, he picks up his plunder, tells the girl of choice it's time, and he starts farming a parcel of land that belongs to his family, or a piece as close as he can get. But not Americans! No self-respecting Yankee can ever be satisfied until he knows what lies beyond the far hill, and then the next, and the next. I reckon there isn't enough space in the whole world to cure some of the wanderlusts in Americans, but there's enough land between the Mississippi River and Pacific Ocean to put quite a dent in them.

"After President Monroe laid down the law for the Europeans in his 1823 Doctrine, a whole lot of folks decided it was safe to move west, and most of them heard that Natchez was the best place to head for. I guess the idea of fresh land makes folks forget or ignore the Indian danger, as well as the hot and dry summers on the Great Plains, with their terrible sand storms. They either forget or ignore freezing winters in the high mountain passes, and terrible blizzards that sap everyone's strength. But physical hardships are not as bad as mental anguish. Until you've lived through that sort of trip, you can't begin to imagine the awful loneliness that descends on human beings as they prod placid yokes of weary oxen, hour after endless hour, day after dreary day, across mile after empty mile of bleak wasteland that is broken only by an occasional clump of buffalo grass. Each morning, the western horizon seems closer, yet each night it seems farther away. Some settlers hang on for dear life and get by. Some lose heart and turn back. Some simply give up and perish along the way."

Bowie paused for a moment, and a look of concern, or pity, came into his eyes for a few moments.

"Getting back to Natchez—it lies along the inside

bend of a sweeping curve of the Mississippi, against a high, rocky cliff bank the river's been carving out since God's Creation. The Natchez waterfront, from one end to the other, runs for a couple of miles along the eastern bank. When we arrived in early '25, flatboats were moored three and four deep along the shore. Each one of 'em was stuffed with trade goods that scores of western bound travelers needed. That winter, there seemed to be no end to a line of wagons coming down Natchez Trace, which is a lot easier to travel on winter's hard ice than in spring's soft mud. Freight wagons and big prairie schooners piled up with every single possession families had, each one carrying a parcel of tow-headed, freckled-face kids, and two starry-eyed parents, hungry for tillable land. In agricultural nations like ours, wealth is measured by land holdings, not bank accounts. Financial panic can ruin national economies. Currencies can become worthless overnight. Not so land! Did you ever ask a farmer how much land he wanted to own? They all give you the only answer they know. More! Western expansion in America is as inevitable as the setting of the sun every evening. There's no way it can be stopped."

Rezin took a sip of coffee, gazed around his circle of rapt listeners, then continued.

"For smart investors, Natchez was a treasure trove.

People were pouring down the Trace, floating down the Ohio and Mississippi, and driving wagons along those riverbanks, all bound to Natchez. Natchez was the last marketplace, the last outpost of the East, and the first outpost of the tens of millions of acres that began across the river on the Mississippi's western bank. Empty land stretched for a thousand miles, and half a thousand more, all the way to the Pacific, to a new Promised Land where everyone was equal and only a man's ambition controlled his destiny, a land where families could dream, where hard work, tears, blood, sweat, and time could make any dream that a man, woman, or child dared to dream come true.

"Settlers could simply cross the Mississippi and head west until they found a likely homestead, squat on the land and defend it by force for as long as they could. But the wiser heads soon realized that at some point in the future, all of the land would be surveyed, apportioned, and sold by federal agencies. Then the land squatters had developed and cultivated might be legally transferred to new owners, and all their years of effort would be thrown away.

"The only smart way to acquire land was to buy it from the legal owner. Change of ownership could be recorded at the land office, the deed signed over, and proper entries made in the patent book. Then no one could show up years later and dispute the title. Jim and I decided to buy as much land as possible along both riverbanks with all of the money we could pool together, and plunge into the land business. But there turned out to be a fly in the buttermilk. The only way to get cheap land was to buy up huge tracts, and that cost a ton of money. Jim and I scouted around and discovered that there were two big land syndicates in town competing to see who could corner the market before all of the available land was gone."

"Since you couldn't hope to beat 'em, I'm guessin' you joined one of 'em." Will Riley ventured.

"We sure did," Rezin agreed, "but before I tell you about those land syndicates, I want to tell you some more about the two towns of Natchez."

"Two towns are named Natchez?" Hawk asked.

"Yep! One of them is called Natchez-under-the-Bluff. It's filled with saloons, gamblers, rivermen, drunks, knife-fighters, and petty thieves who would steal the coins from a dead man's eyes. And they're the best of the bad lot! The rest are thimbleriggers, murderers, and most other varieties of guttersnipes and human trash. Each morning, the previous night's victims are found in muddy alleys with their pockets emptied and their throats cut. Bargemen, eager to spend their hard-earned pay after weeks on the river, are no match for riffraff who are ready to pounce like hungry tigers. Natchez-under-the-Bluff is one of hell's substations. No crime is outlawed. No act is too vile. No deed is beyond acceptable limits."

"It sounds like an awful place," Daniel concluded.

"It's even worse than it sounds. The women are as bad as the men, strumpets and street walkers who are ready for any depravity. Desperate practitioners of debauchery, hard and brazen, giving no quarter to men, asking none in return, greedy for gold and willing to commit any act to get it. That narrow strip of mucky ground that lies beneath the bluff holds a vicious, violent population, crowded into a row of flimsy shacks and a few crumbling brick buildings. People who live there give the town its own rancid personality. Natchez-under-the-Bluff reeks of evil."

Rezin shuddered as he remembered.

"Silver Street bisects the cutthroat colony. It starts at the Mississippi and then, crisscrossed by several dark, menacing alleys, it winds up through the center of the hamlet before it finally arrives at the face of a cliff. But it doesn't stop there. In a steep slant, it ascends the face of the cliff and provides the link between an evil world below and a prosperous world above. A world of tumult and chaos is traded for a world of peace and security. Under the bluff, human life is cheap. On the hill, nothing is cheap. Dozens of white-pillared mansions bear mute testimony to the immense wealth of their cotton-planter owners. The evil world of ruffians is gone! The world of gentility is at hand, an indulgent world of well-manicured lawns, well-mannered, courtly gentlemen, in richly colorful garb, carefully coifed hair, and carefree manners. Six days a week, they stroll along with pristine, dainty ladies. On Sundays, they make a point of being seen worshipping in high-steepled churches with neatly crafted rows of stained-glass windows which they publicly donated. Natchez-on-the-Hill is a place of indolent luxury, which cannot function without a retinue of black servants whose only d'etre is to serve, attend, flatter, and cajole their idly-rich masters."

A few listeners, less familiar with Rezin than Daniel, thought he was putting on airs with his rich and colorful language. They were wrong. Well-read and principally self-educated, this was Rezin's normal vocabulary.

"You mentioned there were two land syndicates in Natchez. How did you decide which one to join?" Daniel asked.

"It was far easier than you might imagine. Jim ran afoul of a man in one of the groups. I don't know the whole story, but Jim and this fellow, Major Norris Wright, had both been intent on currying the favor of the same lady in New Orleans some years earlier. Wright left the city before a duel could be arranged, but he still harbored a grudge against Jim. Wright's group included Judge Robert Crain, Doctor Thomas Maddox, and the Blanchard brothers, Alfred and Carey. They sat around King's Tavern each evening plotting new under-handed schemes that would yield large profits."

"They sound like difficult adversaries," Daniel observed.

"They were," Rezin agreed, "but we were no easy marks ourselves. Our Connelly Tavern coalition was headed up by General Richard Cuny and his brother, Doctor Samuel Cuny, Colonel Samuel Wells and his brother, Jefferson Wells, Major George McWherters, and, of course, Jim and myself. I should add that Doctor Maddox and Colonel Wells were also bitter enemies. They had already fought one duel in which Maddox was slightly wounded."

"Sounds like everybody had to sleep with one eye open," Will Riley commented.

"Not quite," Rezin replied, "but we knew a powder keg could blow at any moment. Early that summer, it finally did."

He took a sip of his drink, then chuckled as each of his listeners leaned forward expectantly.

"Late in May, both syndicates were trying to buy a big tract of land on the western side of the river, a few miles south of Natchez. Our group was strapped for cash, but since this was a choice piece of land that could be divided up and resold for a huge profit, we put everything we had left into our bid, but we came up $50,000 short of the King's Tavern group.

"We thought we'd lost out to them until Jim went down to the river to play poker at Thomas Grady's Tavern, the most notorious place under the bluff. Grady's Tavern boasted a cast of evil characters led by a murderous gambler and knife-fighter named Bloody Jack Sturdevant. During the course of such evenings, Jim won tidy sums of money, and found it amusing to watch as Bloody Jack fleeced the poor unsuspecting, inexperienced gamblers from the top of the hill who frequented Grady's for an evening of excitement and adventure. Jim never interfered. If a man is dumb enough to play in a crooked game, he deserved whatever comes his way. This game ended at midnight after the gullible fools had been relieved of all their money, and Bloody Jack and Jim were the only winners. As soon as the others left, Bloody Jack made an interesting announcement."

"'Mister Bowie,'" Bloody Jack said, "'I won a wager with a Nashville gentleman named Joseph Levington last week. It left me in possession of a racehorse that hasn't been beaten for over two years in more than twenty races. Perhaps you heard of him? His name is Steel Duke.'"

"'No, I can't say I have.'"

"'Not surprisin'. He's well known in Nashville, but not way down here.'"

"'What does this have to do with me?'" Jim asked.

"'It occurred to me that the Duncan Cup will be run in three weeks. Any gentleman who posts a $5,000 entry fee can enter a horse in that race. As pleasant a fellow as I am,'" Bloody Jack grinned maliciously at his own joke, "'nobody around here thinks I'm much of a gentleman. You could enter Steel Duke. He'd be a long shot against Kerry Isle, Major Wright's horse. He won last year, and is sure to be a strong favorite again. Besides winning the big purse, you could pick up a bundle of money on side bets. Since I can't race Steel Duke, I'll sell him to you for $1,000.'"

"'When can I see him?'"

"'Right now. He's stabled in Grady's cellar.'"

"'Let's go.'"

"Tom Grady and Sturdevant lit a pair of lanterns and led the way down a steep flight of stairs to the cellar. As soon as he saw Steel Duke in the dim light, Jim knew he was the best looking stakes horse he'd ever seen. Jim said he could see strong muscles rippling under Steel Duke's dark dappled coat as he shifted nervously. Jim made a decision on the spot."

"'He's everything you said he was, Sturdevant. I'll send a boy down in the morning with the money. He can ride Steel Duke up to Connelly Tavern.'"

"'We'll have him saddled and waitin', Mr. Bowie. It's a pleasure doin' business with a man who knows horse flesh.'"

"Jim met with all of us at Connelly's early the next morning. We all agreed that it was worth risking the money to buy Steel Duke. If he was as good as Jim suspected, we would enter him in the Duncan Cup Race. We had three weeks to decide if we wanted to risk anything beyond the thousand-dollar sale price."

"How good was he?" Hawk asked excitedly.

"Since Peewee rode Steel Duke, I'll let him answer that."

Peewee Potts shuffled in from the fringe of the crowd that had gathered and sat down next to Rezin.

"If I say he's the fastest horse I ever rode, the most willing to run, and the most determined to win, all of that would be true, but it wouldn't do him justice. Steel Duke has the longest stride I ever saw! He just lopes along in that casual way of his until another horse threatens to pass him, then he kicks his speed up to another level. It's as if he doesn't want to show slow horses up, so he only runs fast enough to win."

"So he beat Kerry Isle?" Hawk queried.

"I'll let Rezin tell you the rest of the tale."

"Peewee rode Steel Duke only for a short distance before he realized what he had. So instead of coming up to Connelly's, he headed directly out to General Cuny's farm. Steel Duke hadn't run at all since they brought him down from Nashville, so it took about ten days for Peewee to work him into his best racing condition. Tell them what you found out, Peewee."

"Steel Duke," Peewee told them, "is hard to beat in a mile race. At a mile and a half he's even harder. At two miles, I doubt that any horse in the world can catch him, and the Duncan Cup is a two mile race."

"Since the race was to be run on Saturday," Rezin picked up the story, "Jim didn't enter Steel Duke, or post a $5,000 entry fee until Thursday morning. By Friday evening, ten horses had been entered and the odds were posted. Kerry Isle was two to one. Rip Tide, a rangy bay filly owned by Andrew Marschalk, the editor and publisher of the Natchez Herald, was five to one. Trooper, a big, black stallion owned by a retired cavalry officer, was six to one. All the other horses were ten to one."

"Ten to one on a horse that couldn't lose! No doubt you made a fortune," Hawk surmised.

"Unfortunately, as I mentioned earlier, our group was short of cash. We scraped up every dollar we could, and bet the high odds, but our main goal was to go after Major Wright and his crowd who knew nothing about Steel Duke, and thought Kerry Isle would win handily. On the morning of the race they

197

agreed to put up $50,000 against $10,000, our last $10,000."

"Those are only five to one odds." Hawk said

"True enough, lad, but we were glad to get them. We were sure Wright and his friends were becoming overextended, and $50,000 was far more than they could afford to lose. When you add that wager to the money we'd already bet at ten to one odds, plus the Duncan Cup purse, we would realize a profit of over $100,000. Wright was so confident Kerry Isle would win that he offered to wager his own cotton farm and $5,000 against Jim's $500. Of course, Jim took him up on the wager. Now it was all up to Peewee and Steel Duke, but I'll let him tell you about the race."

"In case some of you have never seen the Natchez Fairground Racetrack," Peewee began, "it's a one mile oval. Since the Duncan Cup is a two mile race, it means two trips around the course. Parts of the track are bumpy, but bumps don't bother Steel Duke. The night before the race, rain started peltin' down at midnight. It kept on until late morning. An hour before the race started, most of the track looked like a big swamp. Jim went to the race committee and suggested the race be postponed until the next day. By then most of the water would have had time to drain away. Al Blanchard was committee chairman, and since Kerry Isle was noted for being a good mud runner, Blanchard refused to delay the start of the race for a single minute."

"How did Steel Duke handle mud?" Daniel asked.

"We had no idea! It had been as dry as a desert for the past month, so we'd had no chance to test him. All I could do was wait and see."

"All the rest of us could do was wait and worry," Rezin added. "Steel Duke stumbled at the start, and we thought we were in a lot of trouble."

"Aye," Peewee said, "but he righted himself soon enough and regained his stride. But no sooner had the one bit of trouble ended, another began. That slip at the start put Steel Duke in the middle of the pack. Meanwhile, Kerry Isle had made a clean break and was drawing farther away with every stride. His tiny Jamaican rider was all but hidden from view in the big bay's long, flowing mane. Fortunately, it was a two-mile race, so instead of trying to force my way through those slower horses, I pulled Steel Duke up and skirted toward the outside rail. As it turned out, it was the right thing to do. It gave us farther to run, but we were all alone. The other horses were still running together in the middle of the track. And the turf along the outer rail, being higher than the rest of the track, had begun to dry. Steel Duke flew past the others as if they were standing still, but by then, Kerry Isle and that Jamaican were nearly a quarter of a mile ahead of us."

"How far were you from the finish line?" Hawk queried.

"A mile and a half, but as soon as Steel Duke ran past the other horses, he eased up. He wasn't aware that Kerry Isle was pulling away. It was a desperate situation that demanded desperate tactics, so I reined my horse off the firm ground along the outer rail and guided him back into the slush that covered the rest of the track, hoping that Steel Duke would spot his rival."

A rush of color testified to Peewee's excitement.

"Suddenly he did! He burst forth with such a rush of speed that I was almost thrown off his back. If I hadn't been lucky enough to grab a handful of his mane, I would' a fallen. From then 'til the finish, all I did was hold on for dear life. Steel Duke needed me as much as a hurricane needs some more wind. He was consumed with running down that flying bay horse."

"He was so far behind Kerry Isle, we didn't think he had a chance," Rezin admitted. "Never in my life did I ever expect to experience such speed. As he sped past the finish line the first time, Steel Duke was a hundred yards behind, a huge distance to make up in a mile. But as incredible as it seems as I look back on it, Steel Duke gained a jump for each dozen he made, and slowly reeled in the bay horse. He came into the homestretch being pelted by heavy clots of mud being thrown up behind Kerry Isle's thundering feet, but Steel Duke didn't waver. On he ran, racing through the stinging mud shower until, in the final fifty yards, he pushed his nose in front of the bay, and then his neck. By the time he flashed across the finish line for the second time, Steel Duke was more than a full length in front of the soundly beaten and staggering Kerry Isle."

"So, in addition to winning the Duncan Cup, your syndicate now had plenty of cash, and Major Norris and his group were nearly broke," Hawk assumed.

"That was the way it should have been, but it didn't quite work out that way."

"We should' a known those scalawags would try to weasel out of their debts!" Peewee suggested.

"What happened?" Daniel asked Rezin.

"As soon as the race was over, Doctor Maddox filed a protest on behalf of the King's Tavern group, which questioned Steel Duke's ownership. Since the Duncan Cup rules say his legal owner must enter the horse, Maddox and the others were demanding proof of Jim's ownership. Until ownership was verified, no winner would be declared, and no wagers would be paid. Andrew Marschalk dispatched a messenger to Nashville with a letter to Joseph Levington, Steel Duke's last known legal owner, asking him to submit an affidavit explaining the horse's sequence of ownership. The messenger returned a week later, and the letter was published in the Natchez Herald. Levington's letter, which confirmed that he had lost Steel Duke in a wager with Jack Sturdevant, was followed by information Marschalk had obtained in an interview with Sturdevant, in which he asserted that he had sold the horse to James Bowie. The final paragraph of the editorial revealed that Duncan Cup officials had met in closed session and declared Steel Duke the winner. Therefore, all gentlemen who had wagered on the race should settle their wagers."

"How did Norris Wright and the others take that bit of news?" Daniel queried.

"Bitterly, as one might expect. Norris Wright sent an envelope to Jim that contained a $5,000 draft, the deed to his cotton farm, and a letter acknowledging Jim's ownership of Steel Duke, but denying his right to enter a race limited to gentlemen's horses. When he read the letter, Jim vowed to kill Wright on sight. The day after the letter arrived, the situation got even worse when Colonel Wells chanced to meet Doctor Maddox on the street."

"General Cuny had warned all of us to stay away from all the King's Tavern people until they cooled off," Peewee recalled. "I guess Colonel Wells didn't heed the advice."

"Actually, he did," Rezin told him. "When Wells saw Maddox coming toward him, he crossed the street in an effort to avoid a direct confrontation, but Maddox followed him. According to Wells, Maddox had come simply to provoke a fight. I'll recall as much of the exchange as I can."

"'Well, Wells, what do you plan to do with your thirty pieces of silver?'" Maddox began.

"'What are you implying, Maddox?'"

"'I'm not implying anything. I'm saying right out that you won the race with underhanded tactics.'"

"'That's a lie. But it is what I'd expect from a man who is dumb enough to be outsmarted by a notorious gambler and a fast horse.'"

"'Those are insidious, insulting words, Wells!'"

"'Make whatever you will of them, Maddox!'"

"'In that case, I demand satisfaction. My friends will call on you!'"

"'I shall eagerly await them! It's time to settle a lot of old scores with you, once and for all!'"

"And that's how it happened. The next day, Judge Crain, acting as chief second for Maddox, met with General Cuny, acting for Wells. They chose Andrew Marschalk to act as referee, and arranged the duel a week ahead at the Vidalia Sandbar, a day that I rank among the worst I have ever lived through.

"For the next six days, Jim worked with Samuel

Wells on his marksmanship, which I must admit was quite poor. The day before the duel, Wells was able to put one shot out of every three in a man-sized target—a-not-so comforting average for a man who within hours will confront an enemy with nothing in his hand except a single shot dueling pistol."

"So, Wells was almost certain to be killed." Daniel reasoned.

"Fortunately, Thomas Maddox's shooting abilities were almost as poor as those of Sam Wells. Jim was hopeful that they would both miss, or at worst, just inflict minor flesh wounds. I learned the same day, that Maddox had been practicing with Al Blanchard, but we all did our best to conceal our concerns the following morning when we were rowed out to the Vidalia Sandbar. When we arrived, a skiff that had transported the Maddox party was already beached on the sand. They had chosen the south end of the sandbar, so we moved up to the north end. A few moments later, Andrew Marschalk motioned for the seconds to join him. I remember every word and act that occurred from then on as if it happened only yesterday.

"'For one last time,'" Marschalk began, "'I ask both parties if this quarrel can be settled peacefully, without loss of blood?'"

"'My principal will reluctantly accept an apology,

made in public, and in print,'" Judge Crain replied.

"'My principal will never agree to a demand of that sort,'" General Cuny assured Marschalk.

"'In that case, bring your principals to me. They will stand motionless, back-to-back until I say ready, begin. At that time, I will start the count to ten. At each number, they will take one step forward, away from their antagonist. On the count of ten, they may turn and fire at will. Any questions, gentlemen?'"

"'None!'" General Cuny said solemnly.

"'No,'" Judge Crain answered softly.

"And so," Rezin continued, "Maddox and Wells walked up, and Marschalk positioned them back-to-back. I swear, for the few seconds they stood there, before the count began, the birds quit chirping, and the Mississippi River slowed down, as if to maintain the stillness the moment demanded. Then Marschalk began."

"'Are you ready, gentlemen?'"

Maddox nodded. Wells nodded."

"'Very well, then. One... Two... Three... Four... Five...'"

"The silence was all but unbearable. It seemed to roar in our ears. We all waited expectantly. No one seemed to breathe. No one moved except the duelists themselves. The only sound was Marschalk's calm voice, as he intoned the numbers."

"'Six….Seven…..Eight……Nine…….Ten!'"

"In the blink of an eye, both men spun around and fired, seemingly without aiming." Rezin continued. "Their poor marksmanship was borne out. They both missed. Marschalk summoned the seconds."

"'Honor has been satisfied. Both of your principals have redeemed themselves. Can this unpleasantness end now?'"

"'I insist on a second shot,'" Judge Crain demanded.

"'Very well,'" General Cuny agreed.

"Once again the ritual began, but this time it was different. Birds found their voices, the Mississippi once again went swishing past. Along the riverbank, choruses of frogs began happily croaking as if they knew that another shot would be just as futile as the first.

"We listened to Marschalk's instructions, watched the nervous steps of the duelists, and listened to the wasted second shots rushing through the empty air. Andrew Marschalk recalled the seconds."

"'Gentlemen, nothing in the Code Duello demands a third shot. Your principals have acted in a manner that will become the envy of all men. Let us shake hands and end unpleasantness once and for all.'"

"Having just seen the glassy-eyed stares emanating from the chalk-white faces of the two principals, the seconds hastily agreed. Unfortunately, bigger trouble was just about to begin. At first, it seemed things had been smoothed over, at least for the present. The foresighted Andrew Marschalk had brought several hampers of food and beverages out to the bar in the hope that the duel would be peacefully resolved. When it was, the opposing parties talked quietly and mingled together in an almost friendly manner. I even observed Judge Crain and General Cuny, bitter enemies for many years, exchanging a few wooden-faced pleasantries.

"Then we saw a tall man approaching through the bushes that grew along the bank. As he entered the clearing, we were surprised to see Norris Wright, whom we thought had gone to Nashville. As he neared the group, Marschalk walked out to meet him, surely in an effort to smooth the bad feelings that existed between Wright and Jim. But for once, Marschalk blundered in his choice of words."

"'Major Wright, to make this festive day complete, will you take a glass of wine, and drink the health of James Bowie, whom you surely will acknowledge is an admirable gentleman.'"

"'I acknowledge nothing of the kind!'" thundered Wright. "'He is a witless, knife-fighting blackguard. Bowie's the same as the Cunys, the Wells', and all the rest of that crowd. Each one of them is more foul and lower than pond scum!'"

"Before Jim had time to react, Judge Crain pulled a small, double-barreled derringer from his pocket and pointed it at General Cuny. For an instant, time froze. General Cuny's face was ashen with fear and ferocity as he struggled vainly to draw a pistol from his own pocket, the hammer of which had caught in his coat. We all heard a sharp double click as Crain cocked his weapon."

"'This will end our quarrels for all time, Cuny!'"

"In another second, General Cuny would be dead. But in the knick of time, Jim sprang forward and leapt between them. The bullet intended for Cuny's heart slammed into Jim's hip. His leg suddenly went limp, and he tumbled to the ground. But Jim's intervention gave General Cuny the time he needed to withdraw the stubborn pistol from his pocket and hastily fire a shot at Judge Crain. In his nervous excitement, all he managed to do was put a second bullet in the same arm he had wounded before. Jim tried to rise, but fell back and lay prostrate on the ground

"Crain now produced a second pistol from another pocket. This time he aimed very carefully and fired a heavy bullet into the center of General Cuny's chest.

A look of surprise enveloped the old warrior's face for a moment, then he slumped heavily to the ground. His brother, the little doctor, raced to his side, but it was too late. The general was dead. Furious at the death of his friend, somehow Jim pulled himself erect with the help of a small sapling, drew his pistol, and fired at Judge Crain. In Jim's shaken condition, it was no surprise when his shot missed. Suddenly, it seemed as if everyone was firing at everyone else. Several of us were wounded, but fortunately, no one was killed. Only the general lay dead.

"Since he had failed to kill Crain with a bullet, Jim pulled his knife and staggered after him. When Judge Crain saw the terrible specter of my wounded brother, he hurled his empty pistol at Jim and then fled in panic. Haste was unnecessary because the heavy pistol struck Jim on the forehead and knocked him down a second time. Andrew Marschalk and I started forward to help Jim, but Norris Wright got to him before we could."

"I'll bet he had mayhem in his heart," Hawk ventured.

"Indeed! Wright was carrying a gold-headed cane, and just as he reached Jim, he withdrew a long, slim sword that had been concealed inside. Wright stood over Jim for a single instant, then plunged the blade into his chest, all the way up to the gold-headed hilt! We were all sure that Jim was dead. So was Wright. In an effort to retrieve his blade from Jim's body, he tugged and strained so hard that he lifted the body

209

off the ground, but the strong steel held firm.

"Again and again, Wright yanked on that golden hilt, trying to free the steel with brute force. Finally, he savagely jammed his boot against Jim's quivering chest and yanked with both hands. The hilt came off, but the blade remained, buried deeply in Jim's body. We all heard Wright curse with frustration. Then we heard him issue a second oath, but it was different. Now there was a note of fear and panic in his voice. Despite the blurred vision that the bullet crease over my eye had caused, I could plainly see the reason for Wright's sudden panic. His helpless victim, the man he presumed to be dead, had clamped a hand around Wright's wrist, a hand as strong and unyielding as a vice. Norris Wright leapt violently backward in an effort to free himself, but a Roman galley slave, chained to an oar, had a better chance of success. Wright's struggles to free himself were in vain. He was abruptly yanked down to his knees, then pulled across Jim's body. In his final moment of life, Wright felt an excruciating pain as the great knife slipped between his back ribs and into his heart. He choked back the blood, and used his last breath to say, "'Damn you, Bowie, you've killed me!'"

"The words ended in a gurgle of blood. Then we all saw Jim roll Wright's corpse aside, and with unearthly strength of will, rose slowly off the bloody ground and staggered to his feet. There he stood, covered with Wright's blood as well as his own, unmoving, glaring about, heavily pondering his next move. He looked down at the steel blade protruding from his chest, and absently tried to pluck it out, but he quickly gave up the effort as futile, and once more glared about.

"Jim started moving forward, a blood covered specter, swaying as he came, mortally wounded, but lethally dangerous until the moment of his death. A panicky Al Blanchard fired from twenty feet away. The heavy bullet struck Jim's arm and spun him around. He recovered his balance and, dragging his injured leg, struggled on to reach his antagonist. A strange, ethereal silence descended on the battlefield for a moment, then was broken by the pop, pop, pop, of gunshots. Everyone except Jim dived for cover as pungent, acrid gunpowder filled the air, attacking the eyes and shriveling the nostrils.

"Jim reached Blanchard and lunged forward with his razor sharp blade poised to strike. Seconds later, Jim turned away, leaving Blanchard staring stupidly at the great bloody gash that had opened his forearm to the bone.

"I heard more firing as I rushed to Jim and covered him with my own body, determined to die myself rather than allowing him to suffer another wound.

"Common sense quickly prevailed over hot blood.

The firing stopped. Crain, Maddox, Blanchard and the rest of their crowd hastened into their skiff and crossed the river. Doctor Cuny extracted two bullets from Jim's body with relative ease, but the sword was more difficult. He said the cold metal bent when it struck the sternum, and then followed the rib cage around to Jim's back, held in place all the way by a strong sheath of muscle. As soon as he had removed the long blade, the doctor filled the gunshot wounds with unguents to promote healing and closed both of those wounds. The wound from the sword blade was a far different matter. The doctor could only treat the entrance and exit wounds, which he did, but the terrible wound that encircled the left side of Jim's chest would be in the hands of nature and the Almighty."

"I saw him after you crossed the river," Peewee remembered. "He looked more dead than alive."

"None of us, not even Doctor Cuny, held out much hope. That night, he lapsed into a coma, and began burning up with fever. For the next two weeks, Jim held on to life by a thread. During those perilous days, the loss of so much blood, the high fever that dehydrated his body, and the insidious infection that Doctor Cuny had feared, ate away a great deal of his musculature, so much in fact that every one of his ribs could be counted through his wasted flesh. On the sixteenth day after the duel, the fever broke and the brave Jim Bowie regained his senses. Nearly two more months passed before he was strong enough to get up and walk around for a few minutes at a time. It took well over a year before Jim regained most of his strength."

"I read an account of the Vidalia Sandbar episode in the Washington Watch," Daniel recalled.

"Yes, during those long months of his recovery, Jim Bowie gained nationwide fame. Dozens of newspapers wrote reviews of the Vidalia Sandbar event. I saved some columns from the Washington Watch, the New Orleans Argus, Philadelphia Times, Richmond Whig and Charleston Courier. But Andrew Marschalk's eye witness account in the Natchez Herald is the one I memorized, even if he is given to rococo."

"...It was Bowie, terrible and bloody, scorning wounds, a steel shard protruding from his chest, yet striding in spite of a wounded leg, with berserk fury into the teeth of the pistol fire, animated only by his deadly ferocity, who drove the Crain party into retreat. To the beholder, he seemed almost superhuman: a terrifying, invincible Achilles, an avenging demon, the knife he wielded like a modern Excalibur, irresistible against any human defense."

"It sounds like one of the tales Sir Thomas Mallory recounted in Le Morte d'Arthur, about the Knights of the Round Table," Daniel said in awe.

"I had the same thought. I read the Malory epic during my first year at sea." Hawk added wistfully. "By the way, Rezin, were any of the others killed at the sandbar?"

"No. Everyone recovered from their wounds, but there was too much bad blood for any of us to stay in Natchez any longer than necessary. Crain, Maddox, the Blanchard Brothers, and all the rest of them left town a fortnight after the duel. Our own syndicate was disbanded and the profits were divided. As soon as Jim was well enough to travel, we headed back up to the bayou country where things were much more peaceful and quiet. In the year-and-a-half it took Jim to recover his strength, he suffered even more from the peace and quiet than from his occasional pains. By the time the winter of twenty-eight/twenty-nine rolled around, he had cabin fever because he craved excitement. As soon as travel was possible, Jim took a trail every other American man eager for adventure seemed to be taking. He headed for Texas, and some bittersweet years."

XI
WAR PARTY

CELERY CREEK CANYON
MARCH 15, 1835

The cerargyrite vein had finally played out. Each day, for four-and-a-half months, they had labored mightily to extract cerargyrite from the bowels of the earth. Now the horn silver had been separated from the raw ore by amalgamation, and a king's ransom of nearly pure silver lay in the mine's outer chamber.

The men were gaunt and aching after the extended gargantuan effort they had expended, but euphoric at the incredible success they had enjoyed. They had spent their last day at the mine loading the silver into forty-pound rawhide sacks the pack animals would carry back to Bexar.

"General Houston won't believe his eyes," Daniel predicted to Hawk. "According to Riley and Berry, there's enough silver here to buy as many cannon and rifles as we need to arm every Texican, and enough more to hire a large mercenary force. The Good Lord and the Celery Creek Canyon have been very good to us. If our good fortune continues for one more week, we'll be back in Bexar with a pocketful of miracles."

"Let's hope it does," Hawk said. "There's a lot of country between here and Bexar. A lot of dangerous country. I won't feel safe until I'm back at the Leon de Oro, eating good food and drinking good wine."

"There are two dozen seasoned frontiersmen in our party. We're far too strong for most raiding parties to come after us. Comanche, Apache, and Cheyenne war parties with less than fifty warriors will swing a big circle around us. Old Ben and Deaf don't believe the tribes will go on the warpath before all the snow melts out of the canyons."

"I hope none of them are partial to snow and cold weather, at least not many of them!"

The next morning, by the time the sun had risen a mere hand width above the eastern horizon, they had eaten, loaded all the pack animals, and saddled their own horses. They were ready to quit Miranda's mine and leave Celery Creek Canyon. Only one more task remained to be done, one that was left to Daniel and Hawk. They mounted the rock chimney that led to the cliff's summit, and swung Miranda's rudder back to its original side. Celery Creek was diverted again, and a waterfall that had concealed the mine entrance for nearly eighty years, concealed it once more.

"If I live to be a hundred, I'll never know how you solved this great enigma," Hawk marveled.

"I was lucky enough, with God's help, to discover

how all the clues fit together. That's all."

"Tell it to the aborigines. There was nothing lucky about it. It was brilliant logic. Do you suppose we'll come back here again some day?"

"Will Riley thinks there may be more silver, but most likely it's buried in formations that require very heavy mining equipment, and a lot of hard work to dig it out. But you never know! Maybe some day."

They descended the rock chimney and followed the path Old Ben had discovered that led to the front of the cliff. Once again, cascading water completely hid the entrance from view. As they mounted their horses, Rezin recounted a part of the process that Daniel and Hawk hadn't seen.

"The ramp leading into the mine rose up and shut the entrance as neatly as a door in a house. For a few seconds the waterfall stopped in one spot and started in the other. It was as close to magic as I ever hope to come."

They rode down Celery Creek along a wide path bordered by a gently sloping riverbank on the right and a thickly forested area on the left. A thin film of ice, the final residue of winter storms, covered many shadowy places along the trail that lay hidden from the sun. In such conditions, experienced riders gave the horses their heads and allowed them to find the best footing.

Since the column consisted of twenty packhorses, each one of them heavily loaded with raw silver, as well as two dozen saddle horses, the pace was only as fast as the least sure-footed animals could travel. It was almost mid-morning by the time they covered the first three miles. Here they left the gentle slopes of the shadowy, tree-bordered path, in favor of a steep trail that plunged into a long, narrow, boulder-strewn gorge, whose sheer walls rose to a rim sixty feet high.

Daniel guessed that for the past several thousand years, Celery Creek had been carving its persistent way through soft rock. The channel here was deep and very narrow. The wide trail they had followed in the upper canyon had ended. Now there was barely enough room for the pack train to pass between the steep riverbank and the towering canyon walls.

Suddenly Raven began shifting nervously, then her ears pricked forward as they always did if she sensed danger. Daniel peered anxiously up at both canyon rims. He wasn't surprised when Hawk said.

"Great spot for an ambush."

The next moment they heard a rifle's sharp crack. Ben Berry cried out, clutched his chest, fell from his saddle, and then lay sprawled in a motionless heap. An instant later, a torrent of gunfire poured down on them from the northern rim. The human cries of pain and surprise, and the screams of the wounded horses seemed louder than the gunshots or their long string of echoes.

Daniel heard a bullet fly past his ear, buzzing like an angry hornet. A second bullet tugged his sleeve before a third ricocheted off his saddle and screamed off into space.

"We're easy targets in this deep canyon, Hawk," Daniel shouted, whirling Raven around and urging her forward. "If we're going to survive, we have to reach that grove of oak trees back there. Let's go!"

Twenty-three men and horses started a wild dash back up the canyon to a big stand of oaks that grew along the bank of Celery Creek, a bank that was low and gently sloped. Only seventeen men survived to reach the cover of the trees, leaving Ben Berry and six more of their friends behind.

Only one packhorse was killed. The others began milling about in a confused group near the canyon's mouth. Suddenly, one wise old mare decided to run. With a burst of speed born of panic, she raced away from the chaos. Down Celery Creek Canyon she fled, toward the far end that opened into San Saba Valley. All the other horses followed. Minutes later, humans were the only living creature left to be killed in the terrible valley of death.

Several men who reached the oaks were wounded,

some slightly, some seriously, two critically. Peewee Potts and Matt Clancy had been shot in their chests. Only superior horsemanship had kept them in their saddles long enough to reach the trees. Matt smiled weakly at Daniel and Hawk as they ministered to his wound, knowing that he was dying. When they went to check on Peewee, he was already dead. The little man with the big heart and a lion's courage, Peewee had faced his last challenge, thought Daniel sadly.

Hawk and Francisco Miranda stayed on watch near the western fringe of the trees, while Daniel moved around, checking on the others. Old Ben had already fashioned a sling for Rezin's broken arm, and was winding a rawhide strip around Deaf Smith's bullet-gouged forehead.

"You'll be a mite groggy fer a spell." Old Ben told him. "Dang good thing that yer head ain't soft. Most fellers would a been dead by now."

Daniel couldn't believe the terrible misfortune that had befallen them. His body slumped in despair as he contemplated the loss of the precious silver, and the loss of his friends' lives. He had been so elated when he managed to decipher the cryptic clues and deduce the general location of the mine. The weary weeks they had spent in their saddles, searching the endless canyons without a glimmer of success. Then the almost certain divine intervention when Raven's stumble had disclosed the skull. Being able to solve Miranda's enigma and finding the rock chimney, and finally, gaining entrance to the mine. All the months of back-breaking work they had expended extracting the silver from the bowels of the earth. During those months, men who had been strangers became friends and finally brothers, brothers who were now dead. They had dreamed an impossible dream and made it come true. Now their dream had ended. Even if they could somehow escape from this canyon of death, which at this point seemed highly unlikely, since the attackers now outnumbered the survivors by more than ten to one, judging by the volume of fire that had poured down on them from the canyon rim, the fortune in silver the stampeding horses had carried away was gone for good. It belonged to a war party of Dog Soldiers that had chanced upon them, and they would have to whip the whole Cheyenne Nation before they saw their silver again. A heartbroken Daniel, thinking once more of the men who had died in vain, was so overcome by despair that he covered his face with his hands, and wept bitter tears.

"Daniel," said Old Ben, gently touching his arm, "we're bottled up tighter than a jug of moonshine with a plug in the neck, and we don't know who they are, or how many are doin' the bottlin'. The shootin' was comin' from the north rim, but that don't mean them bushwhackers won't shinny up the south wall."

"What do you propose we do?" Daniel asked as he struggled to regain his outward composure.

"By dark, Deaf'll be fine. So, him, you, me, Jorge Garza, 'Cisco Miranda, and Louis Rose, will split up into a couple of groups, and scale both canyon walls. There's plenty cover along those cliffs, so we won't be seen. We need to know who, how many, and what they seem to be plannin."

The last daylight disappeared in the late afternoon. There was no moon, and the deep darkness of night that matched a sad darkness in their hearts, obscured the canyon floor by early evening. Ben decided that the time to reconnoiter had come.

"Deaf, you take Jorge and Alvin with you. Check the south wall all the way down to the San Saba, if you don't find 'em closer in. Me, Daniel and 'Cisco will scout the north wall. The bushwhackers know we're here. They also kin figger we got to scout 'em out. They'll be sure to cover every gully leadin' up to the canyon rim tween here and where they ambushed us. So we gotta slicker 'em. We need to sneak along the canyon walls, 'til we get a long way past 'em, then we kin double back once we find a way ta the top of the wall. Maybe we kin ketch 'em nappin'. Deaf, whadaya think?"

"It's a good plan, Ben. Jist one more thing. There's bound to be sentries somewhere up thar. So don't do no shootin! Give 'em Green River, boys."

As he said this, Daniel saw Deaf grin wickedly, hold up his big Green River butcher knife, and make a slicing motion across his own throat.

They split up into three-man teams as Old Ben had suggested. Hugging the walls as closely as possible, they crept slowly toward the open end of the canyon. By now, it was so dark that Daniel could barely see Old Ben, who was only a few paces in front of him. They had gone about a mile, when Old Ben stopped so abruptly that Daniel plowed into his back.

"What's wrong," Daniel whispered.

"I smell Injuns," Old Ben whispered. A minute later Cisco rejoined them. "The bushwhackers are a mite smarter than I figgered. Look sharp when you git to any boulder big enough to hide an Injun."

Cautiously, they started along the wall once again just as the thick clouds that had hidden the moon all evening suddenly opened, then quickly closed again. In that fleeting moment of pale moonlight, Daniel glimpsed a metallic flash on top of a squat rock lying just ahead. His first thought was that it had been the reflection from the blade of a poised tomahawk or knife. If so, the man holding the weapon had been surprised by the sudden burst of light.

He grabbed Old Ben's shoulder to warn him, and waited until Cisco caught up with them, then he led the others toward the safety of the small alcove they had passed moments earlier. Once concealed in the dark shadows, Daniel told them what he had seen, and voiced his conclusions.

"You're right!" Old Ben agreed. "Some hombre hidin' atop that rock was mighty surprised. He was mighty careless, too. He should a been watchin' the sky, not lollygaggin'. He could be alone, but more'n likely, there's a parcel of 'em out thar. So we better be set."

Old Ben mulled over the options, then continued.

"Daniel, you walk past the left side o' that rock, as close to the wall as ya can. 'Cisco, you walk along t'other side, far enuff away from the rock so's he can't jump down on ya. He's gonna have to decide which side to go after. While he's decidin', I'll leap up over the front of the rock and nail him. Now, look sharp! Remember that a whole pack of 'em could be lurkin' out there!"

They left the dark shadows and tiptoed toward the hidden assailant. Daniel's heart was hammering so loudly in his ears, he was certain the bushwhacker could hear it.

As he drew abreast of the front of the rock, Daniel detected a soft scraping sound from above. The next instant he heard a short guttural noise, followed by a brief gurgle, and then silence. Three loud heartbeats later, Old Ben slid down the face of the squat rock and crouched beside him.

"He's done fer," Old Ben whispered. "It was light nuff to see his red, yeller, 'n white warpaint, and a dog sign. Our bushwhackers are a band of Southern Cheyenne Dog Soldiers, the best danged warriors and horsemen on the prairie!"

"Help!"

"Coming, Cisco!" Old Ben and Daniel responded with one voice, as the desperate cry for aid reached them.

They sprang into action and raced forward with the speed and deadly intent of a missile launched from a catapult. In the dim light, they saw Cisco with his back against the canyon wall, slashing at a pair of Cheyenne Dog Soldiers with his tomahawk in one hand and knife in the other. As Old Ben and Daniel neared them, the warriors wheeled around, but it was too late. One died with Daniel's knife in his heart, the other, with Francisco's tomahawk in his back. In his final moment of life, he emitted a shrill war cry. A chorus of whoops answered him.

"There's too many of 'em," Milam shouted, loud

enough for all of the members of Deaf Smith's party to hear him. "We gotta make a run fer it. Let's go!"

Bending as low as they could, and staying close to the rocky walls of the canyon, the three men raced back toward the distant grove of oak trees, followed by Deaf and his companions.

In the pitch darkness, broken only by an occasional moonlit patch, the distance they had to cover seemed more like ten miles than one. The war cries and the shots that buzzed over their heads, or whizzed past their ears, added incentive to an already rapid run.

Just as it appeared that they would reach the trees unscathed, Cisco cried out in pain, staggered, and clutched his hip. Old Ben and Daniel, racing along at his sides, were able to grab his arms to support him. An instant later, Daniel felt a sledgehammer blow in his side. The last hundred yards of their race for life was absolute misery and abject torment. As soon as they staggered past the outer fringe of trees, Daniel and Cisco both collapsed.

Daniel regained consciousness to find Rezin hovering over him, and Old Ben doing something to his side.

"Wish you'd waited another minute to wake up, Daniel," Old Ben told him. "You took a slug under yer short ribs. Nothin' busted, but it was bleedin' a mite. I figgered I'd better sew it up fer ya. Rezin, give the lad somethin' to bite on 'til I finish sewin'.'"

"This'll work, Daniel," Rezin said, as he slipped a thin wad of buckskin between Daniel's teeth.

An instant later, Daniel bit down hard on the wad in response to a sudden jab in his side. A series of sharp jabs followed on the heels of the first, then the pain ended. Old Ben Milam rose, and peered down at Daniel's side.

"It ain't real purdy, but the hole's closed, Daniel. I was gonna cauterize it, but if ya burn flesh to seal a wound, ya make a dead spot that don't ever have feelin' in it again. The wound'll heal fine, if ya don't rip the stitches out."

"Thanks, Old Ben. Do you think the Dog Soldiers will attack again tonight?"

"Nope! They'll crawl in as far as they can tonight, hunker down behind rocks and logs, then start firin' into these trees at first light, tryin' ta soften us up. They're goin' to do some damage, fer sure. Come mornin', lead will be dancin' around like a cricket on a hot griddle! N'other thing. If they kin git to the top o the south wall, they kin throw firebrands down inta these trees, n burn us out. We're in a tight spot. That's fer sure!"

At that moment, Hawk joined them.

"I heard what you said about them burning us out. I found a good-sized cave that will give us plenty of protection in the south wall. The mouth of the cave is just beyond the far edge of these trees. The cave's so long that any shots they fire at us will go back to the end, rather than bounce around and hit us. There are two fallen logs at the entrance that'll make great shooting stands. Then, if they burn the trees down, it will be good for us and bad for them because we'll be able to see them better."

"Good work, Hawk," Daniel told him proudly but painfully.

"Since it'll be a whole lot safer in the cave, we'll start movin' wounded in thar right away," Old Ben counseled. "Since we got water n grub, once we're in thar, we kin sit 'n wait 'til the Cheyenne give up."

"I've been thinking about that, too." Daniel said. "To the Cheyenne, winning this fight means scalps, good horses, and lots of good guns. Short of raiding a settlement, where can they go to get so much loot? We're stuck in an isolated valley where no help will arrive. So waiting is good for them, and bad for us."

Old Ben nodded in tacit agreement.

"You have something more in mind, Daniel! What is it?" Hawk asked.

"Many of our friends are dead, and several more of us are hurt. When our packhorses stampeded, we lost the silver we slaved all winter to collect. The silver's gone for good! In that respect, the whole trip's been a fiasco; but the most important objective remains—getting out of this canyon alive, and saving as many of the wounded as possible. We have to forget about the silver and concentrate on getting away while our scalps are still in place."

"Those Dog Soldiers want them," Hawk reminded him.

"They sure do," Daniel agreed. "As long as they keep the initiative, they're likely to get them. Old Ben, you said we're stuck like a cork in a bottle. Like a cork, we can't push our way out of the bottle. We need somebody to pull it out for us."

"From whence might appear these cork pullers of yours?" Hawk inquired.

"They won't appear," Daniel told him. "They're already here."

Old Ben and Hawk stared at him in awe.

"Let's examine the probabilities," Daniel began. "Most likely, the Dog Soldiers don't know about the chimney leading up to the top of the mesa near the waterfall. If by some chance they do, they know we can't get our saddle horses out that way. They also know we can't get very far without our horses. No warrior worth his salt is going to guard against our escape at a place he doesn't expect us to be. Neither will he sit on top of a canyon wall when he can be part of a frontal attack force on the canyon floor. Are you both with me so far?"

Old Ben and Hawk nodded.

"All right. Since we're bottled up in here, all the Cheyenne need to do is sit, wait, send a few bullets into the trees, and perhaps burn us out. They have nothing to fear as long as we're in front of them. But what if we weren't in front of them?"

"You just lost me!" Hawk admitted.

"Ben, what do you suppose would happen if a few snipers snuck in behind the Dog Soldiers and started picking them off, one by one, while a couple of other fellows ran off their pony herd?"

"I kin almost guarantee they'd gather up their dead n wounded, and race after those ponies like their hair was on fire," Old Ben assured him.

"You sure know a lot more about this sort of thing than I do," Daniel admitted "but let me share a few thoughts. First of all, we can be pretty sure that quite a few members of the war party are gone. By now, they're part way back to their villages with our pack animals and the saddle horses of the men they killed in the first attacks. The ones who remain are hungry for horses and scalps. They undoubtedly believe they have us cornered. The last thing they'll expect us to do is attack them. If you start out right now with every man that's able to travel, climb the chimney, then circle back along the north wall, you should be able to find the same way down the wall the Dog Soldiers did. You can locate the pony herd and finish off the guards. Leave a couple men to run off the herd when the shooting starts. Station a couple of sharpshooters up on the rim, and bring the others down to the floor of the canyon. As soon as it gets light enough to see, you can open fire and spook the ponies. When you start firing from there, we'll do the same from here and catch them in a cross fire."

"I like it, Daniel. Most of the time, a Dog Soldier sleeps with a pony tied to his wrist, but I don't think they'll bother while they're safe in the canyon."

Old Ben shared the plan with Deaf, then the two seasoned frontiersmen wandered through the grove and recruited eight others. The ten men were ready to leave a few minutes later. Hawk was one of them. He stopped to see Daniel before he left.

"Old Ben and Deaf are sure the Cheyenne won't attack during the night but, in case they try, three of the wounded men are strong enough to stand guard. You need sleep, Bucko! Don't worry about missing any of the excitement. We'll rouse you at dawn with a thunderous barrage."

Hawk smiled, turned, and quickly faded back into the trees. Daniel didn't see him go. He was already asleep.

The rescue party stole silently out of the grove,

then remained in the deep shadows along the base of the wall until they had covered the first mile. Feeling safer, they moved away from the wall toward a path they had followed on horseback. The open ground made walking easier and permitted a quicker pace. Still, it took nearly two hours for them to reach the waterfall where Old Ben called a short halt.

"We don't know what we're goin' ta find along the top o the cliff, so we best be ready fer anything. The ten of us er too many to move on cat feet. Deaf, you kin see better in the dark than anyone I know. When we git up to the top o the canyon wall, you work in close, along the rim. The rest of us'll sashay along a little distance away from ya. If ya see Injuns, let us know. Jist hoot like an owl. One hoot means a sentry we kin go around. Two hoots mean fer me to come in. Three hoots mean we all come in real slow and easy-like. Four hoots means we all come a-running."

"Good plan, Old Ben!"

"The rest of us'll string out in a line. Stay back far enough to jist barely see the man in front o ya." Old Ben nodded toward Louis Rose. "Louie, you go last, with Jorge jist in front o ya. Keep yer eyes peeled. If a Cheyenne spots us, Green River him. If not, shoot. Remember, a shot ends the surprise party. Somehow, we gotta sneak up on the Dog Soldiers n make 'em turn tail. If we don't, them fellers in the canyon are goners!

Following Old Ben's plan, they climbed the rock chimney, strung out in a single file, and covered a mile without incident. Suddenly, they heard two hoots. Eight men froze in place, while Old Ben went slowly toward the sound.

"A pair of Dog Soldiers are in those cottonwood trees," Deaf whispered to Old Ben. "I heared 'em palaverin'."

"If we kin hear them talkin', they can't hear us walkin'. Let's skirt out around 'em, and keep goin'."

"Whatever you say," Deaf agreed.

Old Ben returned to the others, and whispered to each man. Then he led a detour around the grove of cottonwoods.

They eased along for nearly an hour. Hawk was, by now, nearly certain they were beyond the place in the canyon where Daniel and the others waited. The stillness of the night was broken when an owl hooted three times. The calls were so realistic Hawk thought it might be a real owl.

The line followed Old Ben, and quickly reached the place on the canyon rim where Deaf waited.

"We're 'bout a half mile beyond the Cheyenne war camp. On the way past 'em, I saw the arroyo where they climbed down. Right next to us, there's a gully that a few of us kin use to climb down to the pony herd. Listen, you kin hear the critters movin' around right below us."

"Good work, Deaf!" Old Ben congratulated him. "I'm surprised ya didn't find anymore guards along the rim."

I found two more," Deaf told him. "They're sailin' down Green River."

"I reckon three of us kin kill the guards and run off the pony herd. Deaf, you, me, 'n Alvin will sneak down this arroyo at daybreak," Old Ben decided. "The rest o' ya find good places with plenty o' cover, 'bout ten feet apart, along the rim over their camp. Stampedin' the ponies will bring every Dog Soldier on the run. Give me, Deaf, and Al a minute to git under cover. Then open up and sting 'em. But don't kill 'em. I want wounded Injuns hightailin' it outta here, but I don't want 'em hunkerin' down, fightin', 'cause they er hurt too much ta run.

"I know you're all hoppin' mad about Peewee, Matt, and all the others," Old Ben conceded. "I'm plenty mad myself! But we have ta look out fer the fellers in the oaks. If we jist sting them Dog Soldiers enuff ta hurt 'em, they'll vamoose when they see we got 'em buffaloed. They won't stop runnin' til they ketch their ponies. By the time they git back, if they come back, we'll all be long gone. Spread out along the rim now. Jorge, you fire the first shot when you figger we're in the clear. Then the rest o' ya open up, and be durned careful what ya hit!"

The three seasoned scouts climbed carefully down into the top of the steep gully that led to the canyon floor, and quickly blended into the darkness. Jorge led the others back along the rim until they were directly over the Dog Soldiers' campfire. This was the center of the firing line. Jorge's stand would be here, while three men would take up positions at ten foot intervals on each side of him.

It was only about an hour until dawn, but the time seemed to creep by. Hawk smiled in the darkness as he remembered a similar night when they had waited on the cliff beside the waterfall, anticipating dawn, and hoping that Daniel truly had solved Miranda's enigma. Then he groaned softly as he thought about losing the fortune in silver they had salvaged from the earth, precious silver that would have helped the Texicans win back their freedom.

Daylight had barely streaked the eastern sky when they heard a chorus of shouts and a sudden clatter of hooves. Old Ben and the others had slain the guards and had stampeded the pony herd.

A peaceful morning in the war camp erupted into instant action as Dog Soldiers leaped to their feet, seized weapons, and raced up the shadowy canyon in pursuit of the pony herd. Picking their shots very carefully, the seven men along the rim, and the three who had found safety in the recesses of the arroyo, opened fire. Their care was rewarded. None of the warriors were killed, but nearly all of them suffered some type of wound. Scars of battle the Cheyenne bore with pride would be visible forever.

The rescue party of ten quickly descended to the canyon floor and returned to the camp in the grove of oaks and were greeted with subdued elation. Four of them had received minor wounds in the skirmish, and two more badly wounded men had died during the night, bringing the total to seven dead and eleven wounded. Only six had escaped unscathed.

"Deaf," Old Ben suggested, "why don't you mount up and trail after those Dog Soldiers fer a while. Jist make sure they're hightailin' it. Keep an eye peeled jist in case any of our pack mules might a wandered off in the brush before the Injuns drove 'em through the canyon. I'd sure love ta salvage some of that silver out a this fandango!"

"Do you think the Cheyenne might come back?" Hawk asked Old Ben as Deaf rode out of the grove.

"Nope! They killed about a third of us, picked off more'n twenty packhorses loaded up with our gut-bustin' silver, got scalps n guns off the first few of us they dropped, n enough battle scars ta brag on fer a lifetime. They got a lot more'n they bargained fer.

Nope! They're gone fer good!"

It was late afternoon before Deaf returned. He had watched the Dog Soldiers round up their pony herd, and then trailed them until he was sure they would not return. He hadn't seen any of the pack animals. Daniel's surmise had been correct. Members of the war party had departed with the packtrain and silver long before the battle had ended. By the time Deaf returned, the able men had attended to the wounded and buried the dead in shallow graves, covered with heavy rocks that would protect the bodies from wild animals.

Five of the badly wounded men, including Rique and Will Riley, were too weak to ride.

"We'll rig a travois for each of 'em." Old Ben said to Deaf.

"What's a travois?" Hawk queried.

"You start with a pair of long poles, tie one end of them together then anchor them to a horse's saddle. A short distance up from the lower end you fasten a platform. It can be fashioned from tree branches or a blanket. It doesn't matter, just as long as it's sturdy enough to keep the poles in place and bear a man's weight," Daniel explained. "Kind of like a horse-drawn stretcher."

"The lower end just bumps along on the ground?" Hawk asked.

"Right. It's not a comfortable way to travel, but it's the only way if a man can't ride."

Hauling the five travois slowed the pace to a walk as they made their way toward the mouth of Celery Creek Canyon. Mounted on the sure-footed Raven, Daniel rode behind the travois carrying Rique and Will, and watched as they pitched and bounced over the rough ground. The five riders who were leading the travois horses were careful as possible to avoid the worst spots, but the badly wounded occupants could not help grimacing in pain from time to time. Travel would be easier when they reached the San Saba River Valley. Riverbanks were much smoother than the rugged canyon's floor.

"This trip has been a disaster," Daniel told Hawk as they rode along. "Seven men dead, seven more badly injured, and a king's ransom in silver we worked our hearts out to get is gone. It's a complete disaster!"

"I can't completely agree with you," replied Hawk. "Sure, men died and some were hurt, and we lost the silver, but life isn't only about winning. It's really more about trying. It's about doing your best, and knowing you did your best! It's about starting over and thinking, 'I lost this time, but I'll win next time, because my heart is pure, and my cause is just.' Most of all, it's knowing that God's Will is all that really counts, not our own."

"Of course, you're right," Daniel agreed. "But if we had gotten out with the silver, we would have been able to buy cannon, munitions, supplies, and hire enough mercenaries to confront Santa Anna's army on nearly even terms."

"'If' is the biggest tiny word in the whole language because it usually introduces an excuse for failure. I suggest that we acknowledge our failure, and replace 'if' with 'since.' Since we failed to get away with a fortune in silver, we'll have to confront the Mexican army on uneven terms."

"You're bubbling over with advice today, aren't you?" Daniel remarked as he grimaced in pain.

"Since I'm on target, I'll add a couple more sage observations. Whether we're well-armed or not, we must fight Santa Anna, or live to regret it. There is no other choice. All we can do, between now and the start of the war, is recruit as many men as possible and develop a tactical plan that will allow us to fight him on our own terms. What you have to do is heal up and recover your strength so that you can go hell bent for leather when the curtain goes up. And it looks like you won't be doing much of anything else for the next few weeks. Life is a series of challenges, Daniel; this is just the latest one in your life."

Bruce T. Clark

PART TWO
JIM BOWIE'S STORY

XII
RENAISSANCE

SAN FELIPE, TEJAS
JUNE 5, 1835

He should have seen and heard the horse and rider thundering down at him, but his befuddled mind was incapable of distinguishing reality from apparition. Fortunately, the animal was far more nimble than the bleary-eyed pedestrian, and veered just enough to avoid a nasty collision. Not until the horseman swept past did he compute the unexpected appearance, the rapid departure, and the serious injury he had barely escaped. Only then did he lurch backward, lose his balance, and fall in a tattered heap in the middle of the dusty street. The horseman's contemptuous shout reached him.

"Borrachon! Bufon! Desvalido zamacuco!" (Drunkard! Buffoon! Penniless oaf!).

A gang of Mexican urchins took up the loud cry.

"Borrachon! Bufon! Borrachon!"

Distrusting himself to stand without a support, the man crawled toward the hitching rail in front of El Diablo Rojo Cantina and slowly levered himself to his feet, then turned toward the urchins and grinned

241

stupidly. They shouted several more stinging insults, then melted away to find more enjoyable pastimes. It was no fun to tease a man too drunk to know he was being insulted.

After clutching the hitching rail for a few minutes, the man gathered enough confidence to try walking. He staggered into the cantina, grunted twice, pointed once, and sank gratefully into a heavy oak chair with sturdy arms.

Flaco, the skinny owner of the cantina, had been unable to understand the man's words, but he knew what the fellow wanted. He picked up an old cracked bottle of tequila, the cheapest rotgut he had, blew off the dust and took it to the man's table. He shuddered as he set it down along with a broken-handled cup. Even the poorest mozos refused to consume the fiery stuff. Local legend said it would make you go blind. He felt a small surge of guilt, but the feeling quickly passed. He probably would not be paid, and he could not afford to waste decent whisky on a drunkard. If the big fellow went blind, it would serve him right.

The man ignored the cup and eagerly seized the bottle, then leaned back and opened his mouth wide. After a number of failed efforts, he finally managed to insert the narrow bottleneck between his lips and pour the liquid fire down his throat. Flaco and his patrons watched in fascination as the tequila gurgled out of the bottle until every drop was gone. They continued to stare, anticipating the big man's collapse, but he did not fall out of the chair. When he finally realized that further sucking on the bottle would be futile, he cautiously leaned forward and stared warily out at them from the depths of bloodshot eyes, buried in a deeply-lined and bewhiskered face that offered mute testimony to the extent of his dreadful suffering. At last, the drunkard carefully laid his head on folded arms, fell asleep, and began snoring contentedly.

"So that's Jim Bowie?" the man at a nearby table sneered.

"Yep! That's him. The biggest drunk in Texas."

"He was quite a famous fellow in his day."

"Yep! Now he's a famous human hog, swillin' and wallowin' in his own slop. He sure stinks, don't he?"

"He does indeed! It's a terrible thing when a man let's himself go to hell like this. I guess famous men hit the skids harder than the rest of us 'cause they got a lot farther to fall."

A roughly dressed man who had just entered the cantina overheard their exchange.

"I'd be careful about insulting Jim Bowie if I were you. Drunk or sober, he's still a far better man than either of you and most other men in Texas. He may suddenly awake, slit your gizzards, and harvest your innards if you're not careful."

243

"Were you a friend of Bowie's in his glory days?" queried one of the men.

"I am his friend! Texas will need all of her fighting men very soon, and Jim Bowie is one of the best. I've come to take him back."

"It'll be a hard row to hoe! He's pretty far gone!" Glints of anger in the stranger's dark eyes compelled the speaker to cautiously add, "I meant no offense!"

"It'll be hard all right, but it can be done. Bowie's no worse than I was when I came back from hell."

"I never laid eyes on you before, stranger, but I believe that if anybody can save Bowie, you can."

"What might your name be?" the second man asked the newcomer.

"Sam Houston," came the soft reply.

Early the next morning, as Jim Bowie struggled to emerge from his alcoholic fog, he heard a voice.

"By thunder, those jackanapes were right. You do stink like a hog!"

Bowie cautiously opened one eye just enough to see the world spinning wildly around him. Unwilling to face a new day, he closed it. His whole body felt like a blazing log in a bonfire, and his head felt like an Apache tomahawk had cleft it in two. Suddenly, a wet towel was pressed to his forehead. Unexpected, blessed relief! Who might the Good Samaritan be, he wondered, but not enough to open his eye again.

He lay still for a few minutes, then slowly opened his other eye. Everything was still spinning, but not as wildly. Throwing caution to the winds, he opened both eyes. As his vision gradually cleared, he made two remarkable discoveries. He was lying on a soft bed in a clean room, and Sam Houston was standing next to him.

"Is it really you, Sam?" Jim garbled.

"It's me, and you've led me on quite a wild goose chase. Goliad, Gonzales, Arcadia, Bexar, Monclova and then all the way back up here to San Felipe."

"Don't go to Bexar any more," Bowie mumbled.

"I know, Jim! There's too much pain in Bexar. But whiskey won't heal your pain. It may dull it for a bit, but it comes back stronger than ever. Only time will heal the pain, Jim!"

"Maybe so," Bowie acknowledged, "but right now I need a drink."

"That's the last thing you need!"

Angrily, Bowie swung his feet out of bed and tried to sit up. The simple movement made him howl in agony. A new tomahawk blade sank into his skull. Raging pain sucked the air from his protesting lungs. Struggling for breath, he pressed both hands against his throbbing temples in an effort to stop his head from exploding.

245

He lay back down on the bed and tried to compose himself, but could not ignore his craving for alcohol, the insidious demon that was destroying his body.

"I need a drink, Sam!" He had to shout to be heard over the deafening clanging in his ears.

"You don't need a drink. You want a drink. I'll give you a drink if you promise to look in a mirror, take a bath, and hear me out. Agreed?"

To get a drink, he would have agreed to anything.

"Agreed!"

Houston reached into his portmanteau, withdrew a whisky bottle, and handed it to Bowie. Only one big swallow remained. Bowie sat up, knocked back the liquor in the blink of an eye, and tried to grin.

"Thanks, Sam!"

"Now, you're going to look in a mirror," Houston told Bowie, helping him up.

With Houston's support, Bowie staggered to the large, cracked mirror that hung over the sink.

"You may be shocked at what you see."

It was difficult to look into the mirror. The bright sunlight shining through the window hurt his eyes. He closed them for a moment and tried again. This time he saw a pair of faces with the same frightening features. They drifted farther apart, came back, merged briefly, separated again, then finally blended together.

Bowie was shocked by his image. He was not yet forty, but he was looking into the face of an eighty-year-old. Deeply sunken, red-rimmed, bloodshot eyes, all but hidden in the shadows of thick, bushy eyebrows—a bulbous, blue-veined nose, and long, dirty, tangled hair. As Bowie watched, the image in the mirror grew blurred again, slowly faded, and was replaced by a hideous, distended mouth. Before his startled eyes, the effigy became the snarling maw of a grotesque carnivore. He waited expectantly for the creature to roar, but it was not a vicious snarl that issued from the hideous creature. It was a piercing, silent scream that only he could hear.

It took over a week for Bowie to emerge from the uncaring, alcoholic stupor that had imprisoned him for so long. Houston talked to him each day. At first, Bowie couldn't understand many of his words, but it really didn't matter. Houston was here because he was concerned about his friend, and Bowie knew it. Throughout each of those long, dark days, Houston's calm voice reassured him, his strong hand steadied him, and his unwavering resolve to bring Bowie out of his pitiful, intoxicated stupor saved him.

During the first few days, Bowie slept fitfully in a hazy, twilight dream world, awakening only when nature required a trip to the backhouse. He was barely able to stagger back and forth with Houston's help, but alert enough to pester him for a drink.

Houston understood Bowie's torment. Mexicans called Bowie Borrachon. When Houston lived with the Cherokees, they called him Ootsetee Arditaskee. Spanish and Cherokee words were different, but they both meant drunkard!

On the third day, Bowie tried to drink a cup of thin soup, but he couldn't keep it down.

"Don't worry, Jim! You haven't had anything to eat for a few days. You have to adjust. After that, you'll be fine."

"I need a drink more than food, Sam!"

"I won't give you one!"

The furious Bowie's hand shot to his hip.

"Put the knife away! Jim, you're sober enough to understand me. Both of us are drunks! We always will be drunks! We'll always crave alcohol. We start drinking to forget pain, and we keep drinking until we can't stop. We justify drunken stupors by telling ourselves we're useless men and no one cares about us, anyway. Many men never find enough strength or a good enough reason to quit drinking. But you and I aren't ordinary men. We have the strength, and I'm going to give you a monumental reason to quit. Santa Anna is coming. He may get here before the snow flies, or he may not come until the spring, but he's coming with one goal in mind, to kill Texicans.

Houston paused to make sure Bowie was listening.

"We have to get ready. Twenty thousand Texicans are scattered all around the countryside. To most of them, Apache, Comanche, Cheyenne, and a dozen other tribes, are bigger menaces than Santa Anna. It's easy to see their point of view. They can't be expected to face the Mexicans while Injun warriors are threatening their wives and kids. So to fight the experienced Mexican army, we need to recruit and train a powerful military force from among Texicans without family responsibilities. That takes time, but time is something we don't have a whole lot of. I'm convinced we'll be fighting before Christmas."

Houston saw stark realization in Bowie's eyes.

"Thank God we're blessed with good leaders and courageous fighting men!" Houston continued. "You were the best of both! You can be again! You must be again! I'm not asking you to do it for me, or even for yourself. I'm asking you to do it for the lives and safety of thousands of settlers, and for the future of Texas."

Bowie was jolted back into a world of reality. The following day, he ate several bowls of soup, and by week's end, he was able to handle solid food. By the middle of the second week, he was out riding around the countryside on horseback. As a result, his skin tone improved and his muscles became stronger. Most important of all, his mind began to clear. Each day, he listened to Houston as he described all the events that had occurred during Bowie's lost months.

"Santa Anna is out of control. As soon as he took the oath of office as president, a revolt, a carefully planned, well-staged revolt, broke out. He marched south to 'stamp out' all the insurgence. As his army moved into place, his own soldiers 'revolted' and joined the 'insurgents' that they had come to fight. Santa Anna made a speech to the entire assemblage, in which he made impossible promises and, lo and behold, soldiers and former insurgents demonstrated in his favor and declared Santa Anna the Dictator of Mexico. That episode was soon followed by a great demonstration in the capital, staged by the powerful aristocrats who support him. Those events, coupled with the uneducated public's gullible willingness to accept blatant propaganda, transformed Santa Anna into a Dictator. He announced a Plan of Cuernavaca, renouncing all of the reforms he promised when he became president. Worst of all, he denounced the Constitution of 1824. Texicans no longer have legal rights. A few men tried to stand up to him. Some were thrown into prison; most were put in front of a firing squad. Stephen Austin went to Mexico City to plead for justice, and was clapped into a cell then and there!"

Bowie listened in growing disbelief. So much had changed since the awful epidemic had taken Theresa and the children away from him. He, himself, had married into the Mexican aristocracy. Santa Anna had been Theresa's godfather. It was understandable because her father had been a high-ranking official.

"Stephen Austin's nephew, Daniel, escaped from their prison," Houston continued, "and brought us bad news. Mexican troops have garrisoned Coahuila. Santa Anna is recruiting and training a huge army! No doubt about it, they'll be at our throats before long!"

"We mustn't wait for them to attack us," exploded Bowie, "we must go out to attack them. We can kill a dozen or more at each river crossing, pick off the stragglers along their line of march, and generally bedevil them. It might not stop them, but it'll sure soften them up."

Houston smiled. He remembered saying the very same words last Assumption Day in Bexar.

"Jim, since you're no longer in an inebriated state, there are a number of things you need to know." Houston paused and then added, "They aren't very pleasant. Shall I go on?"

Bowie nodded.

"After my own terrible months of inebriation, I

had trouble recalling some of the things I had done. Maybe you'll find that to be true. Do you remember a land grant for a man named Mason?"

Bowie searched his memory, but no recollection came forth.

"No. My mind is blank."

"Just before Santa Anna took control, a number of irregularities occurred at the Monclova Legislature's final session. It is said that James Bowie used all of his influence to obtain a grant for John Mason. The grant was for a hundred sitios, nearly half a million acres. Most Texicans are furious about it."

Bowie concentrated, and vaguely remembered the days in Monclova when he had teetered on a razor's edge between deep drunkenness and a faint sobriety. Through the fog of time came faces of the men who had been at the conclave: S.M. William, acalde of San Felipe; Dr. James Grant, a big land holder in Coahuila; Grant's friend, John Cameron, and the smooth-talking, glib, John Mason. Bowie vaguely remembered somebody else, his long time drinking buddy, Old Ben Milam.

"I only remember they were all there to take care of some 'details.' I didn't care about anything other than where my next drink was coming from. What was it all about?"

"Many people believe that sooner or later, Texas

will separate from Coahuila and become a sovereign state. In anticipation of that, political string-pullers have been siphoning off huge tracts of land with the aid of Monclova politicians. They are interested only in lining their own pockets. As a result, great tracts of unoccupied land are being sold to speculators for very little, compared to the value they will have in the future, a future that Texas will have only if the land remains in the public domain. Land represents the only revenue source Texas will have to capitalize and incorporate key ingredients of ensured progress. But as it stands, everything is being thrown away by greedy men who are concerned only with their own futures."

"All I remember is the drinking. Everything else is still dim."

"Do you remember signing any papers? Letters, maybe?" Houston queried.

"I might have, Sam. I just don't know."

"Letters were sent to over a dozen of the principal investors in the land syndicate that you and Don Juan de Verdimente established. The letters asked those men to support the sale of gigantic tracts of land to people who would hold them in trust until the war against Santa Anna ends. The letters, bearing your signature, went on to suggest that, if he were still alive, Juan de Verdimente would support the sales.

Since the men trusted your judgment, they did as you asked, only to discover that the tracts would not be held in trust for the people of Texas, but sold for great profits. Worst of all, forgeries of the original Spanish land grants were substituted. Obvious deception was discovered and quickly exposed, because the false signatures on replacement documents were patently bogus. The entire episode was messy, pitiful as it was illegal."

"They made me a cat's paw, Sam. They got away with it while I was wallowing in drunken self-pity. I've thrown away my reputation for good sense and honesty."

Bowie paused as a new thought occurred to him.

"It's ironic! Those dishonest brigands who imperil the future of Texas can realize huge profits only if Santa Anna is defeated. Folks may conclude that you and I are conspiring to guarantee the rogues' booty by encouraging a war, rather than suing for peace. Of course, we'll find a way to derail their dreams of riches but, until then, many men may misunderstand and mistrust our motives."

Houston stayed for another week to make certain that Bowie had regained control of his life. He left at dawn on the first day of summer.

"As badly as we need to recruit fighting men, I want you to be sure you're rested up and fit before you hit the trail, Jim. Unless I miss my guess, I'm going to wind up as the General-in-Charge of Texan Armies long before any armies exist. Stephen Austin is a prisoner and, even if he were here, he wouldn't want the job. Lot of others would. But when you get right down to it, these Texicans won't follow anyone except Austin or me. So, it's time to select a general staff. Bowie, you are hereby appointed a Colonel of Volunteers. Now you need to recruit the volunteers. Doing that will require a reliable horse and a bit of travelling money."

Houston tossed a heavy rawhide bag onto the bed that clinked as it landed.

"Advance on your military pay, Colonel Bowie."

He heaved his portmanteau to his broad shoulder, and smiled.

"I'll be seeing you, Jim. Until then, take care of yourself."

Bowie rose and shook Houston's hand.

"You, too, General Sam." He smiled, then soberly added. "Don't worry! I won't let you down."

As Houston reached the doorway, he turned back and faced Bowie.

"I know a handful of men I trust enough to cover my back in a fight. I'd trust some of those same men with the lives of my family; but there are only a few special men I would trust with the life of Texas. You

255

are one of those men, Jim. Before this fight is over, that life may very well rest in your hands."

He turned and strode through the doorway. Bowie listened until the echo of his footsteps disappeared in the distance. During his long debauchery, he had lost a good deal of muscle. To regain it, he needed a lot of good food, increasingly demanding exercise, and plenty of sleep. He decided that a nap before dinner was in order. Houston was right; he would spend a few more days recuperating before he left. He might go horse hunting tomorrow, he thought, as he dozed off. That was always an interesting experience.

Tomorrow came and went, and the next day did as well. On the third morning, Jim Bowie rose at the crack of dawn and consumed a big breakfast. He ambled over to the general store as soon as it opened, and was fortunate enough to find two buckskin outfits roomy enough to accommodate the additional weight and muscle he needed to recover. The store clerk said the skins had been tanned and sewed by a local Mexican woman who had learned the special art during the time she'd spent as a Comanche prisoner. The skins were soft and pliable. The lower sleeves, from elbow to wrist, were beautifully fringed but thankfully, there were no beads. Beads glinted in the sunlight, and seemed to snag in thick undergrowth at the most inopportune times, like in the middle of a fight with Indians.

"Have you lived in San Felipe long?" Bowie asked the clerk.

"Most of my life."

"If you wanted to buy a couple of good horses, where would you go?"

"Rancho Arroyo," came a reply without hesitation. "The Arroyo family have the best horses for which they demand the best prices."

"Where is the rancho?"

"A few miles north of San Felipe."

"How do I get there?" Bowie asked politely.

"Ricardo Arroyo is in town. That buckboard across the street is his, Señor."

"Many thanks, amigo."

Dressed now in his new buckskins, a pair of sturdy, well-made boots, and a wide-brimmed, flat-crowned hat, Bowie gathered up his remaining purchases and strolled toward Arroyo's buckboard.

Just as he approached, an elderly well-dressed man walked out of a nearby saddle and harness shop and climbed into the buckboard.

"Señor Arroyo?" Bowie asked.

"At your service, Señor," the caballero replied.

"Good morning. My name is James Bowie. I am told that you own the finest horses in the territory. I would like to buy two of them, a saddle horse and a pack animal."

"My sons and I will be honored to accommodate you," a puzzled Señor Arroyo assured Bowie as he extended his hand. Six weeks ago, he and his son Juan had found Bowie collapsed at the mouth of a dark alley. They tried to rouse him and transport him to a safer place, but their efforts were useless. Bowie was simply too drunk and heavy. The man's rancid odor remained in their nostrils for hours afterward. Yet, here was the same man, sober, clean, dressed in fine buckskins, and in need of a pair of horses. Arroyo wondered how such a miracle could have transpired. It was all but impossible.

"Señor Bowie, please forgive my presumption, but I have no doubt that you will find suitable animals at my rancho. Would it not be prudent to purchase the necessary tack and gear while you are at the saddlery shop?"

"It certainly would," Bowie agreed. "Thank you for your suggestion."

They entered one of the most complete tack shops Bowie had ever seen. More than three dozen saddles were arrayed, from simple work and packsaddles to show saddles that were elaborately tooled and inlaid with costly silver. In short order, Bowie found a comfortable new saddle for himself, and a used, but serviceable packsaddle, as well as a pair of brightly colored saddle blankets. After the gear was stowed in the buckboard, Arroyo made another suggestion.

"If you intend to travel any distance, Señor Bowie, you need weapons, food, and camping equipment. Do you not?" he added politely.

"I will indeed."

Firearms were not abundant on the frontier, but the general store had some in stock. Bowie was lucky enough to find an excellent Kentucky long rifle, and a somewhat rusty, but usable, pistol. He added dry staples, such as cornmeal, beans, flour, salt, and coffee. A kettle, a small pot, a frying pan, four short, thin iron rods, and two spoons completed his cooking and eating needs. Two heavy blankets and a pair of waterproof covers ended his buying spree. One would serve as a ground cloth as he slept. The other would cover and protect him in rainstorms.

"Señor Bowie," Arroyo said, as they drove out of town, "I have been thinking about my saddle horses. I believe Azogue would be the ideal mount for you."

Bowie was familiar enough with horse ranches to know that it was unusual for any of the animals to be named. Azogue, a word that in English referred to the metallic element mercury, must be a very special animal.

Rancho Arroyo lay in a small valley surrounded by

low hills. Bowie's first glance took in the sprawling adobe hacienda and high protective wall encircling it. A wide, tree-lined stream meandered through the center of the valley and provided fresh water and welcome shade for several hundred horses grazing in knee-deep, lush green grass. Behind the hacienda stood several corrals, barns, stables, and sheds. Off to one side, he saw a long, low building with a veranda. He presumed it was a bunkhouse where unmarried vaqueros lived. The valley's perimeter was dotted by at least two dozen small, comfortable looking casas. Outside many of the dwellings, children scampered about. Bowie was impressed by the obvious concern the Arroyos had for their workers, as well as the prosperity that the rancho bespoke. Ricardo Arroyo drove directly to one of the big corrals where a man was patiently working with a skittish sorrel colt.

"Miguel. Can you spare a few minutes?"

"Of course, Padre."

The vaquero tied the colt up short to the snubbing post, left the corral, and walked toward them.

"Señor Bowie, may I present to you my elder son, Miguel. Miguel, this is El Señor James Bowie."

"It's a pleasure, Miguel."

"For me, Señor Bowie, it is an honor. I have heard about many of your adventures, and am one of your unshakable admirers."

"An esteemed member of a diminishing club?"

"Only a member of the frail human race who is no longer worthy enough to throw stones."

"Our guest needs a good horse," Ricardo Arroyo told Miguel. "I have a special animal in mind."

"Azogue?" Miguel queried.

"Azogue." His father affirmed. "Is he nearby?"

"In the small pasture. I'll go down and get him."

"Saddle a pair of mounts for Señor Bowie and me. We'll ride down to the pasture."

A few minutes later, Bowie and his host left the main building and rode a short distance to a pasture that held two dozen horses. As they approached the gate, one of the horses suddenly burst away from the others and raced toward the far end of the enclosure. When he reached the fence, he spun nimbly around and raced back. His flying feet seemed to float above the earth. Bowie watched as he came. Bright silver coat shining in the sun. Long slim legs, deep chest and strong back. The magnificent animal was at least the equal of Steel Duke, who was Bowie's yardstick of horseflesh.

"I hope that's Azogue."

"It is!" Señor Arroyo confirmed. "Now you see the reason for his name."

"Azogue means mercury in English," Bowie said.

"It also means quicksilver. Azogue, who is a four-

261

year-old, is the fastest horse we have ever bred. His sire is our finest stallion, Eperador. Azogue was the last colt of Esperanza. Esperanza is twenty now, but she still runs like a bolt of lightning."

There was a clatter of hooves behind them, and a moment later, a slender young man in his late teens or early twenties rode up beside them.

"Señor Bowie," this is my younger son Juan, but everyone calls him Vaquero."

"Con mucho gusto, Señor Bowie." The youngster had an infectious smile.

"My pleasure, Vaquero," Bowie said as they shook hands.

"Señor Bowie needs a saddle horse. Since there is little doubt that in the perilous days that lie ahead, he will be compelled to go in harms' way. The mount that we select must have speed, stamina, and heart. I thought of Azogue, but since you train all the horses, I would be pleased to hear your suggestion. I'm sure Señor Bowie would as well."

"Most assuredly," Bowie agreed.

"Azogue would also be my choice. He's big and strong, and unlike most other young stallions, not aggressive by nature. Azogue is easygoing unless another horse tries to rough him up, then heaven help that horse. He's also incredibly fast. Azogue is the only horse to ever beat my Listo," Juan said, rubbing the head of the sorrel filly he was riding. "As her name implies, Listo is always ready to run. The only other horse on the rancho that can run with those two is Cojera."

Bowie was puzzled. He had seen the burst of speed Azogue could muster. In English, cojera meant limp, or hobble.

"You've piqued my curiosity, Juan. How can any horse named Cojera compete with lightning streaks like Listo and Azogue?"

In response to Bowie's question, Juan spread his mouth apart with two fingers, and emitted a loud, shrill whistle. At least a dozen horses in the pasture stopped grazing, and looked toward the vaquero.

"Cojera!" Juan called.

A smallish, dainty looking strawberry roan filly began walking slowly toward the fence. Each time her left foreleg came down, she lurched forward.

Juan dismounted and met the animal at the fence.

"This is Cojera," he told Bowie, stroking her ears. "When she was a two-year-old, she got a big cactus spike imbedded in her hoof. We removed it and doctored the wound, but it took a long time to fully heal. She got around by learning to keep as much weight off that foot as she could. That was nearly a year ago, but she still limps when she walks. When she runs, the limp disappears. Hopefully, I can get her to stop the habit because a man would go crazy trying to ride her as long as the habit persists."

"You train the horses to respond to your whistle?"

"The special ones," Juan acknowledged. "I teach them a few other tricks as well. I'll demonstrate."

Juan whistled, and once again the heads came up.

"Azogue!"

Azogue trotted up to the fence and stopped. Juan reached between the rails and stroked the animal's foreleg. The result was astonishing. It was almost as if Azogue had been shot. He toppled to the ground and, aside from breathing, lay absolutely motionless. When his foreleg was stroked again, he bounded back to his feet.

"It occurred to me that a horse lying flat behind a log, or some similar cover during a gunfight with marauders is a lot harder to hit than one that stands up and provides an easy target. If you're ambushed, or if your horse is killed, it's just a matter of time until you are, too."

"No doubt about that," Bowie agreed. "There is also no doubt that Azogue is a horse that any man would be fortunate to own. I'm sure that you'll feel reluctant to let him go."

"Our business here at Rancho Arroyo is raising, training, and selling fine horses, Señor Bowie. It is, as you say, hard to part with the special ones, and

Azogue is a very special horse." Juan paused, smiled and then added, "Together, you will make a good team, for you are a very special man."

Bowie, blushing at the sincere praise, reached out and gently squeezed the young vaquero's arm.

"Azogue will serve you well, Señor Bowie," Juan said confidently. "The presence of the packsaddle is the reason I mentioned Cojera. Because of her speed, she would be an ideal running mate for Azogue. She will outgrow her habit, and when she does, you can ride her occasionally and give Azogue a rest."

"A great idea," Bowie responded enthusiastically.

A price for the horses was quickly agreed upon, and then Bowie spent the remainder of the afternoon familiarizing himself with the animals and learning several other tricks that Juan had taught them.

Bowie left early the next morning, well mounted, and completely certain about the Arroyo family's firm support in the fight that lay ahead. As he rode northward, he wondered how many Texicans would be willing to fight for justice, and how many would settle for peace at any price.

XIII
WINDS OF WAR

Two months of hard riding had taken Jim Bowie to most of the Texican towns and villages, as well as a great many of the far-flung frontier outposts. It was a saddle-weary rider who guided his foot-sore pair of horses into this river port on the south bank of the Rio Grande, just as the sun began sinking below the western horizon.

Those months had burned his skin a rich shade of brown quite common to Mexican vaqueros. The dark skin, coupled with a well-worn Mexican saddle with its broad tilted horn and square skirts, as well as his authentic Mexican clothing replete with serape and wide-brimmed sombrero, identified the man as one of their own to the other riders and strollers in each of the border towns that he had visited in the past few days. Only the horses that the stranger rode and led were worthy of a second look, but the flinty eyes and firm jaw of their owner served to quell curiosity and discouraged either conversation or questions.

Bowie was in a sour mood because he bore bitter

news. A Mexican army was on the march, but it was unlike any army most Texicans expected, much less one they'd ever seen. This was no column of lancers with a horde of weary dusty peons masquerading as foot soldiers, sloughing along in their wake. Indeed not! It was a real army with real cavalry and real infantry, several dozen artillery pieces, and a supply train more than a mile long. Santa Anna's brother-in-law, General Martin Perfecto de Cos, who was also a trusted and able subordinate, commanded the three-thousand-man army.

Bowie had ridden into Matamoros because he was almost certain that this Rio Grande port would be a strategic location for Cos as he moved north, since a few barges could carry more supplies than a train of wagons. There were several men in town who might be able to verify his suspicions, but would they offer him the kind of help a friend could expect, or reject him as an outcast that should be shunned?

Reports of his part in the Nacogdoches fiasco had made him unwelcome in many of the settlements he had visited on his long journey. How quick people were to judge without all of the facts, he thought. He was just as unpopular with the Mexican authorities. Colonel Piedras called him an uncouth barbarian, the most dangerous Texan enemy Cos would face. They were dangerous times all right, Bowie mused, as he dismounted at the town livery stable. Cos would stand him before a firing squad if he were caught, and a whole flock of Texicans would shoot him in the back if he weren't careful. But Houston believed in him, and that was all that really mattered to Jim.

He was fortunate that after stabling his horses, the first hacienda he chanced to call upon was that of Felipe Seguin, the brother of Juan Seguin, the acalde of San Antonio de Bexar.

An elderly mozo in wine-colored livery answered Bowie's knock, then, shuffling ahead, ushered him into a large paneled estudio. Racks of books covered the walls and big, comfortable chairs were scattered about the opulent room. Still reluctant to assume a cordial greeting, Bowie remained standing near the door. He had not long to wait before a well-dressed, middle-aged caballero entered, his face wreathed in smiles.

"Don Jaime," Felipe Seguin beamed, "you cannot imagine the joy that your presence brought to Dona Constanzia and me when Carlos announced you. Dona Constanzia will join us for our evening meal which the servants are preparing. But first, will you join me in a refreshment?"

"Con mucho gusto, Don Felipe. You and Dona Constanzia are most gracious to receive me."

"How else would we greet an old and dear

friend?"

Bowie accepted the goblet his host offered and sank gratefully into one of the large, soft chairs. He was relieved when he sipped and discovered that the goblet contained a tangy fruit punch rather than the wine he had expected. His new resolve to end his drinking had obviously preceded him.

"Delicious and most refreshing," he complimented his host. "What is the word along the river about the approach of General Cos, Don Felipe?"

"Every vessel has been commandeered to transport the soldiers across the river, along with their artillery and supplies. A notice forbidding foreigners to leave the city under any circumstances has been posted in the plaza. This morning a vaquero arrived from the south. He said Cos was in Saltillo with over three thousand troops."

"That's correct," Bowie agreed. "I just came from Saltillo."

"Señor Guillermo Travis," Don Felipe continued, "spent some time with us about three weeks ago. He helped to establish a committee of safety and set up a company of volunteer soldiers. They meet each evening to practice the things Señor Travis taught them. Oh," he suddenly exclaimed, "I almost forgot. I have two letters for you. One from Señor Travis, and one from Señor Houston. They are here on this bookshelf."

Don Felipe went to the bookshelf, and took two envelopes off the shelf, then handed them to Bowie. Houston's note said he would be in Nacogdoches around the middle of September, and hoped to meet Bowie there. Bowie opened the letter from Travis.

Dear Bowie: The truth is that the people are much divided here. The local peace party, I believe, is the strongest and makes the most noise. Unless we can unite, had we better not be quiet and settle down for a while? There is no doubt a Centrist government will be established. What will Texas do in that case? Dr. Miller and Chambers from Gonzales are, I believe, for unqualified submission. I don't know the minds of other people on that subject, but if they had a bold and determined leader, I am inclined to think they would kick against it. General Cos writes that he wants to be at peace with us, and he appears disposed to cajole and soothe us. The same is true of Urgartechea. Only God knows what we are to do. I am determined, for one, to go with my countrymen: "right or wrong, sink or swim, live or die, survive or perish," I am with them! Buck Travis.

Unfortunately, things weren't as clear cut for most men as they were for Travis.

Bowie departed early the following morning, and once again headed north. His destination was Bexar.

The thought of returning to the place where Therese and he had enjoyed wondrous happiness was a red-hot coal in his brain; but go he must, since he carried dispatches from the Matamoros Safety Committee to Travis, and letters from Felipe Seguin to his brother, Juan.

He made several detours along the way to check out various remote ranchos. He was welcomed by some, and treated with abject disdain by others. The attitudes about a proper course of action against Cos were just as divided. Travis's evaluation was correct. The Texicans were badly splintered.

Because of his zigzag path, it was late evening on September 1st by the time he reached Juan Seguin's spacious hacienda and was welcomed by his host.

"A hundred thousand greetings, Don Jaime. This has indeed been my day to welcome great men," said Seguin, gesturing toward a dim figure who stood in the doorway of the hacienda.

"Good evening, Mr. Bowie. As you can see, I'm a little worse for wear, but I'm back." Stephen Austin smiled weakly as he stepped into the courtyard. The two men were too different to ever be friends, and Bowie was a Houston man.

"You've returned none too soon, sir. The Texicans

are badly divided. Many of them are in favor of war. Some want a negotiated peace. A few will settle for a quick peace at any price! Most don't know what they want! They need leadership, and need it now!"

"This is not the time for disunion," Stephen Austin replied. "It's a time for every Texican to stand up for constitutional liberties. The task ahead will require many bodies, but they must feel the beat of only one heart, a true heart that longs for justice. I shall send out that word at once."

"I agree, sir. That's the kind of decisive message, the kind of rallying call that will end the disunity. It will also make it abundantly clear to Cos that we are prepared to fight him rather than knuckle under. He is in Saltillo, but I expect he'll march just as soon as he knows your intentions."

"I concur, Mr. Bowie, but Santa Anna would send Cos after us soon enough in any case. Our weakness, our lack of resolve, would simply make him stronger and more resolute. Bye the bye, I'm surprised to find you here. I'd supposed you'd be with Mr. Houston."

"I left Houston a couple months ago. He sent me down here to recruit men while he went off to other areas. I'm scheduled to rejoin him a couple of weeks from now in Nacogdoches."

"Well, if you gentlemen will excuse me, I must go to my room and write some necessary letters before I retire for the night. My months in prison and journey from Mexico City have wearied me. I trust Daniel, my nephew and scribe, will be able to join me soon."

"Daniel has become quite a celebrity since you last saw him," Seguin smiled. "I won't spoil the surprise. I'll leave the recounting of his adventures to Daniel when he arrives."

"I shall look forward to seeing Daniel again and hearing all about them. Once again, Don Juan, many thanks for your kindness. I shall see you at breakfast."

Seguin then turned to Jim Bowie. "Will we have the pleasure of your company as well, Mr. Bowie?"

"I'm afraid not. I plan to make an early start."

"What a pity," said Austin, as he turned and left the room.

Juan Seguin turned just in time to see a dark scowl disappear from Bowie's face. Seguin thought there had been a hint of disdain in Austin's voice. Now he was sure of it.

It was late afternoon on October 12. Daniel Austin and Ken Hawkins were seated on rickety campstools in Stephen Austin's command tent. The tent had been pitched in the middle of what Daniel imagined misguided folks might call an army camp. The tents, stretching along the Guadalupe River, not far from

273

Gonzales, portrayed it as a military encampment, but all the old shabby tents were haphazardly placed in a crooked line, and the men looked like a ragtag bunch of civilians. Almost a hundred men wore uniforms, but very few looked remotely alike.

They had arrived an hour ago in response to a message Daniel had received from his uncle with the welcome news that he was back in Texas. Daniel's first glance at Uncle Stephen made it clear that the long months in prison had taken a toll on his health. His eyes were deeply sunken in a pale, haggard face. A chronic cough shook his entire body each time it climbed out of the pit deep within his chest. Stephen Austin obviously was a sick man. He was impatient as well, and his confidence seemed to have deserted him. He was explaining the current situation in an effort to sort the data out in his own mind as much as to inform Daniel and Hawk.

"I am the empresario. The Austins are responsible for most of the Texicans being here. I and my father before me. I owe much to these Texicans, even my life if it would set things right. I returned twelve days ago, and sent messengers with letters to the settlements throughout Estado de Tejas, extolling them to stand up for constitutional liberty. I hoped my summons might be the genesis of a new military campaign. Now, I sit in this camp two weeks later, with four hundred men who are eager to be soldiers, and not having the slightest notion how to go about it. They have only three things in common. Tattered clothing, filthy skins, and blind willingness to follow me. I don't know where I'm going! How can I lead them? I'm no military oracle. I'm only the man who called on the Texicans to stand up for their liberties! There are a dozen men in camp with military ability, but if one of them is chosen over the others, it will create an enemy far stronger than Santa Anna, and it will foster disunity."

He shivered and sighed deeply. The sigh triggered a coughing spasm that shook his frail body. His face turned a bright shade of crimson that remained until the spasm ended. As the color slowly ebbed away, it was replaced by a sickly, chalky white. Austin rose unsteadily, shuffled toward the open flap of tent, and peered out at the encampment.

"I didn't know there were this many kinds of guns. Kentucky long rifles, smoothbores, jaegers, shotguns. Even a few old horse pistols! We're going to war but there isn't one bayonet in the whole wretched camp. Flies around the offal from the cattle that have been slaughtered are thick as clouds. Each day in a filthy camp is a day nearer sickness and disease, yet there they sit without a care in the world. Just look out there!"

Daniel and Hawk walked across the tent and stood beside Austin. It was a sorry sight sure enough. Men lounged around, playing cards, wrestling, swapping stories and tall tales, laughing at this, cursing at that. All of them seemed to be chewing tobacco. Streams of foul liquid filled the air as they spit out the juice. Twice while they watched, a careless chewer failed to look before he let fly. The result was the same in each case. The man who'd been assailed by tobacco juice threw his assailant down and began pummeling him. Officers, when they could be identified, were no different.

"With this rabble, I'm expected to confront a well-trained, disciplined army, led by competent officers and armed with real weapons of war. An impossible task, gentlemen! An absolutely impossible task!"

As he finished speaking, they all saw a new arrival enter the far side of the camp. He was a large man, riding a silver horse, and leading a strawberry roan.

"That looks like Jim Bowie!" Daniel exclaimed.

"It's Bowie, all right," his Uncle Stephen agreed, frowning. He had wondered what else could go wrong and now he knew. A man he disliked more than any other he had ever known had just arrived. But Stephen Austin was polite to a fault. He concealed his displeasure and greeted the newcomer warmly.

"Mr. Bowie, your presence is as welcome as it is

unexpected."

"General Austin, I have come to offer my services in any capacity that you may choose."

"I gladly accept them, Sir! Please dismount and come inside."

Bowie entered and stood just inside the tent flap.

"I believe you know my nephew, Daniel. Are you also acquainted with Kenneth Hawkins?"

"I have not had that pleasure yet, General," Bowie said, striding forward, his hand extended. "It's a pleasure to meet you, Mr. Hawkins."

"Meeting you is my honor, Sir!" Hawk exclaimed, pumping Bowie's hand.

Bowie turned to Daniel and squeezed his arm in a friendly gesture.

"It's good to see you again, Daniel!"

Austin needed some time to think, and he needed to talk with Bowie alone.

"Daniel, our guest must be hot and weary after his dusty ride. How about you fellows fetching a pail of water from the spring?"

"Sure thing. If you're not in a hurry, we'll see to our horses on the way back," Daniel replied, aware of his uncle's desire to speak privately with Bowie.

"Take your time, Daniel. Perhaps you would care to clean up a bit before we talk, Mr. Bowie. There's a washstand and basin behind the tent."

Bowie nodded and followed the others outside.

Austin considered the dilemma Bowie presented. Bowie was well liked by many of the Texicans, so he couldn't be asked to serve in the ranks. On the other hand, some of the men distrusted him because of his land speculation and his soiled reputation. To place him in command of troops would be the height of folly. Bowie returned just as Austin formulated a decision.

"I'm going to attach you to my staff as a volunteer aide, Mr. Bowie, with the rank of Colonel."

"I don't want a staff job! I came to fight, General Austin!"

"I'm sorry!" Austin scowled. "A staff position is all I can offer you at this time, Colonel Bowie. That is all for now. I'm sure you want to attend to your horses and find space in one of the tents. I'm holding a council of war in an hour. Please come back then."

"Yes, Sir!" Bowie snapped, turning on his heel. He was not pleased, but he had expected nothing more from Austin.

When he returned an hour later, the command tent was crowded. Colonel Edward Burleson, the portly, graying, politician-soldier and staunch Austin ally, slumped in a chair, already feeling the stress of field service. Deaf Smith, comfortable in buckskins, one hand cupped behind an ear, listened attentively to

Captain William Barrett Travis. His military bearing and impeccable clothing made Travis the sort of man that would appeal to Austin's vision of what a leader should look like. The heavily mustached and jowled Colonel Joseph Neill was speaking with Austin; the dark scowl Bowie had come to expect was in place. Captain J.W. Fannin, hard-featured and hardheaded, but like Bowie, a good fighting man. Near the back of the tent stood another man dressed in buckskins. Old Ben Milam. Bowie was glad to see him. It had been rumored that Milam was a Mexican prisoner.

"Gentlemen. Your attention, if you please!" This came in a loud voice from Colonel Neill.

In the sudden silence, Austin began.

"Good news! Captain George Collinsworth struck a force of Mexican Lancers near Goliad. He finished off several of them and drove the rest back to Bexar. He also captured two pieces of artillery and three hundred firearms. More good news! Old Ben Milam, who managed to escape from the prison in Coahuila where he was held, aided Captain Collinsworth in the attack. In view of these developments, I would like to hear your views on the best course of action for us to pursue."

"Order Collinsworth to join us at once," Burleson advised. "We need the cannon and small arms!"

"In my opinion, we are not prepared to launch an

aggressive operation with untrained men and lacking organization." Austin countered. "We certainly can't consider marching on Bexar in our present state!"

"Why not?" Bowie demanded.

"As you can plainly see for yourself, we are not an army. The men lack discipline and professionalism."

"I plainly see born fighting men! I plainly see men who are ready to defend their families and homes! I don't see the spit-and-polish soldiers that you dream about, General, but I have seen victories determined Texicans with rifles in their hands have produced. It's the wrong time to worry about close order drill, straight ranks, and neat campgrounds! It's time to go after the enemy and look at them over rifle sights!"

Positive nods and words greeted Bowie's opinion.

It was obvious to Austin that the majority of those present agreed with this distasteful knife-fighter. He had hoped they would recognize the wisdom in his words and accept his recommendations. But since a majority seemed to be in favor of immediate action, he felt compelled to accede to their demands.

"Very well, gentlemen. If that's the decision of the war council, we'll move out in the morning."

XIV
FIRST BLOOD

TEN MILES WEST OF BEXAR
OCTOBER 27, 1835

Daniel and Hawk rode into camp and dismounted.

"Good Morning, Colonel Bowie," Daniel smiled respectfully.

"Mornin', Daniel. Hello, Hawk. You two must have ridden all night to get here this early."

"We brought fresh news and an important message from General Austin," Hawk told him. "About three weeks ago, a Mexican column marched on Gonzales and ordered the villagers to surrender the old cannon they bought to repulse Indians, maybe figuring that the cannon might be used against them. A short fight ensued and the Mexicans were driven off without the cannon. Ten days ago, Old Ben Milam's scouting party attacked a Mexican patrol at Cibolo Creek and drove them back toward Bexar."

"Old Ben always was a bearcat in a fight!"

Bowie opened the sealed envelope Daniel handed him, and examined Austin's over-abundant verbiage in the pale light. In six paragraphs, Austin ordered him to proceed, with Captain Fannin and his ninety men, toward Bexar, and select a bivouac site for the army on the river as close to the town as practical. He also detached Daniel and Hawk to act as couriers for Bowie. The final paragraphs held special interest.

You will also reconnoiter, so far as circumstances and time permit, the situation of the town's outskirts and the approaches to them. You will send a dispatch with as little delay as possible, so that the army will have sufficient time to *march and secure a position before nightfall. Should you be attacked by a superior force, send a dispatch immediately with all the particulars.*

"As you probably already know, you've both been assigned to me. As of now, you're my aides with the rank of lieutenant. Lieutenant Hawkins, please find Captain Fannin and Lieutenant MacComb. Ask them to join me here as soon as possible."

"Yes, Sir!" snapped the new lieutenant, turning on his heel.

"Daniel, while we're waiting, build up the fire and brew a pot of fresh coffee. Meanwhile, I'll try to find some hardtack without too many weevils in it."

Bowie was pleased. It was only a reconnoitering patrol, but at least it was a command that might lead to some action. No one knew Bexar's outskirts better than he did. A string of Spanish missions built many years before encircled the town: San Juan, San Jose, San Francisco, Concepcion and the Alamo. All of them were deserted and in ruins, but each of them could be used as a fortress, and staunchly defended, if the approaching Mexican army chose to do so.

An hour later, Bowie's new command was ready to ride. He ordered Fannin to form his men up in a column of twos, and dispatched Deaf Smith, Daniel, and Hawk as outriders.

"Deaf, you scout about a mile ahead of us. If you see or sense danger, hightail it back here. If we hear firing, we'll come up pronto. Daniel, since you and Hawk are so well mounted, you can both move out a bit farther on our flanks. You heard what I told Deaf. At the first sign of trouble, hightail it! If you get cornered, fire a shot, and we'll come a-runnin'."

He mounted Azogue and reined in beside Captain Fannin, at the head of the column.

"Ready, Captain?"

"Ready, Sir."

"Okay. Let's go start this here war!"

Fannin turned in his saddle and roared the order.

"Column of twos! At a trot! Forward!"

Bowie led them directly to the closest mission, San Juan. Aside from a few mozos who lived in the tiny adobe huts near the mission, San Juan was deserted.

He wheeled his detachment and led it to Espada, and then four miles northeast to the Mission San Jose. A mile down the road from San Jose stood the stone and adobe hacienda that he had built for Ursula. He dared not look that way lest his heart should break.

A short ride ahead, they spied the tall twin towers of Mission Concepcion. Except for the Alamo, it was the closest mission to Bexar. Five hundred feet from the mission, the San Antonio River made a big sweeping bend. Within that curve, the land was nearly flat. Fresh water, availability of firewood, and an inviting grove of pecan trees, as well as a proximity to Bexar, made this area an ideal camping spot for the army.

"Hawk, find General Austin. Tell him where we are. Unless he needs you to guide him, scurry on back. I'd send Daniel with you, but he and I have another job to do."

Bowie turned to Fannin.

"Captain, I want you to set half the men to digging a long ledge in the riverbank. I want them to be able to stand on that shelf and fire over the edge of the bank without exposing anything but the tops of their heads. If a Mexican force jumps us while we're here, they'll be in for a big surprise. The other half of the men can picket the horses and start gathering wood for cooking fires. No green wood! We want to cook, not send up smoke signals."

Fannin began assigning men to different duties and Bowie turned back to Daniel.

"Daniel, unless I miss my guess, our army won't get here until late tonight. So, after dark, we're going to sashay into Bexar and snoop around a bit."

Bowie was right. An hour after sunset, there still was no sign of Austin. Leaving Fannin in charge, Bowie and Daniel started toward the distant lights of Bexar. Before they reached the first of the outlying haciendas, they left the road and guided their horses through the fields until they came to a deep arroyo that led toward the center of town. Since Azogue and Raven were trained not to give away their presence by either sound or movement, Bowie decided to leave them tethered in a large stand of cottonwood trees a short distance from the mouth of the arroyo, and then proceed on foot.

At first, the nearest dwellings were far enough to preclude their being heard. As they neared the town, the arroyo grew shallower. From that point on, they were forced to crawl along on their hands and knees in the shadow of the walls. Nearly an hour after they left the horses, they reached a spot close enough to a small cantina to hear a guitar strumming a mournful tune and patrons talking. But they heard no singing or laughter.

"General Cos or a large part of his army must be

in town to make people this quiet," Bowie whispered. "Peons love to laugh and sing, and when they don't, something's wrong. Rise up far enough to look over the edge of the wall, Daniel. You should be able to see the main plaza from here."

The top of Daniel's head and his eyes were visible for only a few seconds before he dropped back to the floor of the arroyo, but it was enough.

"There are no local people strolling around. The plaza is full of soldiers and horses."

"We've found out what we needed to know. The soldiers you saw are Lancers. That means their last patrol already has returned. Cos, or whoever is in charge, won't be attacking us tonight, but General Austin and the others better be here before our patrol is discovered!"

They quickly retraced their steps, remounted their horses, and galloped back to camp. Austin had not come. They shared the results of their visit to Bexar with Captain Fannin and Lieutenant MacComb, and then Bowie consulted his orders.

"The General's orders make it quite clear that he expected the army to be here by now. Hopefully, they won't be delayed much longer. This is an ideal place for a big army, but it could be a mouse trap for a patrol the size of ours. Obviously, General Austin intended for us to hold this position until he arrives. So, here we will stay! I just hope our boys get here before Cos and his people do."

Four sentries walked the camp's perimeter in two-hour shifts throughout the night, while their luckier companions slept. Bowie did not walk or sleep. He lay awake hoping he hadn't led his men into a lion's den.

Dawn on October 28th was like the 27th , bitterly cold with a heavy fog that obscured the entire area. Daniel and Bowie were crouched at a fire, sipping the dregs of last night's tepid coffee, when the crack of a rifle brought them to their feet.

"Where'd that shot come from?" Bowie bellowed.

"From the mission tower," came a shouted reply.

Daniel whirred toward the sound of the voice and saw a number of indistinct, ghostly figures weaving in and out of the ragged morning mist. Suddenly, the air was filled with the smell of gunsmoke as a chorus of shots ripped through the camp. Charlie Heiskell shouted a warning loud enough to carry over the din.

"They're on us, boys!"

"Hold your ground and stay down, boys! Wait 'til you have a target!" ordered Bowie loudly.

The fog lifted as suddenly as a stage curtain being raised. One moment it was there, the next moment it was gone. The Texicans saw a long line of men in blue coats with white crossbelts.

"Open fire!" Bowie commanded. "Pour it on 'em."

Frontier code advised everyone to keep his powder dry. It was obvious that the Texicans had obeyed the code as the first volley opened jagged gaps in the once orderly Mexican battle line. The blue-coated soldiers began moving slowly backward, but as the Texican rifles claimed more lives, the pace increased until it became a pell-mell race into a handy nearby fog bank.

"Let 'em go," Bowie shouted. "They were only an advance patrol."

A moment later, from deep within the bank of fog, there came several scattered shots that whistled over the heads of the Texicans.

"Don't worry," Bowie advised them. "They're shooting blind and wasting lead. This open field in front of us is the only place the Mexican troops can maneuver. It's flanked on both sides by thick woods and the river with a steep bank which runs along the base. While there's time, we need to divide the patrol and set up a three-sided crossfire. Fannin, take thirty men and take cover in that grove of trees on the left. When you start firing, make sure you don't shoot into the trees on the other side. Daniel, take thirty men and move into the grove of pecan trees on the right. The rest of us are going to climb down to the ledge we cut in the riverbank last night. Get ready to sting 'em, boys!"

Bowie and his men raced to the riverbank, slid over the edge, and spread out along the ledge. Dispersal into three sections was accomplished none too soon. The men in Daniel's unit had just reached the cover of the pecan trees when the fog lifted and revealed a big force of Mexican infantry and cavalry stretching across the open plain.

"There's a parcel of 'em, sure enough," Charlie Heiskell observed. "How many ya figure, Jim?"

"Maybe three hundred infantry, five companies of Lancers. About five hundred total. Of course, when you figure one Texican rifleman equals ten Mexican soldiers, we got them outnumbered two to one."

Heiskell and the others chuckled and relaxed.

"They're bringing up an artillery piece, Colonel," reported one sharp-eyed Texican.

A small brass cannon was being moved forward by the Mexicans. The Texicans heard loud commands being shouted. Bayoneted rifles were slanted across blue uniformed shoulders as the Mexican infantry marched in two long ranks, one behind the other. A bugle call was sounded, and the double ranks began moving toward the waiting Texicans.

Bowie was impressed. These were obviously well-drilled troops. Perfect cadence. No sign of hesitation.

Suddenly, from the grove of pecan trees shielding Daniel and his men, there came the sharp crack of a rifle. The effect was instantly apparent as one of the Mexican soldiers clutched at his stomach, doubled over, and crumpled to the ground.

The advance halted, and the front rank knelt down. A single command was all that was needed to raise three hundred rifles to three hundred shoulders. The Texicans all heard the order to fire.

"Tiran!"

A cloud of smoke appeared, and a moment later they heard the sounds of hundreds of angry hornets racing overhead, then buzzing off into the distance. None of the bullets hit its mark, but one kicked dust down on Bowie. A minute later, they saw another burst of furious activity in the Mexican ranks, and then another cloud of smoke, followed by another mass of angry hornets as a second volley was fired.

"Hit 'em now, while they're reloading!" Bowie commanded.

A hundred deadly Texican rifles cracked while the Mexican troops were hunched over their muskets. The result was devastating. Gaps, like missing teeth, appeared in the once orderly blue-coated ranks. It was apparent to all the combatants that infantrymen, standing in the open, firing short-range muskets, were no match for the Texican sharpshooters firing their superb Kentucky rifles from protected places. Despite the long range, a fierce crossfire continued, and dozens of Mexican soldiers were wounded and killed. After what must have seemed like an eternity to them, a new order was given, and the infantrymen dropped into prone positions. The Texican crossfire stopped. The distance now was much too great to hit a figure lying nearly flat on the ground.

Then, through one of the gaps in the Mexican line, a small cannon was moved toward the forward edge of the infantry formation. The gun crew swiveled the field piece around and aimed it at the closest group of Texicans, Daniel Austin and his men in the pecan grove.

"Get down!"

Daniel's command came an instant before the brass cannon bellowed, and a long tongue of orange flame leapt toward them. The effect was immediate but not lethal. The four-pound load of grapeshot the cannon held ripped through the branches of the trees sheltering Daniel and his men. Nobody was hit by grapeshot, but pecans pelted down on all of them.

"Let's go help 'em boys," shouted one of the Texicans.

"They're all right. Stay down!" Bowie ordered.

It was too late. Four men scrambled over the lip of the riverbank, and raced across the open ground between them and the pecan grove. A new volley of musket fire burst from the Mexican ranks, but this time the result was far different. One man staggered, pitched forward, and fell heavily. He slid along, his face buried in the grass, until two of his companions seized his arms and dragged him into the cover of the trees.

Bowie was furious. His order had been disobeyed, and a fighting man Texas couldn't spare was either dead or badly wounded. This would never do. That cannon had to be silenced. He sidled along the ledge to the end that was closest to the grove of pecans and scrambled up over the top. Staying as close to the ground as possible, he inched his way forward until he reached the protection of the woods. Just as he arrived, a new charge of grapeshot rattled through the branches, showering him with leaves and pecans.

When the debris stopped falling, Bowie looked up and saw the three men who had disobeyed orders. They were huddled around Jim Kelly, the man who had been shot. The bloody hole in the middle of his chest told the story. Bowie was so furious at this needless loss of life that he didn't say a word, but simply walked passed the trio.

As Bowie reached Daniel, another blast exploded overhead.

"Wow! These pecans really sting! I'll never eat

pecan pie again without thinking about this day!" Daniel observed.

"We've been stung enough!" Bowie told him. "We're going to put an end to this business! Daniel, you, Bill King, and Cisco Miranda are all excellent marksmen. Find the others and I'll tell you my plan!"

It took only moments for Daniel to locate Bill and Cisco and return. Bowie quickly explained his plan.

"The four of us, and two others, are going to move out to a point in these woods closest to that cannon. There are six men in the gun crew. I want you three to fire at them. As soon as you do, the other three of us will hand you fresh rifles that you can fire again before they can react. It's still a long rifle shot, but all of you are good marksmen, using fine weapons. I expect at least half of those gunners to go down. Let's go!"

Five minutes later, the six of them were crouched in a fringe of the woods that faced the cannon.

"I want each of you to pick a primary target and secondary target," Bowie ordered. "Make sure you all don't fire at the same gunners. I'll give the order to fire your first shots. Fire the second ones as soon as you're ready."

Daniel, Cisco, and Bill King consulted among themselves, and then nodded at Bowie.

"All right! Get ready," Bowie ordered.

Three rifles were raised.

"Aim!"

Three rifles steadied.

"Fire!"

Three shots sounded as one. Seconds later, three more shots sounded in nearly perfect unison.

The effect was even better than Bowie had hoped it would be. Three men lay crumpled on the ground. A fourth lay draped over the breech of the cannon. The fifth and sixth, obviously badly wounded, were stumbling painfully back toward the main body of the Mexican force. Here and there, along the once steady blue-clad lines, men were pulling back, Mexicans who had witnessed the slaughter of their comrades, fearful men looking for some means of escape.

Bowie immediately saw this quickly spreading lack of resolve.

"C'mon, boys! Let's drive "em while they're wavering!"

Bowie suddenly jumped up and raced from the cover of the woods. He charged forward, racing over the ground in long strides, wielding his great knife like the sword of an avenging angel. Behind him stormed three bands of Texicans, nearly a hundred men, converging on the brass cannon. One ill-aimed volley issued from the Mexican ranks, but the Texican swarm couldn't be stopped.

"Swing 'er round, boys," Bowie ordered, as he reached the cannon and grabbed the cannon trail.

A score of eager hands twisted the cannon around, pointing the muzzle directly at the infantrymen who were now a hundred yards away. A fuse lighter was still clutched in a dead gunner's hand. Bowie seized it and held it against the vent.

Thunderous roar! Blinding smoke! Ghastly cries of anguish!

The smoke cleared, and the Texicans could see the gaping hole that the grapeshot had torn in the human wall. The Mexicans' spirit was torn asunder as well. Discipline lost, the formation began to shred as the infantrymen turned and fled in panic. The eruption of the cannon was followed by another eruption of buckskin and homespun as Texicans, shrieking like frenzied banshees, raced forward after the soldiers, adding to the Mexicans' mass hysteria.

Mexican officers did their best to stop the rout with stern orders and the flat sides of their swords, but to no avail. The fleeing foot soldiers engulfed the mounted Lancers waiting behind, and the frenzy spread. The Lancers wheeled their horses and raced away from their slower mates. Battle over! Rout complete! Minutes later, the only Mexican soldiers in sight were dead.

Stephen Austin was nervous, irritable, and also a bit squeamish after viewing the sixty-seven Mexican soldiers who had been killed in the battle. He would have much preferred the quieter, simpler life of a merchant or perhaps a banker. He was unhappy in the role of the commander-in-chief, but accepted it as a necessary cross to bear. Austin needed a daily bath and shave to feel human. He knew he was a misplaced indoorsman in an era of outdoorsmen. To mask his uneasiness, he spoke sharply to Jim Bowie.

"If they were routed as you say, you should have pursued them into Bexar and finished them off!"

Bowie flushed bright crimson at the accusation. If Austin had acted with alacrity, and the army had arrived on schedule, a complete victory could have been achieved. Texicans could be sitting in the Main Plaza at this very moment, and each man in Bowie's command knew it. As he waited for his pique to fade, Bowie studied the fidgeting, scowling Austin, and realized the man's scowl was hiding feelings of helplessness. Austin knew he was responsible for the incomplete victory, but he was unwilling to face his inadequacy to fulfill the role of military leader that destiny had thrust upon him.

"Aside from the fact that we were outnumbered five to one, I had your written directive ordering me to do the exact opposite, General," Bowie reminded

Austin softly.

Austin was in no mood to hear about orders that had proved to be unwise. His white-knuckled hand gripped his saddle horn even harder. He tried once more to save face.

"You misinterpreted my orders," he snapped. "I intended for you to return to the main force as soon as you selected a campsite. I'm extremely displeased with your decision. By remaining at Concepcion, you might well have had your entire force annihilated."

Bowie remembered a line in his orders. Make your report with as little delay as possible, so the army can take up a position before night. He decided that it made no sense to annoy Austin any further.

"As you can see, General, we weren't annihilated, but a fair number of Mexicans were."

A chorus of snickers that rose from the ranks made Austin far more uncomfortable. If the confrontation with Bowie were to continue, he would look and feel even more foolish. It was time to act, not talk.

"As soon as we can form a column, we'll move forward."

"That might not be a very good idea, Sir!" Bowie spoke as deferentially as he could.

"And why not, may I ask?" Austin's tone was sarcastic, as well as demanding.

"Let me begin by saying that I have utmost respect

297

for your position as commander-in-chief. I was a resident of Bexar for years, and I'm familiar with the town's defenses. I have no doubt that they have been greatly strengthened since the Mexican occupation. Storming a fortified town that's ready to repulse you is simply a suicide mission."

Austin's dislike for Bowie reached new heights. It was unpleasant enough to match wits with another gentleman, but to bandy words with a brawling lout was more than he could bear. Desperately, he turned to Fannin in hopes of finding an ally.

"What do you think, Captain?"

"I agree with Colonel Bowie, General."

"For the time being, we'll wait. This is no place for the main army. Bowie, you will remain here with your command. I'm going to lead the rest of the men to the mill north of town. I intend to hold a council of war. I will send for you in due course."

Austin wheeled his horse, and returned to the head of the column. Behind him, Bowie grinned. He'd really gotten under Austin's skin. He hadn't realized how furious Austin was until he called him Bowie rather than Colonel Bowie. For a man who cherished titles, that omission was tantamount to a confession acknowledging his overwhelming frustration.

An hour after dawn, a courier rode into Bowie's

camp on a horse covered with lather, indicating a long, hard run.

"Is General Austin here, Colonel Bowie?"

"No. He's up north of Bexar, with the main force," Bowie told him. "What's the all-fired hurry?"

"Dispatch from the meeting of delegates. They've issued a proclamation. Want to read it?"

"Absolutely," Bowie said, accepting a scroll. He started reading it aloud.

"Declaration of Causes. Whereas General Antonio Lopez de Santa Anna and other military chieftains have, by force of arms, overthrown the federal institutions of Mexico and dissolved the social compact which existed between Texas and the other members of the Mexican confederacy; now the good people of Texas, availing themselves of their natural rights Solemnly Declare: 'That they have taken up arms in defense of their rights and liberties which were threatened by the encroachments of military despots, and in defense of the republican principles of the Federal Constitution of Mexico, 1824.

'That Texas is no longer morally or civilly bound by the compact of union; yet, stimulated by the generosity and sympathy common to a free people, they offer their support and assistance to such members of the Mexican confederacy as will take up arms against military despotism.

'That they hold it to be their right during the disorganization of the federal system, and the reign of despotism, to withdraw from the union, and to establish an independent government.'"

"The Declaration says it clearly and well," Bowie began. "We are willing to fight and die for rights the Constitution of 1824 guaranteed us that now have been usurped." The crowd yelled approval as Bowie summed up the Declaration for the crowd.

An hour after the courier's departure, the courier returned and handed Bowie a message, summoning him to a council of war to decide on a course of action.

The council of war convened that afternoon. It was followed by another council that evening, and a third the next morning. Debate followed oratory, oratory followed debate, nothing was accomplished, and a great deal of precious time was lost. Finally, in the hope that a swift victory could be won, Austin ordered Bowie to form a column and parade his men in sight of the enemy force they had routed. Austin reasoned that their earlier terror might return to such a degree that they would surrender. Bowie complied with Austin's silly order and naive notion, but made sure his column stayed well beyond cannon range.

Of course, none of the Mexicans surrendered. No one except Austin had expected them to surrender.

However, he kept Bowie and his men in their isolated position, far from the main army camp.

"We're sitting ducks out here," Bowie told Fannin, Daniel, and Hawk. "Either General Austin is unaware of our imminent danger, or he feels that he made a mistake giving me this command. Daniel, I want you to take my letter of resignation to General Austin, and tell him that I can't defend this position with the men I have."

Daniel returned an hour later with Austin's reply. They were ordered to rejoin the main force, and Bowie would remain in command.

Wasted dreary days became wasted dreary weeks as the stalemate continued. Men who had left their families somewhere out on the dangerous prairie and had come to fight, began drifting away and heading back home. Some new arrivals came in, but they did not balance out the ones that were gone for good. One new arrival was a tall, raw-boned fellow with a long nose and tobacco stained lips. Colonel Ben Milam grabbed Bowie in a bear hug.

"It's good to see you, Hoss!"

"Good to see you, too, Old Ben."

Milam nodded at Daniel and Hawk.

"You two infants look fit and ready to go at it. Jim, I hear there's somethin' brewing in these parts. You all know I'm a peace-lovin' man, but I sure would admire to watch you fightin' men for a spell."

Bowie's laughter boomed. No one enjoyed a fight more than Old Ben Milam! He'd spent his whole life fighting against the British, the Spaniards, Emperor Iturbide, a dozen Indian tribes and, most recently, against Santa Anna's troops at Goliad.

"Jim," Milam exploded, "why are we sittin' here instead of attackin' Bexar? We keep losin' men, and the Mexicans keep getting in more. Sittin's good for them and bad for us. The Declaration of Causes told them we were comin' to git them. Let's go do it!"

Another new arrival joined them, Dr. James Grant, the Scottish transplant whose hacienda in Coahuila had been confiscated.

"I overheard what you said, Ben. What we ought to do is attack Matamoros, instead of wasting any more time here or attacking Bexar. The river port of Matamoros is the most logical place to resupply the Mexican army before they march north again. Jim, Ben, doesn't that make sense to the two of you?"

"It makes sense, all right, but I'm not the one you need to convince!"

Bowie's reply was cordial; but he remembered that Grant had played a major part in the Monclova land speculation fiasco. For that matter, so had Old Ben Milam! Yet, Stephen Austin didn't seem to hold the episode against them or treat them with the rampant bitterness he exhibited toward Bowie. There was no point in wondering why. Bowie didn't understand a lot of the things Stephen Austin did.

Near the end of November, a cavalry detachment arrived. Well-mounted and armed, they were dressed in spotless new uniforms with tight white breeches, dark gray coats sporting shiny brass buttons, and small, flat gray hats worn at jaunty angles. Members of the New Orleans Grays had outfitted themselves and bought weapons at their own expense. Youthful, adventurous, and somewhat vainglorious, they rode through camp staring in open disdain at the slovenly ragtag bunch peering back at them. But they had come to help, and that was all that really mattered.

On the heels of their arrival, Austin summoned his staff officers to another council of war.

"Timely arrival of the New Orleans Grays prompts me to contemplate an assault on Bexar. I would like to have your input, gentlemen."

Their input consisted of various opinions, both pro and con, running the gamut from reluctant to rabid, but the overall consensus was negative.

"Very well! I bow to the majority opinion. Such being the case, I shall take my leave. A provisional government has been formed and Henry Smith, a very able man, is governor. The commander-in-chief of the army is Sam Houston. I have been appointed commissioner to the United States. My first duty is to seek the assistance of that nation."

Austin spoke matter-of-factly, but every man there was shocked. Despite his dislike for Austin, Bowie felt sorry for him. Austin should be the governor. He was as well-suited for that office as he was ill-suited for military command. By ignoring Austin, members of the provisional government had not only insulted him, they had also foolishly deprived Texas of his extremely capable statesmanship.

Austin ignored the injustice as he took his leave.

"I will only say that I am ready to perform in any manner that the new Texas leaders consider useful."

Austin, regardless of his other shortcomings, was a true patriot. He was also a much bigger man than Bowie and many others had ever realized.

XV
THE BATTLE OF BEXAR

OUTSKIRTS OF BEXAR
NOVEMBER 26, 1835

Deaf Smith thundered into camp on the dead run. His horse was covered with white lather, and Deaf was coated with alkali dust. He pulled his staggering mount back on her haunches and slid to a halt beside the tent of Colonel Burleson, the officer Austin had left in charge. Burleson and Bowie emerged just as Smith dismounted and pointed toward the south.

"Big column of horsemen comin' up from Laredo," Deaf managed to yell while trying to get his breath. "They're Ugartechea's men! Reinforcements for Cos, sure nuff!"

Burleson quickly turned to Bowie with a command.

"Colonel Bowie, take your mounted squadron and try to intercept that column! I'll follow as quickly as possible with my infantry! If you circle around to the southwest, maybe we can pinch them in between us."

The Texicans' camp was at the north end of a bivouac that stretched for over a mile along the riverbank, but the area was almost deserted. After a monotonous string of boring idle days, most of the Texicans, including the men in Bowie's mounted squadron, were widely scattered. They were out visiting friends, gambling, or simply loafing. Bowie found Daniel and Hawk feasting on the roasted ribs of a wild boar Daniel had chased down and tomahawked earlier that morning.

"Time to go, boys! You can finish your pig meat while we ride!"

"Where are we going, Colonel?" Hawk's voice was muffled by a mouthful of pork.

"We're going to have some fun for once! Hawk, round up as many of our boys as you can find while Daniel and I round up the horses. I want to leave as soon as possible."

Hawk returned a few minutes later with sobering news.

"I rounded up only about half of them, Colonel! If we ride south through the camp, we're sure to find a few more."

"We'll have to settle for the ones who are here. We don't have time to delay, and we're heading north."

Bowie, Daniel, Hawk, and forty other men left ten minutes later. They made a swing along the northern perimeter of Bexar, then circled southwest until they intercepted Laredo Road. They trotted south for five miles, and halted at a place where the road crossed an old covered bridge that spanned a deep arroyo. Beneath this bridge, and for a hundred yards on each side, the arroyo formed a right angle with the road before it began angling sharply away and sloping up toward the distant hills that bordered the valley.

"Dismount! Take all the horses along the arroyo to a place beyond the first curve and picket them. Tie them tight! We don't want them getting away when the shooting starts. Once that's done, come back and cut a ledge you can stand up on and shoot from into the bank on both sides of the road. Do it fast because we're going to have visitors before long."

The tasks were completed in record time without a question or a complaint. There were only forty-two in his command, but it was apparent that every man put his absolute trust in Bowie.

They had just moved into position, rifles laid out on the edge of the bank, and powder horns and bullet pouches conveniently close at hand, when suddenly a big dust cloud appeared.

"Hawk, take a gander through your spyglass and tell me what you see," Bowie ordered.

Hawk peered through the telescope for a moment.

"How many?" Bowie asked.

"Enough of them to make me think Burleson and his boys had better hurry!" Hawk told him.

"Give me the glass, Hawk," Bowie requested.

As the dust cloud drew closer, Bowie peered at the approaching column and counted the horsemen as they came into view. Fifty, a hundred, a hundred n twenty, a hundred n fifty! A hundred fifty Lancers, and a string of pack mules! Bowie's heart pounded.

"They ain't Ugartechea's reinforcement after all," Deaf Smith whispered. "Not with pack mules."

"Those mules can't be haulin' grub," reasoned Old Ben. "Already got plenty o that in Bexar. Why do a dozen mules haulin' heavy loads need a hundred and fifty Lancers along? Only thing I kin think of needs that much protecting is dinero, money. I bet it's the payroll train comin' up from Laredo."

"Old Ben," Bowie agreed, "I think you've hit the nail on the head. Boys," he called loud enough for the others to hear. "I think we're looking at a whole parcel of Mexican silver! It'll sure sting the troops in Bexar if we grab the dinero and confiscate the whole shebang as spoils of war. After losing all that silver from the mine to the Indians, let's make this our payday!"

As the Lancer vanguard closed to a hundred yards, Texican rifles began to roar. A dozen saddles were emptied. Horses screamed. Men shouted and then fell to the ground where many remained motionless. The sudden and effective attack caused a momentary panic in the Lancer ranks before discipline returned.

Then the surviving Lancers found cover in a nearby dry riverbed and opened fire on an invisible enemy.

"Hold your fire until you have a clear target," Bowie ordered. "No sense wastin' powder and lead."

For the next half-hour, with the exception of a few random shots, silence blanketed the opposing forces. Between them lay more than a dozen dark shapes. Time and again the eerie stillness was broken by soft moans of pain and, on one occasion, a fretful voice that begged for the mercy of the Lord.

At length, the Texicans heard the welcome sound of marching feet. Burleson was coming! But what was this? Burleson and his men weren't marching down the road! They were cutting across the open fields!

"Where in thunder er they goin'?" Deaf pondered.

"They don't see us or the Mexicans yet," Bowie reasoned. "Yell at them! Warn them!"

It was too late. Following one of the many arroyos that cut through the plain in various directions, the infantrymen had gotten quite close before they were seen. Now they were coming forward at double time, closing the distance in a sudden rush. The Texican warning shouts and deadly Mexican shots sounded together. The shots did what the shouts failed to do. They stopped the infantrymen in their tracks. Several men were caught in the first musket volley. Dead men, wounded men, and alert men all hit the dirt. A few men, under enemy fire for the first time, whirled and dashed off, scattering, running, falling, only to rise and run again, faster than before, driven by fear and panic.

A new volley produced more wounded and dead.

This was the perfect opportunity, Bowie realized, while the enemy was consumed with the destruction of Burleson's troops, to attack the Lancers and drive them from cover.

"C'mon boys," he shouted. "Let's hit 'em while we can!"

The Texicans scrambled up the cut bank and then, led by Bowie, Daniel and Hawk, they dashed toward the dry river that sheltered the Lancers, screaming like mad men. A few of Burleson's men stopped in the midst of their flight, reversed course, and joined the charge. The sights and the sounds of these wild men convinced the Mexicans that their only chance of survival was to remount, abandon the packtrain, and flee. They rushed out of the suddenly unpopular riverbed, threw themselves at the horses, and dashed away. Since the Texicans were on foot, they had no hope of catching the Lancers. They had to be content with firing several disdainful shots to speed them on their way.

"Daniel," Bowie ordered, "fetch one of the mules. Let's see how rich we are."

When Daniel returned with the mule, Bowie drew his knife and sliced open its bulky cargo sack. Eager men leaned forward, expecting to see a cascade of silver spill out but they were saddened and surprised by what they saw. The pack was stuffed with grass. They had captured a forage train. Dreams of instant wealth evaporated. The episode was so completely absurd that Daniel began to laugh. It seemed to grow even more bizarre with each passing moment. One-hundred-fifty Lancers to protect bags of grass! He laughed harder. The men near him began laughing. It spread to all the others. Great gales of laughter, men holding their sides, some, no longer able to stand, rolled on the ground in uncontrolled delirium. This was the sight that greeted the Morales Battalion that General Cos sent to rescue the departed Lancers.

A new long-range battle began, a battle that once again went badly for the Mexicans. Although there was an occasional soft snicker or loud guffaw from Texican riflemen, merriment did not seem to affect their marksmanship. The second battle also proved to be disastrous for the Mexican troops. Forty more of them died. No Texican was killed, and only four were wounded. Bowie's cavalry unit, in league with Burleson's infantry, had fought twice and won twice against vastly superior numbers.

"It was a good day after all," Bowie told Daniel and

311

Hawk, "even though our bags of silver turned out to be bags of grass."

Texicans at the main camp hooted and laughed at the thought of men fighting to capture bags of grass, momentarily losing sight of the fact that a substantial victory had been won. Fifty enemy soldiers would not live to fight another day, and Burleson's big blunder had been erased by the courageous charge of Bowie's men, a charge that snatched victory from the Mexicans.

The Grass Fight soldiers, as they came to be known, patiently endured stinging rebukes and stupid pranks for nearly a week before they began to retaliate. It took several fights, bloody noses, and lost teeth but, aided by a passage of time, the teasing finally ended. Then began again their daily journeys from tedium to boredom, with stopovers at apathy.

Dr. James Grant, the rich landowner with the glib tongue and grand ideas, spent his days going from one group to the next, suggesting as forcefully as possible, that they all quit this useless siege at Bexar, and attack and seize Matamoros. Then a rumor began circulating that the attack on Bexar was at hand. This was followed by a new rumor that the army would pull back and go into winter quarters at Gonzales.

Men who had been patiently waiting for so long

went berserk. They began taking Dr. Grant's words seriously. Maybe mutiny wasn't a bad idea after all. Men became indifferent to orders. They refused to drill or to tidy up the camp. They did not want to be cheated out of the fight they'd come for. If they could not fight at Bexar, they would fight elsewhere. All they needed was a leader. Into that void stepped a long, lanky, buckskin-clad figure they all knew, respected, and trusted. He stood before them and asked a question they longed to hear.

"Who'll come into Bexar with me, Old Ben Milam?"

Almost every man in the camp answered Milam's challenge. They gathered around him, whooping like Indian warriors, howling like lobo wolves. It was obvious to Burleson that these men would wait no longer. They were bound and determined to fight. In an effort to maintain some semblance of discipline and order, Burleson split the men into two fighting forces and appointed five commanders for each one: Milam, Patton, Llewellyn, York, and Hurd for one group; Johnson, Edwards, Swisher, Cook, and Benavides for the other. Burleson made no mention of Bowie.

"I guess Colonel Burleson doesn't want to remind everyone that Colonel Bowie saved him and his men at the Grass Fight," Hawk told Daniel disgustedly.

"It seems like a snub, all right, but maybe Burleson wants Colonel Bowie with him because he knows a lot more about the layout of Bexar than Burleson."

Hawk nodded, but he didn't buy Daniel's theory. He didn't think Daniel did either.

The temperature began plummeting at midnight on December 5th. Two hours before dawn, it was bitterly cold. The men's teeth were clicking like castanets as Milam and Johnson formed their warriors into long columns of twos and led them out of camp. They halted in the large wooded area on the northern edge of Bexar and ordered the men to dismount. The leaders gathered their troops around them. It was Old Ben who gave the orders.

"Boys, we ain't gonna need our horses fer this shindig. I want every sixth man to be a horse tender. The other five men will go in with Johnson and me. Nobody wants to miss the fun, so we'll rotate horse tenders twice a day. Johnny," Milam asked Johnson, "you want to go down Soledad or Acequia Street?"

"We'll take Soledad, Old Ben! My favorite cantina is there. I may stop off and buy my boys a drink," Johnson chuckled.

"Good idea! Bring some firewater along. We'll drink it in the plaza after we capture the town."

Milam and his men reached the end of Acequia in

the first streaks of the cold gray dawn, but they had gone only a short distance when their presence was detected by a sentry. He raised his musket and fired through the morning mist at the ghostly figures. The bullet whistled past them, but the shot was sure to alarm the Mexican foot soldiers, the Lancers, and the artillerymen who manned the cannon in the Military Plaza.

"Pat," Milam ordered Patton, "take half the men over to the far side of the street. If they get that big cannon lined up on us, we'll have to stay out of the street and fight from house to house."

"You mean break through the walls?" Patton asked.

"Yep! Adobe walls ain't gonna stand up fer long against crowbars and pick axes," Milam reasoned.

Milam's wisdom of moving forward and capturing sections of the town while remaining under cover all but negated the cannon fire from the heavy weapons located in the Military Plaza and the Alamo. There were only a few casualties during the day, but the steady roar of the artillery, coupled with the danger from exploding shells, was unnerving for the Texican men who had not faced such firepower before.

Mid afternoon saw both streets in near-shambles. While Johnson's and Milam's men pounded and cut their way slowly through the adobe walls, any well-aimed cannon ball simply disintegrated the adobe on contact. Flying chunks of adobe wounded far more men than cannon fire! Throughout the day and into the early evening, they smashed through the walls, often diving to the floor as the unmistakable whistle of a cannon shell screamed toward them, only to rise and attack the adobe once again. But in the end, the strategy worked just as Milam had predicted. By nightfall, the attacking forces had reached the end of both streets, had occupied well-fortified positions, and were in control of the northern section of Bexar.

Daniel and Hawk had volunteered as couriers. They kept Bowie and Burleson updated on the house to house advance. Since Burleson was unfamiliar with Bexar, Bowie sketched a map that depicted the areas, progress, and likely objectives.

On the second day, the advance continued. During the afternoon, as Daniel and Hawk reached Bexar's outskirts, they noted a definite slowdown in artillery fire. When they reported this to Milam, he agreed.

"We're wearin' 'em down, boys. Tell Burleson I expect to reach the palacio by sundown, and tell Jim Bowie we kin use his help in here if Burleson will let him come."

Hawk and Daniel decided not to deliver Milam's message. Bowie had done everything he could to get Burleson's permission, other than getting down on

316

his knees and begging, all to no avail. Milam's jibe would have been the unkindest cut of all.

Another courier arrived in the deepening dusk. The Veramendi palacio and the property of Antonio de la Garza, the Padre's brother, were in Texican hands.

Burleson summoned Daniel.

"At first light, I want you and Hawkins to ride into Bexar and find Milam. I need to know what he plans to do next."

A first faint glow of dawn had just begun to appear in the eastern sky that wintry December 7th morning as Hawk and Daniel mounted Raven and Sovereign and raced toward Bexar.

"We'll most likely find him at the palacio!" Hawk shouted over the thunder of pounding hooves.

"I agree!" Dan shouted back. "We had better cut through town rather than ride along the river. The Mexicans must know couriers are coming back and forth. I have a feeling they may try to pick one of us off."

Hawk nodded in agreement but said nothing.

They left the river and circled around so as to approach the patio of the palacio from the opposite side, and arrived without incident a few minutes later. This was the patio where Uncle Stephen and Daniel had been welcomed when they first arrived in Bexar. At this very spot, he'd met Monica Granados.

They had danced and laughed, and had a wonderful day. That afternoon, the entire patio had been gaily decorated with ribbons and bows and piñatas. The cobblestones had glistened in the sun. Now the patio was the site of torn trees and lifeless plants, and the cobblestones were covered with debris and dried blood.

They dismounted and tethered the fillies. Turning, they saw a lone figure walking toward them from the side of the patio closest to the river.

"Here comes Old Ben now," Daniel remarked.

"That's him all right!" Hawk agreed.

Milam saw them at the same time. He started to lift his hand just as a rifle cracked. Milam clutched his chest, and then slid slowly toward the cobblestones.

By the time they reached him, Old Ben Milam was dead, felled by a sharpshooter's bullet. Daniel's premonition had come true. Mexican riflemen had been lying in wait along the riverbank. Sadly, they carried Old Ben's body back to the main camp.

Old Ben Milam was dead, but he had won his final battle. Two days later, on December 9th, General Cos sent a flag of truce to the Texicans, asking for terms of surrender. Bowie reflected that Old Ben and his four hundred men had whipped the Mexicans. They had done what every military expert, including Sam Houston himself, said could never be done without a large number of reinforcements and a dozen heavy siege cannon.

Burleson reasoned that the defeats the Mexicans had suffered at Mission Concepcion and along the Laredo road had undermined their morale. By the time Milam and his attackers penetrated their inner defenses, desertion and insubordination had been commonplace. Faced by probable defeat, Cos had simply capitulated.

Bowie wasn't so sure. It was true that he and his men had administered those first two defeats. Twice he had led howling Texicans in wild-eyed charges against overwhelming odds. In an effort to raise the morale of his men, he had joked that a Texican with a long rifle was the equal to any ten Mexicans. But, of course, that was bravado. The Mexican Lancers were the equal of any light cavalry in the world. Bowie had dozens of good Mexican friends. He had wooed and won a Mexican bride. He himself was an adopted son of Mexico, a proud part of a Mexican family. His children had been half-Mexican. It was true that, for the most part, Mexicans were easy-going men and women who loved the joys of today, and spent little time worrying about the woes that tomorrow might bring. But they were not cowards.

Several of the men in his own command were Mexicans. They had been in the vanguard of every

319

battle. Why, then, would professional soldiers, who were experienced, well-trained, well-armed fighters, turn and run when they faced danger?

His thoughts drifted back to the Mexicans who had been killed during the Concepcion fight, and then thought of one dead Mexican soldier in particular. At first glance, he looked like a soldier with his long, blue uniform coat with crossed white belts, and military trousers with a stripe running down the side of each leg. His tall plumed infantry shako lay beside his body. Every inch a professional soldier, it seemed. But the feet were bare. Big, brown, flat, thickly-callused, sturdy feet of a Mexican mozo, feet that might have at some time known rawhide sandals, but they certainly had never been encased in shoes. They were feet that belonged behind a plow, feet that were at home in a small, peasant hut that housed a hard-working wife and a flock of happy children. He had knees that were far more accustomed to kneeling in church rather than on a firing line, and herein lay the answer. Santa Anna's conscription had ruthlessly whisked farmers from their farms, dragged peons from their villages, and stripped the prisons of their inmates, all in an effort to fill his army's ranks. Dazed and uncomprehending, these poor Mexicans were herded into rough barracks like so many sheep being led to the slaughter. They were issued uniforms and weapons, quickly welded into cohesive units, and taught to follow simple commands by brutish, abusive officers. How long would they serve? Until they died or were seriously wounded. But it took far more than a uniform and a bayoneted musket to make a soldier. There was no pride here, no morale, no tradition, no incentive to win. When a deadly enemy confronted them, it made much more sense to turn and run than to stand and fight. There was no shame attached to retreating when the alternative was to remain behind and die.

Santa Anna was aware of the situation. Bowie had heard that he often referred to Texicans as intruders, ruffians, warmongers, traitors, ruthless barbarians, and filibusters. He was right about the filibusters. Hundreds of articles in newspapers across America had spurred an influx of adventurers. Willing to fight and eager for profit, they had joined the Texicans' cause. Santa Anna called men like himself, who had become Mexican citizens and professed Catholics, traitors for standing against him. In Bowie's opinion, Santa Anna had negated his oath of allegiance when he denounced and rejected the Constitution of 1824 and combined the states of Tejas and Coahuila. He had slandered and cursed the Texans, gambling that he could engender enough hatred among the poor peons to spur them into action, but it seemed that he had lost his gamble. The love of life and family had prevailed over manufactured hatred of fellow men.

What would Santa Anna do now? Bowie wondered.

Stirring up hatred against the Texicans was not only meant to motivate the Mexicans and Tejanos. Santa Anna no doubt hoped that new feelings of bitterness would mask the uneasy discontent that so many men and women on both sides of the border had toward him. Bowie decided that if Santa Anna couldn't lead an army into Texas, he would drive it. Originally, he had reasoned that Santa Anna would not march north until the end of the winter. Now he believed that the Mexican army would start out much earlier; perhaps soon after the New Year. The loss of Bexar to hated enemies would stick in Santa Anna's craw. Desertion by so many would be avenged, as would the surrender of General Cos, Santa Anna's own brother-in-law. Blood lust in Santa Anna, born in the Bexar defeat, would smolder until it could no longer be controlled. A firestorm would follow, Bowie knew in his heart, and the blood-red flag, the symbol of no quarter, would be raised, and Santa Anna's bugles would intone the Deguello, the cutthroat song.

XVI
THE LINE OF DUTY

GOLIAD
JANUARY, 1836

Soon after the Battle of Bexar ended, Jim Bowie asked Burleson to relieve him from duty. He rode away from Bexar without having entered the city. He had no desire to renew friendships or rekindle memories of the happy days he and Ursula had spent together.

Christmas was at hand. This was the worst part of the year. Time had not filled the emptiness in his life or dulled the terrible ache in his heart. He still lived in a state of misery, but now it was unrelieved. He no longer drowned his sorrows in alcohol. To add to his distress, chest pains that had begun some months ago as dull aches had blossomed into constant stabs of agony each time he breathed. It was like having his own Bowie knife thrust between his ribs. He decided to visit a doctor in San Felipe, an old friend he trusted. The medico was honest and direct.

"You have lung fever, Jim. Tuberculosis. One lung is worse than the other, but both are very bad."

"What can you do for me, Doc?"

"Not much, I'm afraid! I can give you something for pain, but that's about all. This sickness will wear you down until you reach a point that you can't stand up anymore. After that, it's just a matter of time."

"How long do I have, Doc?"

"A few weeks. Three or four months. Maybe more. Maybe less. I'm more sorry than I can say, Jim!"

"Do me one favor, Doc."

"Sure! If I can."

"Don't mention this to anyone."

"I won't, Jim! But people are bound to suspect that something's wrong. You've already lost a good deal of weight. Your skin is pale and waxy looking, and your harsh cough will get worse."

"I don't care what people suspect, Doc. I have a job to do before I cash in, and I intend to finish it."

The doctor handed Bowie several vials.

"This is laudanum. It's the strongest painkiller I have. It's habit forming."

"I wish that was the worst worry I had, Doc!"

They both laughed.

Bowie left the doctor's home and wandered slowly along until he arrived in Goliad ten days later. Now he sat in the town's best fonda, trying to eat supper. In the past few days, he had begun to feel his strength oozing away. His appetite had all but disappeared, but he knew that food was vital in his battle to keep going as long as possible.

Bowie looked up as the door of the inn swung open, and the bulk of a large man filled the opening.

"Innkeeper! Aguardiente! Pronto!"

There was no mistaking the bulk or the voice.

It was Houston.

"General Houston! Please join me!"

Houston squinted in the dim candlelight.

"By thunder!" he roared. "Jim Bowie! This is the best news I've had for quite a spell."

A muchacho brought a bottle of aguardiente and two mugs to the table.

Houston poured a full measure for himself, started to pour a second, but paused.

"Jim?"

"No! I haven't had a drink since you left me!"

"Good man! I'm proud of you!"

Houston reached across the table and squeezed Bowie's shoulder fondly. He was startled by the frailty he encountered.

"I'm surprised you haven't regained some of the strength and muscle you lost during your siege."

"I did for a while, but I've been under the weather lately. Don't worry, Sam. I'll be fine."

Houston raised his drink to his lips and sipped, and looked more closely at Bowie. The buckskin shirt seemed to be hanging on his bare bones rather than covering his once robust body. His skin was pale and sickly looking. Deep-sunken eyes and an ashen face gave him a bleak, cadaverous appearance. When Bowie noticed Houston's concerned expression, he smiled, but his eyes couldn't disguise his intense suffering.

Suddenly, Bowie turned away, covered his mouth with a bloodstained handkerchief and began a series of coughs that wrenched his whole body. Houston watched with concern and pity for his friend. There could be no doubt. Bowie was a very sick man.

At last the coughing ended. Bowie tried to smile, and took a gulp of water.

"I guess I caught the winter croup, Sam."

"It's sure the right time of the year for it," Houston agreed, becoming a co-conspirator in Bowie's game. Fate's hand had maimed Bowie, but Houston still trusted him more than any other man in Texas.

"I see the army's gone." Sam Houston's words were partly question and partly accusation.

"Marched away yesterday with Grant, Fannin, and Johnson, heading for Refugio, on the border," Bowie informed him. "Here's one of the recruiting posters."

Bowie handed Houston a small placard.

It invited volunteers to join a fighting force that would attack Matamoros. It went on to promise that the volunteers would "share in the spoils of war taken from the enemy." It was signed, Colonel J.W. Fannin, Acting Commander-in-Chief.

"I am the Commander-in-Chief, and I gave Fannin no such authority! It is simply an unauthorized raid with the obvious intention of looting for profit. This is insanity! We strive for enlightenment and support. This tyrannical action will have exactly the opposite effect! Can you account for this?"

"Fannin and Johnson went along with Dr. Grant. During the siege of Bexar, even as the battle was being waged, Grant belittled the effort as unworthy of losing time and lives. He persisted in his claim that Matamoros was more important and valuable. He called it the gateway to the interior of Mexico, a city where support against Santa Anna could be rallied, and men to fight with us could be recruited."

"Utterly fantastic! Completely illogical!"

"Fantastic yes, but not illogical," Bowie offered. "I've had some unpleasant dealings with Dr. Grant in the past. Remember that all of his estates and land in Parras were confiscated. The road to Parras leads through Monterrey, and the road to Monterrey leads through Matamoros."

"So Grant is using this force of brigands to recover his own former holdings! What incredible gall!"

"Well, as you know, Grant's pretty glib, and he's a

sure enough spellbinder when he has an audience."

"And he had an audience."

"He sure did, Sam. With every one of those wide-eyed New Orleans Grays standing in the front row, hanging on every word."

"That's just plain wonderful!" Houston blustered sarcastically. "You know as well as I do that Santa Anna's pride will compel him to avenge the awful whipping his army took at Bexar. We need fighting men to oppose him, and the only sizeable force we had is on a wild goose chase, guaranteed to incite more hate and discontent. How many men are still here?"

"Thirty. Men from my former command whom I talked into staying, although I had no authority to do so," Bowie added bitterly.

Houston understood. In the little time that Bowie had remaining, he wanted to spend fighting. Many of his peers were convinced he had harmed the future of Texas. Helping to give it a new life as a republic was the only way he could recover the respect of his peers and, of even more importance, his self-respect.

Equally as important was the fact that the only time he could forget his sorrow about Ursula's death was in the midst of battle, with bullets whizzing in every direction. He needed a command. It was his single reason to stay alive. Austin had promoted

Travis to the rank of colonel after he stole a herd of horses. Fannin received a similar promotion for his service under Bowie at Concepcion, but there was no recognition for Bowie who had done far more than either of them. Houston saw the injustice, but he understood why. The men in control of the new government at San Felipe were colonists. Bowie was not. Marrying into a leading Mexican family had made him a Mexican, a foreign aristocrat, a man who adopted a Mexican life-style. To many, Bowie was an enigma, to many others, he was a renegade. To Houston, he was the best fighting man in Texas.

The door behind Houston opened and Bowie saw a familiar face under a thick coating of trail dust.

"Daniel Austin!" Bowie exclaimed. "What brings you to Goliad?"

"Good evening, General, Colonel. I bear extremely unwelcome news from Bexar!"

Daniel handed a small dispatch case to Houston.

"Muchacho," thundered Houston while opening the case. "Bring this tired young man a drink!"

"With utmost respect, General, what I need most is water, inside and out. I'll be back in a moment."

Daniel turned and walked toward the wash area in the rear of the fonda, as Houston scanned the papers.

"Young Austin was right. It is grave news indeed!

Colonel Neill desperately needs reinforcements. He has only eighty men fit for duty, and Santa Anna is in Laredo with over four thousand men!"

Houston handed the message to Bowie, as Daniel rejoined them.

"I must catch the army that's heading for Refugio. I also need to be in San Felipe, to ward off trouble, to organize overall resistance, and effect a defensive strategy. Now I'm needed in Bexar. I wish I could be in all three places at once. What I need most is time, a few miserable weeks to get ready. But there is no time. Santa Anna is on our doorstep!"

"I can go to Bexar for you," Bowie offered. "Santa Anna won't leave a fighting force behind him. His pride will force him to retake Bexar before he heads farther north. If I can round up a few hundred men, we can stop the Mexicans like a cork in a bottleneck for a couple of weeks. If we sting them enough, it'll take another week or two to lick their wounds. What do you say, Sam?"

"I say you're the only man who can pull it off! Daniel, is Hawkins with you?"

"No, Sir. Colonel Neill sent out a half dozen of us, since he didn't know where you were. Hawk went to Gonzales, but he'll return to Bexar when he doesn't find you."

"Good! All right. You go with Colonel Bowie. I want

you and Hawkins, and a couple of others, to keep me up to date for as long as possible. Round up as many men as possible, Jim. Can you leave first thing in the morning?"

"We can leave tonight. While Daniel washes out his throat and eats a hot meal, I'll start rounding up the men. We can be out of here by midnight."

"Use your own judgment when you get there. If defending Bexar is impractical, demolish all of the fortifications and blow up the Alamo. Put a torch to the food stores and everything else that would aid an army on the march. If you stay ahead of them as they march north, you can ambush them at river crossings and campsites. Whatever you think best! It's your call, Jim. Just buy me as much time as you can."

"I will! We will, Sam!" Bowie assured him.

"I know you will! Well, I'm heading for Refugio, boys, to recover a missing army. Good luck and God Speed."

It was a swift, bone-jarring ride into Bexar. Bowie pushed his small, thirty-man force and their weary horses to the edge of their endurance. Daniel Austin and Jim Bowie, serving as outriders, scouted ahead and along both flanks of the column, and covered much more distance than any of the others, but Azogue and Raven seemed to suffer no ill effects.

331

Colonel Joseph Neill met them in the Main Plaza when they arrived.

"Tarnation, Bowie. You brought thirty men when Santa Anna has five thousand! What can we do with so few?" Neill's tone suggested desperation.

"I won't have an answer to that until I look around. I'll let you know presently."

Neill was a regular army man, and a friend of Sam Houston's. He was not particularly smart or insightful, but he was honest and conscientious. Bowie's reply to his query had been a gentle way of letting Neill know who was in charge. He mounted Azogue and faced his men.

"Well, boys, I reckon the first place we need to check out is the Alamo."

The Alamo looked exactly the same as it had the day that General Cos abandoned it. Two enclosures surrounded by walls eight feet high and three feet thick. In the smaller of the two was a convent yard that housed the convent, now nothing more than a long row of two-story dormitories that had been used as barracks by both the Mexicans and the Texicans. At the southeast corner of the enclosure sat a chapel or, more accurately, the ruins of the chapel. The roof and some of the hewn walls had fallen down, leaving only a room on either side of the door. The sacristy the Mexicans had used as a powder magazine; and the baptistry had become the dispensary. Daniel guessed that the entire area enclosed within the walls was just a bit less than three acres.

"What do you think, Colonel?" he asked Bowie.

"There's not much here," Bowie replied. "Let's go into Bexar before we make a decision."

They rode slowly into Bexar. It was the first time that Bowie had entered the town since the night Don Jose Navarro shared the tragic news about Ursula and his family. He had not intended to stop at the de Verdimente Palacio, but something drew him. The spacious courtyard and beautiful garden where he had spent so many wonderful hours with Ursula, her parents, and her younger sister, were a shambles. One of the two huge oak doors that opened into la sala de estar had been smashed. The other hung by a single hinge. Nearby, a hole large enough to permit an easy entry by many men had been hacked through a side wall. He gazed past the opening and saw that the room had been stripped of all its carpets, furniture, paintings, and statuary. Looters had damaged this beautiful home. Bullet holes pockmarked many of the windows and shutters. The carnage and chaos of war, and the greed of men, had left a demolished palacio in their wake.

Sick at heart, Bowie turned away and rode toward the Navarro hacienda. They dismounted and climbed the polished steps to the veranda. Once again, Bowie stood at the door of the home that had given him so much joy, and so much sorrow.

Don Jose himself answered their knock. The first thing Bowie noticed were the man's eyes. Lustrous, dark eyes that were the most striking feature of the whole family. Eyes that Ursula had received from her mother and passed on to her tiny daughter. Emotion welled up in his throat so that he could not speak.

Don Jose's firm hand darted to Bowie's shoulder in a gesture that said far more than mere words. It took several moments for him to speak.

"Don Jaime. Daniel, I have not seen either of you for many months."

"It —has been—very hard."

"I understand. Come in my sons, and tell me what special mission has brought you here."

"I need your counsel and advice, Don Jose."

"I give it gladly."

"You know that Santa Anna is on the border with thousands of troops?"

"Yes."

"What, if anything, would the people of Bexar have us do about that?"

Navarro looked wistfully for a moment before he answered Bowie.

"I cannot speak for all the others, but I helped to

formulate the Declaration of Causes, and I am going to a March first meeting in San Felipe as a delegate."

"Are you going to discuss independence again?"

"More than that! We shall declare independence, elect a president, and adopt a constitution. This time, for better or worse, we will take that giant step."

"And you are in league with these decisions."

"For the future of Texas, and her people, I must be. If our beloved friend, Don Juan Verdimente were here, it would be he, and not I, who would be going. He hated tyranny bitterly, Don Jaime!"

"I am relieved beyond all bounds that you are with us in this fight."

"Many others are with you, as well! Judge Erasmo Seguin; his son, Captain Juan Seguin who, as you know, is serving with Colonel Neill; his nephew, Blaz Herrera; the acalde, Don Pancho Ruiz. Many men in Bexar are with you, but not all. Propaganda spread by Santa Anna's agents has been swallowed by many people."

"What is the chance of recruiting men in Bexar?"

"Alas, very poor! The fear of Santa Anna is far too great! Santa Anna is a vicious man. No doubt you heard about the massacre in Zacatecas. Hundreds of people were lined up against a wall and shot. He will do that here and everywhere else he goes. He will fly the blood-red flag of no quarter, play a deguello, and put every resistor to the sword. I am certain that he has marked my entire family for death. To protect them, I am sending them into the mountains. If we ever are to know liberty, Santa Anna must be beaten and deposed; but I fear that this is neither the place nor the time to administer that beating. His army is much too strong. I advise you to abandon Bexar and flee to San Felipe with me and the others. If you run today, you surely will live to fight tomorrow. To remain in Bexar means certain death."

With Don Jose Navarro's dire prediction ringing in their ears, Jim Bowie and Daniel Austin rode back to the Alamo.

When they arrived, they took an inventory and a muster. There were fourteen pieces of artillery and one hundred twenty officers and men fit for duty. Both numbers looked pitifully small when compared to Santa Anna's seven thousand men and dozens of cannon. Bowie was loathe to leave the cannon for Santa Anna but, with so few available horses, there was no way to haul them away. He decided to hold a council of war with Colonel Neill, Daniel Austin, a handful of experienced men, and Ken Hawkins, who had just returned from Gonzales.

"Boys," Jim Bowie began, "our mission is to confound Santa Anna. Unless we receive a lot of reinforcements, we won't be able to stop him. But we can hurt him enough to slow him up a bit. Houston asked me to buy him as much time as possible. We can destroy the Alamo, spike all the cannon, and burn up all the supplies and munitions we can't carry. Then we can nip at Santa Anna's heels along his line of march. Ambushes, hit-and-run raids, forays in the middle of the night, attacks at creek crossings. Cut and slash, then duck and run. Killing or wounding a few invaders at every opportunity. That's one way. Our other choice is to stay right here: defend the Alamo and place a huge stumbling block in Santa Anna's path. He can't go around us and leave a fighting force behind, so he will have to finish us off before he marches on. One possible advantage of staying is the very real chance that we will be reinforced when other Texicans and men of courage become aware of our commitment. I would like to hear your opinions, gentlemen."

Counting Bowie, there were ten men at the parlay. They exchanged ideas and opinions for the next hour and wound up divided. Five favored abandonment of Bexar, followed by a long series of hit-and-run raids. The others felt that defending Bexar was the proper course of action. Hawk assured Bowie that a group of men from Gonzales would support his decision regardless of which plan he decided upon.

Bowie wrestled with the most important decision

he would ever make throughout the evening and well into the long, lonely hours of the night. At last, he took pen in hand, and composed a letter.

Relief at this post in men, money, and provisions is vitally important. The salvation of Texas depends on keeping Bexar out of enemy hands! Colonel Neill and I have come to the same conclusion. We would rather die defending Bexar than surrender it to the enemy.

Now that the momentous decision had been made, Bowie left the letter on the desk and strolled into the cool, still darkness of the night. Once, in a deadly duel, he had taken a flesh wound in order to deliver a deathblow to his enemy. Defending Bexar was very similar. Texas could endure a flesh wound, even if it cost his life and the lives of his men. In return, Santa Anna would be forced to sacrifice men, morale and time, most of all time. He wouldn't be able to sweep across the plains of Texas, leaving death, destruction and chaos in his wake. Houston needed time, and no one would ever be able to say that Jim Bowie had not bought every day, hour, minute and second that he could. Any life lost in defense of the Alamo, if it meant delaying Santa Anna, would be a necessary investment in the life of Texas.

Buck Travis arrived a few days later with thirty

men. Bowie was happy to see him. He had always regarded Travis as a friend, but now something had changed. His manner was cool and stiffly formal. Bowie later discovered that Travis was reluctant to come to the Alamo. Twice, he had written letters to Governor Smith asking him to countermand an order that sent Travis and his men to Bexar. He threatened to resign his commission and even accused Smith of sacrificing him. In the end, he controlled his rage and followed orders, with a good deal of undisguised reluctance.

It turned out that Colonel Neill was unwilling to die defending Bexar. The day after Travis arrived, Neill announced that, as much as he wanted to stay, a sudden illness in his family required his presence. Neill departed that same afternoon. His final words were more than a little surprising.

"Colonel Travis, take command of this post!"

As Neill rode away, Bowie grinned.

"I reckon we can sort that out ourselves, Buck."

"You heard Colonel Neill's order, Colonel Bowie! Henceforth you will regard yourself as under my command!"

Bowie's pale face darkened for a moment, but he regained his composure before he spoke.

"Since you've chosen to adopt a hard case attitude, you force me to respond in kind. Colonel Neill had no authority to name a commander. Furthermore, I am your senior in rank, and the commanding general ordered me to come here and take charge. So, until General Houston relieves me, I'll remain in charge."

An hour later, Bowie left the Alamo and rode into Bexar. Unfortunately, these bitter feelings between him and Travis could not be smoothed over. The disagreement was simply an example of the factions that existed in Texas. Houston's supporters opposed Austin's followers. Strangely, Neill was a Houston man while Travis was pro-Austin; however, Travis and Neill were both regular army men. That was another bone of contention: the regular army versus the volunteers. Other divisions included Americans versus Mexicans, colonists versus non-colonists, and land speculators versus farmers and ranchers. To make things even more confusing and hotly divided, many Texicans and Tejanos were members of more than one faction. Lines were not clearly drawn and easily identifiable, but were muddled and volatile.

None of that, Bowie reflected, offered the answer to Travis's strange attitude. He and Buck had always been friends, good friends. Houston had mentioned that Travis had been both vocal and outspoken in his support of Austin. A well-read attorney, Travis had written stirring essays, explaining and strengthening his beliefs. Accolades had flowed from Austin and a majority of his supporters. Perhaps, Bowie reasoned, dreams of fame and high office had endowed Travis with his newly developed arrogance. The loss of this friendship troubled Bowie. His long drunken spree had already cost him most of his friends; he couldn't afford to lose the friendship of Travis during this important battle to buy Houston time.

His activities of the past few days, compounded by his confrontation with Travis, had physically weakened Bowie. He tied Azogue to a hitch rail outside the cantina called Lion de Oro and entered. Bowie hadn't tasted strong spirits since Houston had rescued him. With a strong depressing sense of failure and personal loathing, he ordered ron blanco, a strong, clear rum. He told himself that this was a means of regaining some of his dwindling strength. It was strong healing medicine, not a weak relapse back into oblivion.

He reached for the bottle and poured fiery liquor into a glass. He lifted it to his lips, hoping that the strong smell would sicken him; instead, a craving possessed him and weakness betrayed him. With a shaking hand, he set the glass back on the table. For the moment, caution and resolve overcame longing, but the longing soon prevailed. He lifted the glass again, only intending to moisten his dry, cracked lips and nothing more. He dipped the tip of his tongue in the elixir and, before he knew what was happening, the stimulating balm cascaded down his throat, warming, soothing, and comforting until, at last, it became a screaming warning in the deep pit of his stomach. Take care! Don't become a slave to alcohol again. But the combination of pain, impending death, and awesome responsibilities did not heed the tardy call. Bowie poured and downed another glass with more eagerness and less resolve. The third was even easier. Warm waves of relief coursed through his tortured body and mind. Suddenly, responsibilities, chest pains, even impending death, seemed far away.

Bowie shuttled back and forth between the Alamo and Bexar for the next three days. Travis watched him leave early each morning and return late each afternoon, clinging to his Mexican saddle.

"Colonel Bowie's conduct is disgusting," Travis complained to anyone who would listen, managing to impart an air of sarcasm to the words Colonel and Bowie. "He's been drunk as a skunk for three days already. How long must we endure a drunkard for a commander? The command should be mine anyway! Peril from Santa Anna's army grows more ominous with each passing day! Meanwhile, Bowie leaves all of the responsibility on my shoulders. I deserve the authority that goes with that responsibility."

Not content with vocalizing his displeasure, Travis wrote letters to everyone that he thought might read them, pleading to be relieved of his present duties or, failing that, for more supplies and re-enforcements.

Early one morning a few days later, one desperate plea was answered as eighty Tennesseans, dressed in buckskins or homespun, and carrying long rifles, tomahawks, and knives, arrived at the gates of the Alamo. The leader was a tall raw-boned fellow with iron-gray, shoulder-length hair that was covered by a coonskin cap. No mistaking his identity. Travis had seen that rugged face on a dozen penny novels. He was the legendary Davy Crockett, former Congressman from Tennessee, as well as a noted frontiersman and Indian fighter. His sudden arrival was both a surprise and a delight. Travis told him so.

"Colonel Crockett, I am Colonel William Barrett Travis. It is a joy to have you and your Tennesseans come to aid us at this moment of our great peril!"

"I hear Jim Bowie's here about," Crockett grinned. "Where might I find him?"

"No doubt he's sitting in the Lion de Oro Cantina, getting drunk again, Colonel Crockett."

"It's downright unneighborly to allow a fella to git drunk by himself. I reckon I'll go help him. By the by, there ain't no point of both of us runnin' around

343

callin' each other colonel. Nobody worth his salt has time for titles anyhow. Just call me Crockett. I'll call you Travis!"

Despite a pervasive feeling that he was playing the part of a hat-in-hand lackey, Travis felt compelled to escort Crockett to Bexar personally and introduce him to Bowie. His offer was promptly accepted.

The meeting was a very special moment for both of the two living legends. They shook hands, and looked each other up and down, smiling broadly.

"Bowie, we got a heap of talkin' to do. Let's have a drink, or two, or ten, and get at it."

"Gladly, Congressman Crockett."

"Please, Jim, don't call me that. I'm still tryin' to live it down."

Crockett hung his coonskin cap on the end of his long rifle, leaned it against a wall, and then poured large measures of tequila into two tall glasses.

"Soon as I get washed off on the inside, I'll worry about getting' washed off on the outside."

Travis felt like an intruder. There was obviously no further need of his presence, so he left and rode back to the Alamo. The others didn't notice his departure.

The meeting was unique, Bowie reflected. He'd had a great many acquaintances in his life, but very few friends, even fewer good friends; but he hit it off immediately with Crockett. They sat drinking tequila and swapping stories for several hours. Bowie tried not to cough any more than necessary, and Crockett tried not to notice when he did. In the early evening, as they sat enjoying platters of buffalo ribs, Bowie asked Crockett why he'd run for Congress.

"Well, after General Andy Jackson and the rest of us whipped them British fellers at New Orleans, I'd had my fill o' crowds n blood lettin'. I rode back to Tennessee and set up in the deep woods for quite a spell, huntin,' trappin,' and such. Married me a wife, had me some kids. Then I begun lookin' round at the things that was goin' on that shouldn a been, in Tennessee, n the hull country. Bein' the backwoods bumpkin I was then, I figured an honest man could join up with some other honest men in Congress and set things right. But I tell you true, Jim, I found more nasty critters in Washington City than I ever found out in the piney woods. The hull town's full of 'em. I reckon the last straw was when a big family with a bunch o' kids got burned out a house n home. I voted ta give 'em a few dollars ta help 'em git set up again. Folks back home decided they didn't hanker t'have a spendthrift representin' 'em, so they voted me out. Whereupon, I told 'em to go ta hell, 'cause I was goin' to Texas. I figured that gettin' back in a sure enough shootin' war, beat all the hell outta speechifyin' n congressifyin', so I grabbed up Old Betsy, my rifle, 'n

I come a runnin'!"

Crockett had been looking with great interest at the knife Bowie was using to slice his meat.

"Is that the Bowie knife I heard so much about?"

Bowie handed the weapon to Crockett.

"Thunderation, Jim, it seems to come alive in your hand! Almost like it has a will of its own. Makes me quiver in my boots just ta look at it."

"I've seen a few men on the wrong end quiver a bit," Bowie admitted.

Crockett withdrew his own knife from its sheath and passed it over to Bowie.

"They call this a bowie knife. Made in England. Every man jack in Tennessee's seems ta be carryin' one, but compared to this hog whallopper of yours, they're all of 'em toys. You n this knife are legends. How's about tellin' me some more about yerself?"

Bowie stared past Crockett toward a fast darkening sky for several moments before he answered.

"Growin' up on the Louisiana bayous, I discovered that most men don't have enough sand in their craws to stand up to another man with a knife who's willin' to use it. It's different in a battle when you're firing a rifle, or even looking down the barrel of a pistol in a duel. A lot of things can happen at such times. A pistol misfire, a poorly aimed shot, a shaky hand, all can end a duel or a fight without anybody dying. But sharp, cold, hard steel means personal involvement. A realization that, at best, a winner won't come out unscathed. Closeness betrays a sour smell of fear, as well as steadiness does courage. Skilled swordsmen can keep enemies at bay until they wear them down or weaken them; but the first thrust in a knife fight usually means a mortal blow, one way or another. If an enemy can strike first, and you can't parry him and return one of your own, you're dead. If you can, he's dead."

"I never figured it that way, Jim. Thinkin' about bein' impaled on a pig sticker is enough to turn any man's innards."

"Exactly the point, Davy! The only surefire way to win any fight is not to fight at all. If you do have to fight, you want to have an edge. My Bowie knife's weakened more than one fellow's knees, and let me walk away from quite a few others."

"Who designed the knife and forged it fer ya?"

"I pretty much designed it myself. It was forged with special steel by James Black of Washington, Arkansas."

"I'd admire to hear that story, Jim."

*****

As he began relating the history of the Bowie knife, Bowie's mind drifted back to 1827, to a low-roofed workshop that stood on the bank of a swift stream that powered a big water wheel. A burly slave respectfully nodded to him as he entered the wide doorway and asked for James Black, shouting to be heard over the clang of hammers on anvils.

"In office, Sur," the slave shouted back, indicating a closed door at the rear of the shop.

A heavy door was opened in response to his knock by a tall, lean man with long black hair tied at the base of his neck in a queue. Widely-spaced, piercing dark eyes held Bowie's own.

"Mr. Black? I'm James Bowie."

"Come in and sit yourself, Mr. Bowie."

The solidly built, thick walls of the office muffled enough of the outside noise to eliminate shouting.

"I'm told that you craft a keen blade that holds a cutting edge for a long time, Mr. Black."

"I do my best."

"Does that come from a new tempering method?"

"With all due respect, Mr. Bowie, my methods are a trade secret."

There was an icy quality to the reply.

"My apologies, Mr. Black! I intended no intrusion into your private business. I inquired only because I have a very special knife in mind. I took the liberty of whittling a model out of soft pine."

Black watched as Bowie unrolled a piece of soft

buckskin. It wasn't unusual for men to bring wooden models to be reproduced in steel. Most were poor designs that gave no thought to shape, features, or balance. Black examined Bowie's carefully carved model and found none of the shortcomings he had expected. His dark eyes sparkled as he turned it over in his strong, slender hands.

"I'm greatly intrigued, Mr. Bowie. I apprenticed as a cutler in Philadelphia before I came down here, My hobby was crafting fine knives. Unfortunately, there is little call for them out here. There are several unique features here."

"It's the start of an idea."

Bowie extracted a butcher knife from the sheath on his belt, and handed it to Black.

"As you can see, about all this knife is good for is hacking meat! It's clumsy and lacks balance. It's bad for fighting, and even worse for throwing."

Black returned the butcher knife and began a series of careful measurements on the model.

"The blade is eleven inches long and an inch and a half wide. The back of the blade, at the heel, is just slightly over a quarter of an inch thick."

"I figured that would give it strength. The blade must never snap. Overall dimensions can be adjusted to give it balance. You won't know about that until you know the weight of the blade in relation to the entire weight of the knife. Notice the point is exactly at the center of the blade! That makes an accurate throwing knife. The blade curves toward the point convexly along the top edge, and concavely away along the bottom. Both edges must be razor sharp, so as to make the top of the blade an extension of the lower cutting edge."

"That's an excellent idea, Mr. Bowie! Particularly since the spine will be so thick."

"Once in New Orleans, I met a man who collected ancient weapons. One of his swords was particularly fascinating. It had a long hollow tube attached to the spine. Inside of the tube, a heavy ball called a steel apple, rolled toward the point on downward strokes. Of course, a similar system would be impossible to build into a knife, but I wondered if, somehow, the forward edge of a blade could be weighed to bring about the same added force and striking power."

"An intriguing concept, Sir! I also wonder."

"The cross guard is extremely important. It must be constructed of heavy brass, not steel. I want brass backing on the spine as well, running from the guard down to the end of the curved blade."

"Why brass?" Black asked quizzically.

"When I parry a thrust, the brass, being softer than steel, will catch and hold a steel blade momentarily."

"Very simple. Very logical. You seem to have

thought of everything, Mr. Bowie."

"I have theories. I think you can make them work, if you decide to accept the commission."

"I love challenges, Mr. Bowie. Your project gives me many to solve and overcome. I accept with great pleasure. I will do my utmost to incorporate as many as possible into a knife made from my finest steel."

"We have to settle on the price."

"Not until the knife is finished. Come back in a month. If you don't like the knife, you won't owe me anything. If I don't like it, you won't even see it. By the way, may I presume that you have heard of Damascus Steel?"

"Of course."

"No other steel the world has ever known would take and hold a cutting edge like Damascus, or have the strength and durability. It's easily identifiable by a mottled look it acquires in the hardening process. Would you be surprised to know that I've duplicated Damascus steel?"

"Yes, indeed!"

"It may not be an exact duplicate. I discovered the process by accident, but it's the best steel that can be made with the limited knowledge we possess. Yet, it's possible to produce much higher quality. Let me show you a real treasure, Mr. Bowie."

Black rose and went to a large metal cabinet with

a sturdy lock. He unlocked the cabinet and withdrew a brassbound oak box, also fitted with a key. Almost reverently, he opened the box. On a soft bed of red velvet lay a small, dark, roughly circular object, the size of a man's fist. Black held it out to Bowie.

"Take this."

The object was incredibly heavy for its size.

"What is it?"

"Steel! Pure steel! Finer than any ever made in this world."

"Then how..........?"

"One winter evening, a week after my sixteenth birthday, I was walking home from the farm where I worked, when I saw a fireball racing across the sky. The sound it made was ghostly. A moan yet not a moan. Like the roaring blaze in an open fireplace, yet different. As I watched, the object began descending toward earth, sounding like the wail of a frightened banshee, prowling about on a misty Irish moor. The sky glowed brightly, then suddenly went pitch black. I had just witnessed the death of a shooting star. The visitor from space terrified many that saw it. Some thought it heralded the last days of the world, but it fascinated me. I ran to the place where it had fallen and searched for fragments. This was the largest one. Years later, a famous scientist from the University of Pennsylvania examined one fragment and concluded that it was pure steel. Steel with such a density mass that it can't be cut, even with a diamond. The secret is the alloys that mated with the steel. Alloys that remain a secret that some day we may uncover."

Black took the meteorite and returned it to its bed of red velvet.

"Now you know why I keep it in a jewel box. It is a jewel, a precious jewel from the distant heavens."

Black laid the box aside, picked up the carved wooden model, and once again turned it over, eyeing each curve and feature.

"As I said, you've given me a real challenge. Let me see what I can accomplish in the next thirty days, Mr. Bowie."

Bowie spent the next month conducting business in Little Rock. As soon as it was concluded, he rode eagerly back to Black's foundry. The moment Black placed the knife in his hands, Bowie knew his dream had come true. Here was the strength of three knives in one, yet was perfectly balanced and easily welded. Bowie's eyes reflected his wonderment.

"It's unbelievably fine!" Bowie told Black, unable to conjure up more appropriate praise.

Mounted on a wall of Black's office was a small wooden target.

"Try throwing it," Black suggested. "It's machined

to turn over once in twenty feet."

As the knife thumped into the precise center of the target, the blade emitted an eerie melodic tone that gradually became a soft sigh, a sound the likes of which Bowie had never before heard. It was like a human sigh, yet it had an unearthly quality as well. Bowie shook his head in disbelief at the knife's superior quality and Black's ingenuity.

"I can't believe you crafted anything so perfect."

"There will never be another knife like it, that's for certain! I began with my very best, already refined, wrought iron. My slaves cleaned a small furnace, then cleaned it again, to be certain that not a cinder or the tiniest speck of dust remained. Then they laid a charcoal fire that heated the iron to red, then white, and finally to a molten mass, as the charcoal slowly defused into the wrought iron and produced steel. Crude steel, still imperfect because particles of slag had formed carbonic gas pockets. Being unable to escape, they had formed small molten blisters. I was now ready to further refine the steel through the crucible process until each imperfection was sinered out of it. Since my goal was flawless steel, this process had to be repeated many times.

"As I poured the final molten mass, my heart was in my throat until I knew it was flawless, for only then could I create a perfect knife. The next morning, I examined the steel I had made. It wasn't perfect! So my slaves built a new fire and returned the steel to its molten state. When it was as perfect as possible, I added one more special ingredient to the crucible."

Black paused and withdrew the red velvet jewel box from its place in his desk. When he opened it, it was empty.

"The ingredient I added was the piece of steel that came from beyond the far reaches of our world. It is now part of your blade, Mr. Bowie. Whether it was a part of Heaven, or a part of hell, only time will tell."

*****

In the best frontier tradition, Crockett and Bowie continued to celebrate a new friendship by strolling from tavern to tavern for the next several days. Their apparent disregard for impending danger was all but intolerable to Travis. He shared his exasperation in a letter to Governor Smith.

Dear Sir:

My situation is awkward and delicate. Colonel Neill left me in command, but in an effort to placate the volunteers here and not assume command over them, I issued orders for the election of an officer to command them, with the exception of the one company that had previously engaged to serve under me.

Bowie was elected and, since then, he has been roaring drunk all the time! He has assumed complete command and is proceeding in a most disorderly and irregular fashion.

If I did not feel my honor and that of my country would be compromised, I would leave here immediately for some other place with the troops under my personal command, since I am unwilling to be responsible for the irregularities of any man.

I hope you will immediately order some regular troops here as it is more important to defend this post than I imagined. This is the key to Texas. Without a foothold here, the enemy can do nothing against the rest of the colony.

Stiff-necked, terse, and somewhat childish, the letter bespoke the bitter disappointment Travis felt. He had ordered an election because volunteers were used to electing their own leaders, and because he was confident of the outcome, certain the men would follow him rather than a buck-skinned knife-fighter.

Travis failed to realize that elections are not always won by the best-qualified candidate, but rather by one that men most admired. Many of the Texans, and all of the Tennesseans, including Crockett, admired and liked Bowie. In his cold, honest moments, Travis had to admit to himself that he was not a likeable fellow. Admired as a good fighting man? Perhaps. Liked? No! But Travis was a patriot. The final paragraph of his letter confirmed his patriotism, his willingness to admit the wisdom of Bowie's decision to stay put, and his willingness to defend Bexar.

The next morning, Travis, Bowie and Crockett met to affect a truce and establish order. Crockett's idea won the day.

"To satisfy my Tennesseans, I reckon I should be appointed some sort of high private, but you fellers should share the command."

That afternoon, another dispatch went to Governor Smith.

Sir: As a result of an agreement reached today, Colonel James Bowie will henceforth command the volunteers of the garrison, and Colonel W.B. Travis the regulars and volunteer cavalry. General orders and correspondence will be signed by both.

With the exception of the thirty men commanded by Travis, Bowie was in charge of the Alamo. He could now turn his attention to important issues. The most important issue was strengthening the fortress.

Despite the discomfort it caused, Bowie worked beside the men as they built a palisade of cedar logs and dug an entrenchment in an effort to fortify the opening between the church and the outer wall of the enclosure. The principal defense would come from the Alamo's fourteen cannon, four of which already had been mounted on a platform above the apse of the church by the troops of General Cos. Positioning the other ten cannon in most advantageous locations was vital.

Working in concert with Crockett, Travis, and Captain Almeron Dickinson, Bowie decided to use four cannon to protect the log palisade, the point of the greatest danger; four more were placed on the outer walls, and the final two were installed over the main gate.

In order to accommodate these main gate cannon, a platform of heavy cedar timbers was constructed fifteen feet above the ground, and a block and tackle was rigged to haul the heavy weapons into position.

The first cannon was positioned without a hitch, but as the second was being raised into place, one of the stout ropes snarled in a pulley. Shielding his eyes from the bright winter sun, Bowie looked upward, trying to determine the best way to free it. As he did, for one of the few times in his life, he took a step back without looking and stepped into empty space.

He seemed to hang suspended for a long time before he thudded to the ground. Stunned by the fall, he passed out. The next thing he knew, Crockett was supporting his head and asking if he was hurt.

A sharp, stabbing pain coursed through his chest as he drew breath to answer.

"Musta ... busted... somethin'. Git Doc."

The pain, when he breathed, made the utterance of each word an ordeal.

He fell into unconsciousness once more. He awoke to see the concerned, bearded face of Doctor Edward Mitchasson bending over him.

As the doctor's gentle hands explored his side, back, and hip, Bowie coughed in terrible agony, and on the ground next to him, he spit out a bright splash of blood.

"How bad, Doc?" The words were a groan.

"Bad, Colonel! Your hip is shattered, and at least one of your ribs penetrated your lung."

"How long till I kin git around?"

"I need to put a box splint on your hip, and a firm binding around your ribs. Severity of your injuries, coupled with the advanced state of your lung fever means at least six weeks flat on your back."

As Bowie struggled to reply, he coughed again. This time a bloody froth covered his lips.

"Santa Anna won't wait six weeks, Doc."

"I know, Colonel Bowie! I know!"

Eager hands lifted Bowie as gently as possible and

carried him to an alcove off the makeshift dispensary in the baptistry. In a painful eternity for Bowie, his hip was set and box splinted, and then his ribs were tightly bound.

The doctor gave him a heavy dose of laudanum, an opiate designed to reduce pain and induce sleep. The doctor and all of the others departed and, gradually, stabbing pain gave way to a continuous dull ache. Uncomfortable, but manageable. Nearly impossible to bear was his frustration and disappointment. At a time when Texas needed him most, he had, for the first time in his life, taken a careless step. His very being writhed in despair. He felt like a deserter! The opiate finally brought some merciful sleep, but soon he began to groan again, his face contorted in new pain as he dreamed about Ursula, the great love of his life. What a change she had made in him with her soft, tender ways. Always giving, never demanding. Ever spirited, never questioning. Her patience and will had bound their hearts together with bonds as unseen as the wind, but as strong as steel. Goodness that he could love and admire but never hope to emulate. Ursula was one woman in a million.

The laudanum's effect became more pronounced. He fell into a deep sleep and his dream ended. Three hours later, shearing pain jerked him out of his uneasy slumber and back to the world of torment. A soft groan that escaped his lips brought Mitchasson to his side and a new dose of laudanum to relieve his tortured body.

*****

For a second time, a slight easing of pain propelled Bowie into another drugged trance. Once again, he saw a beautiful, dusky woman as she emerged from the depths of his dream. Had anyone been watching, they would have noticed a grin of pleasure replace Bowie's grimace of pain as he anticipated seeing Ursula again. But it was not Ursula who emerged from the dim shadows in the corners of his mind. It was Catherine Villars. She glided to him and took his hand; then, together, they floated over a wide expanse of time and space. He found himself ashore in a sandy cove on Galvez Island, a stronghold of Jean Lafitte and his Berataria pirates. Here was Lafitte, eager to welcome him and Rezin, leading them past a line of rickety shacks that crowded along the beach just above the high water line, toward a strange, red, rambling structure. This, Lafitte told them, was the Maison Rouge, part fort, part home, part palace, and part storehouse for pirate treasures. Two stories high, it commanded a view of the island, and the barracoon where the slaves were kept, and most of the surrounding sea, but the base of the walls were only about ten feet above sea level.

361

Scattered around the floor of the structure's main room was an impressive collection of oriental rugs and a variety of rich furnishings that included a grand piano. Fine tapestries and oil paintings adorned the walls. The room that should have conveyed an air of wealth and luxury had been arranged with such an evident lack of good taste that it only bespoke an air of barbaric opulence.

"Fernando, you Spanish dog! Bring food for my guests. Be quick about it!"

Moments later a dark complexioned, middle-aged servant shuffled into the room bearing a large silver tray laden with delicacies. For some reason, the man looked strange. Bowie quickly saw why. He had no ears. Tiny stumps were all that remained. It was easy to see why his eyes were full of fear.

They sat down at a long mahogany table to a feast of dried fish, smoked turkey, duck, ham, delicious fresh bread, and vintage wine.

"No doubt you noticed that my servant lacks ears," Lafitte remarked. "He has no tongue, either, but he has one distinction. He is the only Spanish nobleman I ever captured that lived to tell about it. It satisfies a whim of mine to have a slave of noble Spanish birth. Fernando will live for as long as that whim remains. Spaniards killed my bride. I have been paying them back ever since. People call me a pirate, but I am not a pirate! I am a legal privateer, duly licensed by Venezuela, Spain's enemy, to raid Spanish ships and possessions."

Bowie thought it peculiar that Lafitte bothered to mention this, or felt the need to justify his activities.

"I see you're enjoying the food!" Lafitte observed. "You were hungry. Excellent! Good food is one of the reasons my men fight for me. Regular seaman's fare is enough to turn any man's stomach. Salt pork, so long in cask that it's rancid. Watered-down rum, water so long in cask it's alive with green tendrils, and ship's biscuits, alive with weevils. We, the free traders of Galveztown, have the best of everything, from the finest meats and wines to the best cigars. Any man alive would rather share our lot than rot on a stinking naval ship."

The door at the far end of the room swung open, and a young woman entered, such an astonishingly beautiful woman that Rezin and Jim stared at her in silent admiration. Instinctively, Jim rose to his feet, then suddenly noticed that she was a quadroon: one quarter Negro blood in a section of America where one drop of such blood made a man or woman black.

"Please be seated, Sir. You owe no such homage to her." Lafitte's advice was accompanied by a sneer. "She is my housekeeper, Catherine Villars."

Catherine, slim and graceful in movement, was of medium height with smooth and silky skin the shade of golden tan. Her raven black hair fell below the level of her shoulders, that framed an oval face with lovely dark green eyes, a delicate nose, and full lips. Bowie beheld nothing that was not perfection, other than her timid expression.

"Come and sit with us, little one." Lafitte's former tone of disdain was replaced by one of gentleness.

Catherine glided to the chair opposite Jim Bowie, sat, and began nibbling on the array of delicacies, her chin gracefully lowered to avoid eye contact. Lafitte spared her not a single glance. Instead, he continued his droning, one-sided conversation with Rezin.

Jim Bowie couldn't ignore her. She was simply too graceful, too lovely, too exotic. The shadow of her mixed blood was evident. She had inherited the best traits of both races. It was this that gave her a certain majesty and accounted for the luxuriance of her skin and hair, the fullness of her lips, and the tropical warmth of her eyes. Her demure demeanor was visible proof that Catherine Villars had accepted her role in life as a concubine. Her body did not, never had, and never would, belong to her. She was merely a possession, an ornament whose beauty and wonderment were to be acknowledged, but never loved by the men of wealth and importance who owned her. He could see that she accepted her status without resentment because she was only a woman, a quadroon woman at that, although a very beautiful one.

Bowie could not know that at that moment, Catherine was thinking about the baptismal record of her son. *Pierre Villars, son of Catherine Villars, grifa libre, concubine of Jean Lafitte.* She would have preferred "mistress." "Concubine" was a terribly ugly word. She was brought back to attention as she heard soft words from the man seated across from her.

"Have you been on the island very long?"

She raised her hooded eyes just enough to steal a glance at him. He was fair-haired and handsome in a strong and rugged way, yet his voice was gentle and she had glimpsed concerned compassion in his blue eyes.

"Oui, Monsieur," she replied demurely.

"You are from New Orleans?"

"Oui, Monsieur."

"I spent last week in New Orleans."

She raised her head and gazed directly into his eyes before she responded in a voice filled with longing.

"You found it a most beautiful and charming city, did you not?"

Catherine's terrible loneliness and emptiness was so visible that Bowie wanted to sweep her up in his arms, whisk her back to the city that she loved, and protect her from all of the terror and pain of her alien world. This magnificent woman, fit to sit beside an emperor, was consigned to an existence as mistress to an aging buccaneer. Once again his eyes met hers. This time, the air around them seemed to crackle with energy, then envelop them in a private cocoon where no one else was welcome. The next instant, Catherine's expression of wonderment turned to one of fear. She rose and fled from the room without another word. Bowie turned and glanced at Lafitte. What he saw was a stare so menacing and hateful that he instantly understood Catherine's frightened departure.

*****

Doctor Mitchasson checked on Bowie's condition several times during the evening and was relieved to find him sleeping more peacefully. Before he retired for the night, Mitchasson injected enough laudanum into his patient to keep him sleeping and, hopefully, pain free until morning. Through it all, Bowie's vivid dream continued.

*****

Aside for his knowing stare, Jean Lafitte seemed to pay no more attention to the silent exchange between

Bowie and Catherine. He waited patiently until they had finished eating and Catherine had left the table. Then he suggested business.

"Shall we visit the slave quarters, gentlemen?"

The Bowie brothers and Lafitte trudged down to the barracoon where the slaves were kept. They were met by the slave overseer, an evil-looking man with long, stringy black hair, and a hideous knife scar that started high on his left temple, ran across his nose and chin, and ended near the right corner of his jaw. His name, Lafitte told them, was Diego Malo. As they approached, he bowed to Lafitte.

"Bad luck, Captain. Two more of the miserable wretches died this morning."

"Fever?"

"No!" Malo hung his head. "They starved to death. I tried to persuade them to eat, but they refused."

Lafitte's gaze fell to the whip that Malo held.

"No doubt you used that cat-o-nine-tails as your persuader. Your carelessness steals money from my pockets, you Spanish dog! My patience wears thin. Mend your ways, or you'll feel the sting of the lash before you feel the caress of the hangman's halter."

Malo unlocked a gate in the high, sturdy stockade, and led them into a squalid enclosure. He was the only full-blooded Spaniard on the island, except for Lafitte's earless servant. Lafitte had called him a

Spanish dog. The sobriquet was frightening to Malo, who was as fearless as any man. It was time to work his way back into Lafitte's good graces. Malo just hoped an opportunity would present itself before the legendary Lafitte temper did him in.

Several flimsy lean-tos covered with dried brush and patches of sod were the only protection against sun and storms. In the shade of the crude structures lay the most miserable collection of humans that the Bowies had ever seen. Most lay prostrate. A few, apparently a bit stronger, struggled to sit up. Each of them was secured to a post by an unnecessary chain. Five of them were women, so thin that each of their ribs protruded from hideously blotched skin. Like their male companions, they gazed at the white men through dull eyes filled with hopeless resignation.

"They're a disgusting sight!" Rezin lamented.

"Yes," Lafitte agreed. "It's because of the terrible treatment they received from the Spaniards."

"They are far better than they seem, Señors," Malo assured them. "All they need is a little meat on their bones! Most of them are lazy malingerers. Like this fellow."

Malo indicated one of the men with his whip, and slashed him viciously. The unfortunate slave was far too weak to move. In an effort to force a response, Malo continued applying the whip until the man lost consciousness. Suddenly, the whip was torn from his hand, and Malo was hurtled to the ground.

"Is this how you treat your slaves, Captain Lafitte?" Bowie asked, as he towered over Malo.

"No! Of course not, Monsieur Bowie." He turned a glaring eye on Malo. "I'll have your back stripped for this. Go to your quarters and stay there until I summon you!"

Malo hastily withdrew.

"Malo is an able lieutenant most of the time, but from time to time he is overzealous. A good beating will remind him not to be. It is apparent that these slaves are unworthy of your attention. Tomorrow, I plan to intercept an inbound Spanish slave ship. I am certain that they will provide a far better selection."

"We came to buy fifty slaves, Captain Lafitte," Jim Bowie reminded him. Overcome by pity for his fellow men, he added. "We'll buy all thirty-four of these poor brutes, and add the other sixteen from the new slaves before Diego Malo can punish them with his lash. Can we impose on your hospitality until the members of this group are strong enough to travel?"

"Of course, Monsieur! You're welcome to stay for as long as you wish. I regret that I will be sailing on the morning tide, and will be unable to continue as your host. However, Fernando will see to all of your desires." Lafitte paused for a moment and looked directly at Bowie in a challenging manner before he added, "No doubt, Catherine will as well."

As scheduled, Lafitte and his men departed early the following morning in a pair of captured Spanish frigates. For the next three days, the Bowie brothers kept watch on the slaves, feeding them, nursing them back to health, and protecting them from Malo in case he fell into one of his unpredictable rages. Jim saw Catherine only at the supper table. The rest of the time she kept to herself. It was just as well. She would be easy to love. In his twenty-two years, he'd had very little to do with women. He didn't know if his feelings toward Catherine were generated by infatuation, pity, or a young man's desire for a radiant woman. The image of her beautiful face with that frightened expression filled his thoughts day and night. He must not allow himself to fall in love with her. They could have no future together. She was the mistress of Jean Lafitte, a ruthless buccaneer who had men flogged or killed whenever it suited his fancy. Bowie could not even imagine the punishment that Lafitte would invent for a guest that violated his hospitality, much less steal the love of his mistress.

On the evening of the third day, Jim retired early. His time on the island had been traumatic. Not only was he haunted by the image of Catherine, he was becoming evermore conscious-stricken by thoughts of making a profit from the misery of other humans, though they were slaves. In an effort to find solace, he drank a bit more of Lafitte's brandy than was wise.

He dozed off the moment his head reached the pillow, but it was a tormented sleep. Two hours after midnight, he awoke in his still, humid, airless room, drenched with sweat, and consumed by a throbbing headache. For a time, he lay still listening to the drone of insects as they buzzed around his head but, finally, abandoning sleep, he arose and staggered back to Lafitte's social room where every manner of beverage was kept. Seeking more of the hair of the dog that had bitten him, he didn't bother to light the oil lamp that stood on the bar. Instead, he reached for the same brandy flask that he had nearly emptied earlier. Disdaining a glass, he lifted the flask to his lips and gratefully sloshed the liquid down his gullet.

Almost at once, a warm peaceful feeling consumed him. It was then that a tiny patch of dim moonlight revealed a slim figure huddled in the corner of a long couch. A sudden rush of adrenaline lifted him out of the brandy fog so that he became instantly alert.

"Catherine?" He whispered softly.

"Oui, Monsieur," came her soft reply.

"I'm surprised to see you."

"I couldn't sleep. I thought no one else would be

awake."

"I'll leave you alone, if that is your wish."

"Oh, no, Monsieur. Please stay."

He crossed the room and sat down next to her. He could feel her shaking.

"Are you coming down with the ague, Catherine?"

"No. For the first time in my life, I am wishing that things were different. Jean is kind to me, but I am only his concubine. He does not love me. I do not love him. I haven't thought about loving anyone since I was a young girl. That dream returned to me when I saw the tenderness in your eyes. Since that moment, I have thought of nothing else. My thoughts frighten me, and they make me sad, but they also fill my empty heart with nearly forgotten joy."

She covered her face with her hands and began to sob, her body shaking with emotion.

Overcome by pity, he reached out and pulled her into the protective circle of his arms, remembering a long ago boyhood day at the family's homestead on Bayou Boeuf, when a large dog had menaced a small kitten. He'd snatched up the kitten, defying the dog to hurt it. Now, he was defying Lafitte. He could feel Catherine's body trembling. He held her and gently stroked her hair until her trembling stopped. Then, rising, he gathered her up in his strong arms and carried her to her bedchamber. He laid her gently on the bed and started to leave, but, as he did, her arms reached out to him, her eyes imploring him to stay.

"Don't go! Love me! Give me one night of real happiness," she whispered.

The first slivers of dawn were piercing the eastern sky when he finally left her. As he closed her door, he sensed a presence behind him and spun around in time to see the disfigured face of the earless servant just before he disappeared around a corner. Fernando knew. As soon as Lafitte returned, he too would know. Only one question remained: What to do?

Jim roused Rezin and made him aware of their mortal danger.

"Perhaps Fernando will be too frightened to make this known to Lafitte," Rezin suggested. "He's terrified for his life already."

"Perhaps," Jim admitted. "Maybe I can scare him even more than his master by guaranteeing a swift, unpleasant death if he reveals the secret."

"Lafitte's expected to return this morning, Jim! You better find Fernando and silence him right away."

"He was probably on his way to the kitchen to start breakfast when he saw me leaving Catherine's room. Let's look for him there first."

They hurried to the far end of the building which housed food storehouses and kitchen. They searched the whole area, but Fernando was not to be found.

"Let's check on the slaves," Rezin suggested. "We may find Fernando at the servants' quarters."

They checked the servants' quarters enroute to the barracoon, but there was no sign of Fernando. They also passed close to the shack Diego Malo occupied, near the gate of the slave stockade, and heard him moving about inside. As they entered the barracoon, they discovered that another of the slaves had died, the one Malo had beaten with his lash.

Jim Bowie was so furious that he spun on his heel and headed directly toward Malo's shack. Malo must have seen him coming because he was standing in the wide, open doorway, leaning on the jamb, his thumbs hooked idly into the waistband of his leather britches.

"Malo, Captain Lafitte will skin you alive when I tell him you've beaten another valuable slave to death!"

"Bowie, you won't be alive long enough to worry about slaves when the captain hears a story I have to tell him." The slave master's black-toothed grin was the very essence of evil. He stepped back enough for Bowie to see into the shack's dim interior, yet it was light enough for Bowie to see the earless Fernando cowering in a corner. His presence made perfect sense. Fernando and Malo were the only Spaniards on the island. Afraid to face Lafitte alone, Fernando

374

had come to Malo for advice and protection, and had given Malo a way to regain Lafitte's goodwill.

At that precise moment, they heard the sound of the signal cannon, and saw two frigates and a large slave ship entering the bay. Lafitte had returned!

"Come, Bowie. Let's rush down to the beach, greet the captain, and see which of the tales he finds most interesting."

Malo brushed past the Bowies and walked quickly toward the beach. Jim knew he could not allow Malo to speak to Lafitte. If he did, the Bowie brothers and Catherine would die very nasty deaths.

Just as the prow of Lafitte's longboat touched the sand, Bowie ran after him and spun Malo around with one hand, and smashed his other fist into Malo's nose, knocking him to the ground.

"What is the meaning of this, Monsieur Bowie?" Lafitte demanded as he hurried up.

"This stupid oaf killed another one of our slaves. He's not only a bully and a sneak, he's a craven coward as well. I only regret the scum is too yellow-livered to fight me man-to-man, here-and-now."

Malo pulled himself up to his feet and wiped the blood away from his eyes and broken nose with the back of his hand.

"Captain, this man ----." Malo began speaking, but his words were cut off by Lafitte's savage blow that

375

knocked him down again.

"You are a stupid fool, Malo. But it remains to be seen if you are also a coward. You will fight Bowie here-and-now, or I will kill you where you lay."

The damaging news he had been so eager to share with Lafitte vanished from his mind. His hot Spanish blood cried out for vengeance. Damn Lafitte for not listening to him! Lafitte was the real fool, but that didn't matter to Malo anymore. He had suffered an unforgivable insult to his manhood, an insult that would not be erased until the sand ran red with Bowie's blood.

"Pierre," Lafitte called to one of the nearby pirates, "fetch a box of big nails and a hammer."

The messenger raced away and was back moments later. When he returned, Lafitte led the combatants to a heavy driftwood log that lay a short distance away. The log, which was at least three feet thick, once had been a giant cottonwood growing along one of the mighty river's northern banks. Furious storms most likely had toppled it into the current and swept it along for a thousand miles or more. It now lay stripped of leaves and branches, aside from a few short stubs that anchored it in the sand. Lafitte pressed his dirk into the wood to test it, and found solid wood an inch below the surface that had been softened by long immersion. Confident nails would hold, Lafitte ordered Bowie and Malo to straddle the log, facing each other with their knees touching.

"Pierre, nail the edges of their leather breeches to the log. Be careful not to nail one of the legs. I don't want anyone to be hurt before the duel begins."

The man did as he was told. Stretching the leather out, he drove half-a-dozen nails through each trouser leg into the still sturdy areas of the old log. When he was satisfied that the nails were firmly implanted, he turned and nodded. Lafitte approached, holding two sailors' dirks. The blade of one was about an inch longer than the other. Lafitte handed the longer one to his henchman.

"I will count to three. On the count of three, you may strike."

Bowie took the opportunity to strip off his shirt. It made no sense to give Malo anything to grasp. Malo must have seen the wisdom in Bowie's action, since he quickly followed suit.

Malo suddenly had second thoughts in the moment before Lafitte began to count. Strong muscles rippling under Bowie's skin were one cause for his alarm. He'd thought Bowie's young slim body couldn't muster enough power to counter his brute force, but now he wasn't so sure. It might come down to his power against Bowie's speed. He also realized Bowie had planned the duel to silence him before he could speak to Lafitte. This blond, blue-eyed slave buyer was far more cunning than Malo had imagined. He hoped his poor judgment wouldn't cost him his life. He must strike first at all costs, he decided. Bowie would probably be ready to counter a direct thrust, and then strike back, so Malo would trick him. He would swing his knife out in a wide arc the instant Lafitte reached the count of three and plunge it into Bowie's heart from the side.

Satisfied that both combatants were ready, Lafitte stepped back.

"One, two, three." The words blended together.

As planned, Malo brought his right arm around in a sweeping arc, the point of his blade aimed to enter Bowie's left armpit. Most men would have died with steel imbedded in their hearts, but Bowie was not like most men. His quickness saved him from death, but not from a nasty flesh wound that spouted blood.

Since he had not struck his target squarely, Malo's momentum carried the hand holding the dagger well past Bowie's right side, but that was just as well. A backstroke could be just as deadly, and he would be able to deliver it in the space of a heartbeat. But in the space of that heartbeat, Bowie acted. He grasped Malo's knifehand in a vise-like grip, imprisoned it, then suddenly struck. Malo tried to intercept the thrust with his free hand, but that was like trying to capture the head of a striking cobra before the fangs found their mark. Bowie's blade sank deeply into his side. A gush of bright blood was followed by an unearthly scream. The blade was withdrawn, then driven home again. The scream gurgled and died in Malo's throat as life faded slowly from his glassy black eyes. His lifeless body sagged down toward the log, held in place only by the nails.

Bowie waited patiently as the nails were withdrawn and his bloody wound was bound. As soon as he had been freed with Rezin's help, he staggered up to the Maison Rouge. Malo was dead, and if the earless Fernando could be silenced, a deadly secret Bowie and Catherine shared was safe.

Since Lafitte was busy landing the cargo of slaves he'd acquired, Rezin was able to seek out Fernando. He found him in Malo's shack. Terrified by the loss of his protector, the earless man had hanged himself with a length of chain from the barracoon.

When Catherine came to tend Jim's wound a short time later, a look of relief passed between them, but no words were spoken. Their secret was safe! No one would ever learn about their stolen hours together.

*****

Jim Bowie never returned to Berataria, so he never again saw Catherine Villars. Bowie remembered her fondly, but for him their episode was only that, a

379

dangerous episode. It was much more for Catherine. Six months after the Bowies' left Berataria, vexed by Catherine's visible pregnancy, Lafitte tired of her and sent her away. After a brief stopover in New Orleans, she went to live with her grandmother on a remote backwater bayou. Three months later, she bore her second child. This baby bore no resemblance to Pierre, her dark-haired, first-born. Her second son had blond hair and bright blue eyes. She named him James in honor of his father.

*****

A heavy dose of opium allowed Bowie to sleep until mid-morning. In the hours before he awoke, the doctor assumed his restless writhing was the result of his pain, and it was, but not his current pain. Mitchasson would never know that Bowie's physical pain did not torment him half as much as his mental anguish.

380

XVII
UNDER SIEGE

THE ALAMO
FEBRUARY 23, 1836

Moments after dawn lit up the eastern sky, Charlie Heiskell, the lookout in the San Fernando church tower, heard the drumming of hooves on the frozen ground, and soon after saw approaching horsemen. It was an advance patrol of Lancers, about fifty strong. They paused on the outskirts of Bexar, about half a mile from where he stood.

Hastening down from the high tower, he mounted his waiting horse and hastily galloped back to the Alamo

"Officer of the Guard," he hailed James Bonham, a cousin of Buck Travis. "A band of Lancers just rode into town, fifty or sixty of 'em."

Bonham dashed to the flight of stairs that led to Travis's quarters and took them two at a time. A moment later, he reappeared with Travis in his wake.

Bonham went to rouse the sleeping garrison and dispatch messengers to bring back anyone who had spent the night outside the protective walls of the

Alamo. Travis beckoned for Heiskell to follow him, then mounted a parapet to survey the Lancer patrol that had followed Heiskell to a place safely beyond cannon range.

"I count fifty-four men, Charlie. The first of many such units, as the dust clouds in the distance testify. If he's awake, inform Colonel Bowie, if you please."

Bowie was still asleep. The opium allowed him to slumber until late morning. By then, those fifty-four Lancers had been joined by many more cavalrymen.

At noon, Travis, Crocket, Robert Evans, and Green Jameson held a council of war around Bowie's cot.

"Over a thousand men have arrived already. But so far, there are no infantry, siege artillery, or a single commissary wagon. The baggage train could be as much as three or four days' march behind. It allows plenty of time for Texican reinforcements to arrive," Travis announced optimistically.

"Let's send couriers to Goliad and Gonzales. Dan Austin and Ken Hawkins are both well-mounted. Let them run for it before the Mexicans close the circle." The pain killers made Bowie slur his words. "Don't take time to write a message, just send them on their way!"

Ten minutes later, Daniel and Hawk galloped past the Alamo's main gate. Dan headed for Gonzales, Hawk to Goliad. Travis and Crockett watched them until they were out of sight. About a half mile out, they were pursued briefly by a squad of Lancers, but Dan and Hawk asked Raven and Sovereign for more speed and quickly left the astonished Mexicans far behind.

"By thunder and tarnation," Crockett marveled, "those horses are faster than any I've seen lately."

"Faster than any I've ever seen," Travis told him. "Bowie has a pair of horses that that can fly, but the four of them are in a class by themselves."

For the rest of that day and throughout the night, more Mexican troops streamed in. The first infantry regiment and a dozen commissary wagons were the last arrivals of the day, moments before sunset. The Texicans inside the Alamo watched, waited, and wondered what Bowie and Travis were planning.

Crockett had spent the evening at Bowie's bedside, trying to cheer him up with tall tales and Tennessee whiskey. Coupled with more of Doctor Mitchasson's laudanum, the whiskey and companionship did the trick. Bowie slept soundly throughout the night, but awoke early the next morning feeling much weaker.

A short time later, the door of the baptistry opened, and a thin man with a leathery face and wearing a long black cassock, peered in.

"Padre Garza," Bowie called softly, "please come in and sit beside me."

The Padre entered and sat on a stool Crockett had left next to the cot.

"Padre, it is so good to see you again."

"I came the moment I learned about your accident, my son."

"Is my condition that critical?" Bowie smiled.

"No! No! But Santa Anna himself is reported to be only two or three days' march away. I fear there will be a terrible battle here before long. This may be the last time I see you. I thought you might need me."

"I do, Padre. It is more than two years since my last confession. Lack of the sacraments has muddled my thinking. Padre, does God dictate every man's destiny?"

"He certainly knows all that will come to pass."

"I have come to many forks in many roads during my life. Things could have been very different. At this moment, I could be living safely on a backwater bayou with a wife and children. Instead, here I am in Tejas, at a time when my life can be measured in days, perhaps even in hours. Why?"

"Quien sabe? Who knows? No one can answer that question. No human can hope to understand God or His Wonders. I know great historical events seem to pivot around special men. It is in my mind that you may be one of those men. Why God chose you, or why He chooses any man, is beyond our rationality, but we can be certain that it is for good."

"Are all things good, Padre?"

"Everything except sin, my son."

"What good was there in Ursula and my children being taken away?"

"The only honest response I can offer you is that I don't know, because I am not capable of fathoming the workings of God. The only way to cope with any great adversity is to put our faith and trust in God."

"I have been oppressed by sorrow and guilt for many months, Padre."

"Why, my son?"

"I sent Ursula, the children, and all the others to Monclova where they died terrible deaths. It was because of me that they perished in misery. It is that knowledge that torments me and rends my heart. I long for peace. I sought it by numbing my memory with strong drink, but it was useless. My agony does not fade; it grows stronger and deeper every day." Bowie's voice grew steadily weaker as he spoke.

"Now I know why I am here. To bring you peace from your torment. You are a just man, Don Jaime. You would not condemn another man for making an honest mistake. You would understand and forgive. Be as just with yourself as you would be with others. God is perfectly just. You acted with wisdom and judgment when you sent everyone to Monclova, and

God knows that. If they had stayed in Bexar, there is no guarantee they would have lived. Cholera took some people here as well as in Monclova. God absolves you from your guilt. Be at peace with God and be of good cheer, for He is all-merciful. He will reunite you again with Ursula and the children you love so dearly. You think of them as dead, my son; but I assure you that there are no dead. You are not near Ursula and the children in body, but you are together in spirit. They are as surely in His Keeping in Heaven as you are here on earth. God's Splendor, His Justice, His Mercy, and His Peace surround them as surely now as one day soon they will envelope you, and you will be happy with them again, happier than you can begin to imagine. There is no death, my son, only reunion."

The kindly face and warm heart brought a sense of tranquility to Bowie that he hadn't known for a very long time.

"One of the biggest mistakes I have made in my life is that I did not come to you before. Now, Padre, please hear my confession, and bless me."

Bowie's pain diminished slightly, surely more from Padre Garza's penance and absolution than from laudanum. Whichever the case, late that afternoon, he was able to sup half a bowl of beef broth, and eat some bread. Since he was far too weak to sit up and feed himself, Susannah Dickinson, wife of Captain Dickinson, patiently sat beside his cot and fed him. In the early evening, fortified by another strong dose of laudanum, Bowie dozed off and slept fitfully until dawn, awakening only once.

Susannah was helping him with breakfast the following morning when they heard a shrill sound of Mexican bugles.

"What do the bugles mean?" Susannah queried.

"That's the bugle call to parley."

Before the echo faded away, one of the Alamo's cannon bellowed.

"What's going on?" a mystified Bowie wondered.

"I'll go and try to find out," Susannah answered.

She returned a few minutes later.

"A party of Mexicans was approaching the main gate. Colonel Travis fired a cannon at them."

"Good Lord!" Bowie couldn't believe his ears. "Was anyone hurt?"

"Apparently not, but the Mexicans fled."

"Those Mexicans wanted to parley! Travis had no right to fire! He should have listened to them. See what's going on now, if you can, Sue."

Susannah returned with ominous news.

"The Mexicans have hoisted a blood-red flag on the steeple of the San Fernando church."

"The flag of no-quarter! Every defender of the Alamo will be put to the sword. Please summon Benito Jameson for me, and then write a note to the Mexicans."

As Susannah returned, Bowie was ready to dictate his message, which she wrote in Spanish.

To the Commander of the Mexican Army in Texas: Because a cannon was fired from the Alamo at the time when a red flag was being raised in the San Fernando tower, and that a short time later, I was told that a delegation signaled for a parley, a signal that was misunderstood within these walls, I wish to ascertain if indeed a parley is desired. For this reason, I am sending my aide, under the protection of a white flag, which I feel certain will be honored by you and your forces.

James Bowie, commander of volunteers of Bexar, to the commander of the invading force.

February 23, 1836.

Jameson left immediately, carrying the message under a flag of truce. Minutes later, Travis stormed into the baptistry, his face flushed with rage.

"I demand to know why you did that, Bowie!" he bellowed. "It amounts to direct contravention of my orders and my authority. Explain your actions, Sir!"

Bowie tried to rise, but he was too weak.

"Let's wait until Jameson returns," were the only words he could muster.

Jameson returned a short time later with an official reply to Bowie's query.

As the aide-de-camp to His Excellency, President of the Republic, I reply to your communiqué in accordance with the orders of His Excellency, that Mexican Forces will not come to terms under any conditions with the foreign interlopers to whom there is no other course left, if they wish to live, than to place themselves, without delay, at the disposal of the legally constituted and supreme government, from whom they may receive clemency after some issues are considered.

Jose Batres, to James Bowie, Headquarters of the Army besieging San Antonio de Bexar.

February 23, 1836.

Bowie passed the communiqué to Travis.

"Well, that's it, Buck! A fight to the finish with no quarter given or asked. I can't help you much because of the shape I'm in. I will notify the garrison that you're the commander now. From this moment on, you can count on me to loyally follow every order."

"Thanks, Jim. I'm sorry about the recent trouble

we've had. I'm even sorrier about all of this." Travis indicated Bowie's box splint and the bandages. "You know I've always respected you as a man and a true warrior."

Travis reached out and took Bowie's weak hand in both of his strong ones.

"I'd gladly give this right arm of mine if you could be with us on the parapets."

Moments later, they heard a distant, rolling sound of artillery, followed by answering thunder from a nearby cannon. A first Mexican salvo and an answer from one of the Alamo's guns. Mexican cannon fire increased all day and continued throughout the night.

The next morning, Jim Bonham left, carrying the last message the world would receive from the Alamo.

To the People of Texas, and all Americans in the World, Commandancy of the Alamo, Bexar, February 24, 1836.

Fellow Citizens and Compatriots: I am besieged by a thousand or more Mexicans under Santa Anna. I have sustained a continual bombardment for twenty-four hours and have not lost a man. The enemy has demanded surrender at discretion; otherwise the garrison is to be put to the sword if the place is taken.

I have answered the summons with cannon-shot, and our flag still flies proudly from the walls. I shall never surrender or retreat. Then I call upon you, in the name of liberty, of patriotism, and of everything dear to the American character, to come to our aid with all dispatch. The enemy are receiving reinforcements daily and will no doubt increase to three or four thousand in four or five days. Though this call may be neglected, I am determined to sustain myself as long as possible and die like a soldier who never forgets what is due to his honor and that of his country. Victory or death!

W. Barrett Travis, Lt. Col. Commanding

Intense cannonading continued throughout that day and night, and grew even more intense the following day and night. Interspersed were occasional pops of Mexican muskets and the sharp crack of long rifles from the Alamo walls. On the morning of the 25th, Crockett led a foray against Mexican infantry that had infiltrated a long row of adobe shacks about a hundred yards from the wall. Four Texicans suffered flesh wounds. In return, they managed to kill several members of the enemy force, drive the others back, and put all the buildings to the torch. A northerner blew in that night and the temperature dropped more than thirty degrees. It grew even colder the next day.

Defenders slept at their posts both day and night, as continuous musket and cannon fire rattled around them. More and more Mexican troops continued to arrive.

Just before sundown on February 27th, sentries heard a chorus of musket shots break out along the Mexican lines. Moments later, Daniel and Hawk sped out of the gathering darkness, nearly invisible in the thick flowing manes of the flying Raven and Sovereign as they swept across the open ground. They gained the safety of the Alamo before all but a few of the most alert Lancers could offer pursuit. The ones who did quickly veered away from the Tennessee long rifles' deadly fire, but not before four of them lay sprawled and lifeless on the ground. A solitary Lancer officer, perhaps ashamed of their unceremonious retreat, had ridden beyond rifle range when he suddenly stopped and wheeled his horse around. With a bright yellow cape whipping in the wind behind him, he charged back toward the Alamo, brandishing a pistol. Buck Travis, who stood just inside the open gate, called up to the men on the parapet.

"Hold your fire. The fellow may be a damned fool, but he's much too brave to be killed without an even chance."

Travis advanced to a place a few paces outside the gate, and patiently awaited the approaching Lancer.

Suddenly the horseman leveled his pistol and fired. Lead screamed past Travis's ear and slammed into the wall behind him. Travis sighted down along the barrel of his weapon and then fired. For a few jumps, the rider was able to cling to his saddle before he toppled back over his horse's hindquarters, bounced twice, then lay motionless as his frightened mount went thundering away from the madness of men.

Davy Crockett, who admired steel nerves above all else, smiled down at the Commander of the Alamo, and voiced the thought of many observers.

"Travis is a sure-enough bearcat for courage, ain't he?"

As soon as Travis came back through the gate, he motioned for Daniel and Hawk to follow him up to his quarters. They were joined by Crockett, Almeron Dickinson, and James Bonham.

"What's the word from Colonel Fannin in Goliad, Hawk?" Travis queried.

"He seems reluctant to move, Colonel Travis, but he says he'll do his best to reinforce you within the next few days."

"How about Gonzales, Daniel?"

"John Smith was busy rounding up volunteers as I left, Colonel. He guarantees at least thirty men in the next two or three days."

"That is good news. If Fannin moves quickly, we

can hold out for quite a long spell," Travis beamed.

"There are other serious problems, Colonel," Dan added. "Hawk and I skirted along through the woods on the far side of the river as we rode in. About two miles out, we saw a company of artillerymen hauling the biggest cannon either of us has ever seen. Hawk says the barrel is at least twice as long as the biggest navy cannons aboard ships-of-the-line. Between here and the river, we saw a big detachment of Mexicans working to dam up our water supply."

"They're both serious problems, all right," Travis agreed. "I reckon we better stop the ones threatening the water supply first." He turned toward Crockett. "What would you suggest, Crockett?"

"My Tennesseans are just spoilin' fer a fight. If Al Dickinson here and his cavalry kin keep the Lancers off our necks fer a few minutes, we'll sashay out to the hombres doin' the diggin', and wipe 'em out."

"What do you say, Al?" Travis asked Dickinson.

"How soon do you want us, Colonel Crockett?"

"Thirty minutes."

"We'll be saddled up and waiting."

"It's a good plan," Travis concurred. "Hawk, tell us more about the outsized cannon you saw."

"I've never seen a siege cannon, Colonel. Biggest I've seen are naval 32-pounders. A man-o-war with 32-pounders can blow a small ship out of the water with a single broadside. Or it can lay off a hostile shore, outside of normal cannon range, and batter shore installations into submission. The cannon that Dan and I saw was a lot bigger than a 32-pounder."

"It's obviously too heavy for us to haul away, so we have to destroy it, wherever it stands, tonight, before they can use it against us. We'll make final plans when you return, Crockett. There's one more thing. Daniel's report makes me believe that Fannin needs more prodding." Travis turned to Bonham. "Jim, ride over to Goliad and try to get Fannin and his boys moving."

"I'll do my best, Buck," Bonham said back over his shoulder as he raced down the stairs, followed by the others.

"Colonel," Daniel called as Crockett started back toward a cluster of Tennesseans. "How about letting me tag along with you when you hit the diggers?"

"On one condition, Dan. You gotta start callin' me Davy!"

"It will be an honor, Davy!"

"How about you, Hawk?" Crockett asked.

"There is nothing I'd like more, Davy. But should the truth be told, I'm not in a class with shooters like you and Dan. I'd be a liability rather than an asset."

"I admire your honesty, Hawk. One of the most important things a man kin know is his limitations."

Thirty minutes later, a squadron of horsemen burst through the Alamo's main gate without the slightest warning. Each horse carried two riders, one member of Dickinson's cavalry patrol, and a rifleman bent on the destruction of the Mexicans cutting off the water supply. The fight was furious, but brief, less than five minutes. When Dickinson's cavalry reached the Mexicans, the riflemen slid off the horses' haunches, and the cavalrymen thundered on to stop any Lancer that might attempt to intercede. The attack had been so unexpected that the Mexicans had no time to drop their tools or seize weapons before the Tennesseans' rifles spoke with deadly precision. In mere moments, the members of the digging party were dead, and the cavalry had swept back to pick up their passengers. In short order, they were all safely back within the confines of the walls.

The foray went so well that one of the Tennesseans who'd carted a small keg of sippin' whiskey all the way from home was so happy that he tapped the keg and shared the contents with the other participants.

"This is the way to fight a war," declared Andrew Jackson Harrison, the owner of the keg.

"We got bigger fish to fry, Andy!" Crockett told Harrison and the others. "I want every one of you sober enough to do a job before tomorrow morning."

As he spoke, one of the sentries hailed Travis.

"There's a big commotion in the Mexican camp, Colonel Travis."

Travis and Crockett raced to the parapet that faced the Mexicans. Through his field glass, Travis saw a huge throng of soldiers arrayed around something in the middle of the camp. It was several minutes later before the crowd thinned out enough for him to see the object of their interest. Satisfied, Travis handed his telescope to Crockett.

"Crockett, you won't believe what you're about to see!"

Crockett squinted through the glass and grunted.

"I heard the French had invented a new super long range cannon! That's the one Dan and Hawk saw. They can pepper these walls and kill us all without risking a single man! When those Mexicans are asleep, I reckon I better take my boys, kill the sentries, then do something about that monstrosity."

Ken Hawkins and Louis Rose turned out to know more about artillery pieces than anyone else, Hawk, because of his experience aboard ships, and Rose, as an artillery officer with Napoleon. The two agreed that any cannon could be ruined by spiking it.

Hawk explained to Travis that by enlarging the touchhole in the breech of the cannon, which was the only means of igniting the cannon's main powder charge, the weapon could no longer be fired. The only question remaining was how to do it.

"We need to sneak in," Rose summed up, "kill the sentries before they can raise the alarm, destroy the cannon, and get out again in one piece."

"We can't go thundering in on horseback. We need to sidle down to the river in the middle of the night and wade over to the Mexican camp. As long as we don't make too much noise, we'll be all right. It's so cold that the night mist risin' from the river will hide us. When we reach the cannon, we can fill the barrel half full of powder, and fill it the rest of the way with mud we bucket up from the river. Once that's done, I can rig a slow match fuse into the touch hole. We can be almost all the way back here before she blows up. When she does, it'll wake the dead."

"It sure will!" Hawk agreed.

"Good! Then that's how we'll handle it," Travis decided. "Crockett, are your boys ready for another mission?"

"Ready, willin' and able!" Crockett assured him.

"I'd like to tag along this time, Davy," Hawk said.

"I wouldn't think of leavin' without ya!"

Crockett reasoned that because of the bitter cold, the sentries would be changed every hour or two. He decided that the strike force would quit the Alamo a few minutes before 3:00A.M., make their way under cover of darkness and mist. Shielded from view by the high, curving riverbank, they would crawl to a place close to the cannon. Once there, they would ascertain how many sentries were on duty, and wait a short time past the next change of the guard to give the outgoing guards time to settle down in their warm tents. Only then, would their experienced Indian fighters move in to silence the sentries quickly and quietly.

They left the Alamo's sally port on schedule and reached the river without being spotted. The frigid water and icy air made Daniel's teeth chatter so hard that he feared the Mexicans would hear them. It took about ten minutes to reach the position from which they would launch their attack. A few minutes later, the nearest sentry was relieved.

"It's time, boys," Crockett told them ten minutes later. "The dozen men I chose earlier can go out and silence the sentries. Dan Austin will lead his six to the left, my six will go to the right. The rest of you stay under cover for ten minutes before you move. Each of you fill up a couple of these canvass buckets with mud, and follow Louie Rose. We will circle around and meet you by the cannon."

Daniel glided noiselessly through the darkness. At his heels came five deadly specters. There were four sentries on their side of the camp. Each was seized, throttled, and dispatched before he had an inkling that anyone was near. There were four on Crockett's side, as well. They suffered similar fates. The entire episode ended so quickly that the two teams arrived at the cannon before Rose and his mud haulers.

Hawk and Rose opened enough powder canisters to pour at least ten times the normal charge into the mouth of the cannon. Then Hawk, sitting astride the barrel near the muzzle, dropped bucket after bucket of mud down on top of the powder. Rose rammed the mud down the barrel, and then inserted a slow match he had readied into the touch hole, and ignited it with his flint and steel.

"All right, boys!" Crockett whispered. "Back to the river."

Eager to be out of the bitter cold, and buoyed by success, they moved up the river more quickly than before. They had almost reached their starting point near the Alamo when the gunpowder blew up. The concussion was so enormous that the earth around them shook. No doubt the Mexican sentries were not the only ones in camp to die that night. Fragments from the exploding cannon even fell within the walls of the Alamo. Fortunately, no one was injured. As they climbed the riverbank, Crockett whooped like a Shawnee warrior.

"Good work, boys. Santa Anna ain't goin' to have time to haul up another one of them monsters."

400

He's right about that, Daniel thought sadly. Before another such cannon could be brought into action, he and the other defenders of the Alamo would be dead.

Constant cannonading continued throughout the 28th and 29th as Mexican cannonballs hammered on the walls of the Alamo. Although no defenders were killed, many were injured by sharp chunks of flying adobe. Even worse than the falling shells and shards were falling temperatures. After an hour on the wall, sentries were so numb from the bitter cold that they had to be relieved.

On March 1st, thirty-two men from Gonzales, led by John Smith, reached the Alamo after fighting a running gun battle with Mexican Lancers. Morale within the walls skyrocketed.

The same afternoon, however, three more artillery regiments arrived to reinforce the Mexican siege force. In an effort to prevent Texicans from entering or leaving the mission, Santa Anna ordered a total encirclement of the Alamo. During that cold evening, many more campfires sprang up around their perimeter. In their light, the defenders could see shadowy figures of the troops and pinpoints of light as the dancing flames reflected off the barrels of the cannon.

March 2nd dawned, still and cold. A few minutes after first light, Doctor Mitchasson entered Travis's quarters.

"Bad news, Colonel! More than a dozen people are down with stomach sickness this morning."

"They probably had too much to drink last night."

"I wish that's all it was. Most of the sick, including Mrs. Dickinson and her little girl, aren't drinkers."

"What can it be?" Travis wondered.

"It's a barrel of beef they opened yesterday. I just tested it. It's contaminated. So is every other barrel. There are nearly two hundred people here, and we have nothing to feed them aside from a few handfuls of dried corn. In this terrible cold, that wouldn't be enough to sustain them for very long."

"Doctor, please find Crockett and Dickinson. Ask them to join me in Jim Bowie's room."

Dickinson arrived first. He hadn't seen Bowie for a couple of days, and was shocked by his cadaverous appearance. The once ruddy skin was now pale and waxy. Bloodshot eyes in a pain-lined face spoke silent volumes about Bowie's suffering. He tried to smile as Dickinson entered.

"Morning, Jim. You're looking pretty spry today!"

"I'm feeling a lot better this morning, Dick."

Bowie's weak voice contradicted his cheerfulness.

Travis and Crockett entered moments later, and the three men took seats on the stools arrayed around Bowie's cot.

"Bad news, boys," Travis began. "The doctor has discovered that all of our barreled beef is rancid. A few measures of dried corn is all that's left. We can't survive for long unless we replenish our stores. It's patently obvious that the Mexicans are rounding up every available beef cow in this part of Texas to feed their troops. Half our job's already been done for us. All we need to do is to go out, take a herd of those critters away from them, and bring them back."

"I ain't a man that likes to rain on another fellow's parade, Travis," Crockett told him, "but just in case you ain't noticed, ever since John Smith and the men from Gonzales came in, Santa Anna's tightened up a noose round us tight enough to shut off a fella's air. How do you propose we ride out, rustle a herd a' cows, and ride back?"

"Folks that don't have a choice often accomplish impossible dreams, Davy!" Jim Bowie's resolve was evident despite his strained voice. "If a bunch of you fought your way through the Mexican encirclement, they'd figure you were tryin' to break out in order to escape. The last thing they'd expect is for you to roundup a beef herd and stampede them back to the Alamo. Besides, nobody in his right mind will get

403

in front of a stampede! Gettin' out will be the hard part. All you'll have to do comin' back is guide the herd through the main gate, and saunter along in the safety of the big dust cloud."

"Hanged if you don't make a case, Jim!" agreed Crockett.

A few minutes before sunset, eighty well-mounted frontiersmen gathered in a tightly-packed group just inside the main gate. The gate swung open a moment later and the horde of horsemen burst forth. They rode past the first line of sentries before the startled soldiers could react. They swept down on the second circle of campfires, bent low along the backs of their mustangs, partially concealed by the flowing manes, firing from beneath the necks of their mounts as they came. Mexican Lancers, who only moments before had been enjoying the evening meal, were suddenly surrounded by screaming horses and men, cracking rifles, and the swift, silent agony of death. But all of the dead were not numbered among the Mexicans. Several Texicans toppled from their saddles and tumbled down among their enemies as the Lancers recovered from their initial surprise and responded to the assault. Brave men all! No cowardice existed in this place.

The Texican's charge carried them through the

Mexican camp well past the outskirts of Bexar to an area that housed cattle pens. From there, it was an easy matter to round up a manageable-size herd of steers. Then, all that remained to be done was to drive the cattle back through Bexar toward the main camp of the Mexicans, and just beyond into the safety of the Alamo.

When all was in readiness, Crockett called Daniel and Hawk to his side.

"Boys, Travis, Jim Bowie, and I palavered this afternoon, and decided that we need to get word up to Sam Houston. We figured the two of you have the best chance to break through and get it done. Tell Sam how things are down here. Tell him we'll hold out for as long as we can to buy him time. You can also tell him that we won't sell our lives cheap."

Crockett reached out and shook hands with each of them.

"Get goin', boys. Good luck, and God Speed!"

XVIII
MEN OF VALOR

THE ALAMO
MARCH 3, 1836

Raven and Sovereign quickly carried Daniel and Hawk to a high hill north of Bexar. They arrived just in time to turn around and watch the tail end of the cattle herd thunder past the main gate of the old mission. Dan and Hawk turned and rode north, knowing full well that not many more messengers would leave the Alamo.

However, they weren't the last messengers to enter or leave the Alamo. Early the next morning, James Bonham returned from his journey to see Fannin at Goliad. Bonham's red face and furious grimace told Travis something was very wrong. Bonham shook with rage as he reported.

"Fannin isn't coming!"

"Not at all?"

Travis couldn't believe the words he was hearing. "No!"

At that moment, an artillery shell exploded in the compound, showering them with debris.

"Let's take cover, Jim."

The barge continued unabated until late afternoon. After ten days of siege, everyone's nerves were raw, but Travis knew he had to share Bonham's message with the others. He issued an order for the defenders, including the sentries, to assemble on the parade ground. Bowie asked to be carried in his cot to the assembly. It was there that Travis broke the news.

"Men, Jim Bonham has brought news from Goliad. News as final as death. Fannin and his men are not coming to our aid. For the past ten days, you have confronted thousands of enemies from these walls. You have bought ten days for Houston. Ten days he needs to prepare for the fight that lies ahead. You are brave and noble soldiers. Now you each must decide what to do. Escape over the walls, or buy a few more days, or even just hours, in the life of Texas. I shall stay, even if I am alone. My honor will not allow it to be said that William Barrett Travis did not buy every single minute that he could. If you decide to leave, do not go with heads hung low. Be assured that you go with my blessing as well as my gratitude for all that you have done."

He drew his sword from its scabbard and traced a line on the ground between himself and the others.

"I ask anyone who is willing to stay and die with me to step across the line."

Crockett and Dickinson, both standing near

Bowie's cot, started to cross the line. Bowie in a weak voice called to them.

"Boys, I can't make it on my own. Will you carry me over?"

A dozen eager hands lifted his pallet and carried it to a place next to Travis. One by one, or in small groups, the men crossed the line, until only one man remained on the far side. Louis Rose.

"I'm sorry, boys! I wish I could stay, but there's nobody else to watch over my family. I'll slip over the wall after dark."

New artillery salvos began at dusk and continued throughout the long night. An hour after midnight, on Friday, March 4th, the eleventh day of the siege, with the sounds of exploding cannon shells to mask their movements, Rose and John Smith dropped over the wall and disappeared into the darkness, Rose to care for his family, and Smith to make a final appeal to Governor Smith for reinforcements. They were the last men to leave the Alamo.

Many miles to the north, Daniel and Hawk had stopped to rest their horses. After several days of rest and inactivity, Raven and Sovereign had been eager to run. Anxious to reach Houston as soon as possible and return before the Alamo fell, Daniel decided to let them run until they showed the first sign of strain.

They walked the fillies for the final mile in order to cool them down, and then stopped in a dense grove of cottonwood trees that were growing along a small stream. While Hawk fed the horses a portion of the oats they carried, Daniel built a small, smokeless fire and brewed some mint tea. The hot tea and flames drained the cold from their bodies, but did nothing to relieve their fatigue.

"I sure would like to get some sleep before we go on," Hawk sighed.

"We can sleep for a few hours," Daniel told him. "The horses need the rest as much as we do."

"Is it safe for both of us to sleep?" Hawk queried.

"I think so. The horses will warn us before anyone can get close."

No one slept in the Alamo. Shells continued to rain down throughout the night, with very little time between salvos. The two-foot thick adobe walls were nearly battered down in some areas by cannonballs repeatedly striking the same mark, and the heavy log palisade near the room where Bowie lay was badly splintered. In the morning, sentries discovered that under the cover of darkness, several Mexican cannon had been dragged closer to the walls. Crockett and a dozen of his sharpshooters mounted the parapets and began picking off the gunners manning the cannon before they had time to run. For the rest of the day, whenever a gunner approached one of the weapons, he was stopped in his tracks. On one occasion, four squads of artillerymen with teams of horses galloped forward to haul the weapons back out of rifle range. Moments later, all of the men were sprawled lifeless on the ground, every horse had run safely away, and the cannon had not been moved.

"I hope they quit," Andy Nelson muttered sadly. "I've killed enough brave men already."

"Me, too," his friend John Hayes agreed. "I'm proud of 'em! They have courage."

Aware that further attempts to recover the four cannon during daylight hours would be fatal as well as futile, the Mexican commanders made no further efforts until thick darkness shrouded their activities.

Late the same evening, Daniel and Hawk reached Houston's camp, and were ushered into his tent.

"Couriers from the Alamo, General Houston. We left two nights ago. Crockett and about eighty men had just raided into Bexar and driven a herd of cattle back to the mission. So far, all of the attacks have been repulsed, including one attempt to destroy the water supply. We were also able to wreck a giant cannon that the Mexicans hauled in. We've lost a fair number of men to cannon fire and several others to the flying shards of adobe, but most of the walls are still standing and morale is high. Colonels Bowie and Travis know you can't reinforce them in time, but they pledge to buy you every minute they can before the Alamo is overrun."

"Gentlemen, I know the situation's desperate down at Bexar. I would give anything if I could help those brave men who are buying time to sustain the life of Texas. I can do nothing to help them, but I pledge to them and to you, that their sacrifice shall not be in vain. Every dead man shall be avenged, just as every living Texican shall be free. The Texan Declaration of Independence was signed on March 2nd. We are now an independent republic. You've had a hard ride. Get some food and rest. We'll talk more about this later."

"We have no time for food or rest, General," Daniel told him. "We're riding back to the Alamo right away!"

They raced south throughout the long, cold night of March 5th, finally stopping in another riverbank's thick stand of oaks at dawn, still many miles north of Bexar. The frantic pace the fillies had maintained for the past two nights and days had taken a toll. They desperately needed rest. Daniel decided to wait until noon before resuming the journey. Once again, he built a smokeless fire, just big enough to create the allusion of warmth. They rolled up in their blankets as close to the tiny flame as possible, and instantly fell asleep. Raven and Sovereign stood together, tails to the wind, and rested.

Six hours later, they were back in their saddles, fortified by the strong hot tea and dried beef they'd eaten while the fillies munched on bran and oats.

They moved along quickly until late afternoon, as the temperature dropped and the wind velocity grew stronger. Behind them, thick banks of menacing dark clouds began building up. Swift as the fillies were, the weather front was swifter. Daniel was reminded of the *blue norther* that engulfed the wagon train. If the impending storm was anything like that one, the temperature would plummet in short order, making prolonged exposure to the storm potentially deadly.

A few minutes later, good fortune smiled on them.

A short distance ahead, they saw an obscure object rising abruptly from the prairie. When they reached it, they found a substantially built soddy, a building made from squares of prairie sod and grass that had been cut to build walls and a low, slanted roof with a tin chimney. Once the dwelling of a homesteading family, there was no way to tell how long it had been deserted. The doorway that led inside and the soddy itself were both large enough to accommodate the

412

horses as well as the men. Beside the fireplace was a big supply of buffalo chips and other combustibles. The soddy was Heaven sent, and they both knew it. Within a few minutes, heat from the big fireplace had filled the sod homestead with welcome heat. As soon as the storm blew over, they'd head south once more. Until then, they'd be safe and snug. Fatigue and comfort combined to induce sleep, and they soon dozed off. Daniel's last conscious thought was about the Alamo, and how things were going.

Many miles to the south, defenders were enduring their twelfth day of siege. Constant artillery barrages had taken a toll. Wounds of every variety, inflicted by shrapnel from exploding shells and flying shards of adobe from exploding walls, had filled the long barracks with wounded men, reducing the effective fighting force by more than a third. The strain and lack of rest had sapped the strength of the men who were still unscathed or had suffered minor wounds. Most of all, the men inside the Alamo needed sleep.

When the *blue norther* reached them in the early afternoon, artillery fire was halted and the encircling troops, who had been steadily tightening the ring around the Alamo, moved back toward Bexar in an effort to find shelter from the fierce, raging wind. A few fortunate ones might even be lucky enough to find a warming fire.

Within the battered walls, weary Texicans made instant use of the welcome respite. The men rolled up in blankets, buffalo robes, and anything else that might provide a degree of warmth. Each available nook and cranny was soon occupied. Moments later, most of the men were asleep. The only exceptions were Davy Crockett and a few of his Tennesseans.

Davy knew the twelve days of siege, particularly the last three, had demoralized most of the Texicans. Punishing cannon fire, ever-increasing numbers of wounded, growing fatigue, the terrible cold, certain defeat, and the prospect of imminent death had taken a fearful toll on their morale. For the past three days, Mexican bugles had played the haunting strains of *Deguello*, a cutthroat song of no quarter, a guarantee that every defender would be put to the sword. This was no way for brave men to die. He had fought and killed enough soldiers in the past few days to know there were no cowards on either side of the Alamo's walls, certainly no lack of grit in the defenders. They were simply worn out. By golly, Crockett decided, a good meal and a stiff drink would go a long way toward lifting their spirits.

He spent the afternoon dozing intermittently and supervising the roasting of whole beef quarters over roaring fires.

Hours later, as a wintry darkness began creeping over the land and cold-driven wakefulness began to stir the sleeping men into a state of awareness, they could scarcely believe their own eyes when they saw great slabs of meat sizzling over bright flames. They were cold to be sure, and they were surrounded by thousands of enemies, but they had gotten some rest, and soon their empty bellies would be full.

That evening, it could have been the 1836 Alamo or just as easily an 836 Viking mead hall, for the happy banter and strong teeth pulling apart half-raw red meat were the same. So were the wide grins of contentment on the faces as they shared dregs from the last keg of bracing Tennessee sippin' whiskey. Their fatigue seemed to melt away, and many were soon dancing lively jigs to an aberrant sound of John McGregor's bagpipes and the screech of Crockett's fiddle. Once more they were ready to stand and fight for the freedom of their families, the future of Texas, and the precious honor they all so dearly cherished. There was no hope of survival beyond this night, but there was a renewed commitment and purpose. The final battle would begin at dawn. This was a time for camaraderie, a time to remember their loved ones, a time to pray for God's forgiveness and everlasting life, a time to dwell on the good things that life offered, and things worth dying for. Tomorrow, their battle cry of victory or death would be much more than a dare or a challenge. They would look death in the eye with courageous resolve that would earn the admiration of the Mexicans, and stir undying pride in American hearts for generations to come.

They spent their last evening on earth reminiscing, in pairs or small groups, talking of things that had been, and things that might have been. One by one, as drowsiness overcame them, most of them said their prayers, then they said their goodbyes and fell asleep, a peaceful sleep that only the just can enjoy.

At 5:00 A.M., on that final morning of March 6, 1836, the *Deguello* woke the Texicans and brought the Mexican Infantry Regiments to their feet. Every defender who was able to shoulder a rifle was at his assigned post moments later.

The infantry *mozos* charged. Those who showed the slightest bit of reluctance were whipped forward by their subalterns. Across the plain, the defenders could hear shrill commands being shouted.

"Adelante! Seguir adelante!" Forward! Go ahead!

"A la carga! A la carga!" Charge! Charge!

"Vamos, ninos! Vamos!" Let's go, boys! Let's go!

The first assault was gallant but doomed to failure. Three thousand infantrymen, charging from every direction, managed to get halfway to the walls of the Alamo before the ground was littered with dead men and moaning wounded. When bugles sounded retreat the survivors rushed back out of harm's way.

On the walls, there was a mixture of elation, pride, and sorrow. Elation because the charge had been defeated; pride in the courage of their enemies; and sorrow that so many brave men had died. The Texicans did not go unscathed. More than a dozen of them had been killed or mortally wounded.

The second charge came minutes later. This time Mexican infantrymen and cavalrymen came close to the north wall before they were finally repulsed and beaten back once again, with great loss of life. Many defenders on the north wall also died. One of them was the Alamo commander, William Barrett Travis. The man who dared to dream an impossible dream, and dared others to dream with him, died instantly when a bullet pierced his brave heart. Before the third charge, two thousand more infantrymen and Lancers were added to the attack force, and it was this charge that carried the Mexican forces over the north and south walls, and past the log palisade. The cannon on the west wall cut great holes in the white and blue Mexican lines before the gunners were finally overcome and killed.

Fierce hand-to-hand combat, pitting overwhelming numbers of weary Mexican troops against desperate

Texican defenders, swept across the parade ground and then into the buildings. The clubbed rifles and knives of the Texicans worked against infantry bayonets, and the lances and sabers of the Lancers and Dragoons.

Mexican infantrymen now reached the long barracks where fifty wounded Texicans, fighting courageously, took a great many lives in exchange for their own.

Davy Crockett died at the chapel entrance. Long after his rifle was empty, he stood off attacker after attacker like Samson standing against the Philistines, a coonskin cap glued to his head by dried blood. It was not a jawbone of an ass that slew his enemies. It was a long-bladed butcher knife in one hand, and a bloody Cherokee tomahawk in the other that stacked the pile of bodies around his feet. Bullets and blades pierced his mighty body time and again, and yet he refused to yield or to fall. At the end, bearing several mortal wounds that would have killed lesser men, he used his very last ounce of strength to hurl a blazing firebrand through the door of the powder magazine. In the gigantic explosion that followed, another two dozen of his tormentors died with him.

Doctor Mitchasson, attempting to protect the most seriously wounded, was able to finish off two of his attackers before he was overpowered and killed.

The last Texican to die was Jim Bowie. He'd been awakened by the sounds of the battle as it drew ever nearer his tiny room off the dispensary. With every bit of his remaining strength, he raised himself on his cot until his back was supported by the wall. Then, from the small stool beside him, where Padre Garza, Davy Crockett, Buck Travis, and so many other dear friends had sat when they visited him, he took the four loaded pistols he had requested, and his unsheathed knife. He laid them all beside him on the cot, praying that he would live until the enemy found him. His prayer was rewarded a moment later when several Mexican soldiers burst through the doorway.

The first four men succumbed to his pistols. The fifth soldier died as Bowie's knife pierced his heart. More soldiers rushed into the room, led by a Lancer officer who looked very familiar. This officer started toward him, then stumbled and fell forward just as the soldiers opened fire. Bowie was dead before the first bullet touched him, knowing that there was no death, only reunion.

The battle was over ninety minutes after it began. By 6:30 A.M., fifteen-hundred forty-four Mexicans lay dead, as well as one-hundred eighty-nine Texans.

Colonel Juan Almonte, a humane, compassionate man, was the first staff officer to tour the battlefield and buildings. He walked sadly from place to place, finding friends among the Texican dead as well as among the Mexicans. He had hoped that some of the Texicans might survive, including his dear friend, Jim Bowie, but no survivors had been reported. Each step brought more proof that no quarter had been offered or expected by either side. The carnage was complete. Almonte was also worried about his elder son, Alonzo, whom he had not seen since the battle began. His younger son, Estaban, a Lieutenant in the Artillery Corps, had survived unscathed, but Alonzo, a dashing Lancer Captain in General Castrilion's Brigade, had led his company of Lancers in the very vanguard of the final charge.

A great sadness awaited Colonel Almonte when he entered a tiny room near the entrance of the chapel. Still partially propped against the wall at the end of a cot lay the body of his friend, Jim Bowie. Covering Bowie's body in a protective manner was the body of a Lancer Captain. Colonel Almonte knew who it was even before he turned the body over. A glance confirmed his worst fears. Alonzo had given his life in an effort to protect his friend. It was a moment of great sorrow, but of even greater pride. Bowie and Alonzo both had perished with courage and honor for noble causes. He gazed down at the son he had dearly loved and the good friend that he had greatly respected and admired, then he knelt beside the cot and offered a prayer for the repose of their souls.

As Almonte rose, he caught sight of Bowie's knife. He withdrew it from the soldier's body and wiped it off. When his son Estaban wed, he would pass the knife on to him. It would be a lasting tribute to the courage that had been displayed here today, a reminder of what good men owe to God, to their friends, and to their honor. In his mind's eye, the Colonel saw the knife being passed down from one generation to the next on the day the eldest son wed. It was a shame it would not be shared by Jim Bowie's descendents, but, alas, Bowie had left no children to share in the great legacy and tradition.

PART THREE
FINAL RECKONING

XIX
OUT OF THE DUST

THE TEXAS PLAINS
MARCH, 1836

Daniel and Hawk, who had ridden out the fury of the *blue norther* in the comfort and safety of the mud soddy, rose shortly after sunrise. While Dan cooked the last of the traveling rations, Hawk fed the horses, and set about gathering enough buffalo chips and other combustibles to replace the ones they had used to keep warm. They finished their meal, saddled the fillies, and were on their way about the same time as the battle ended in the Alamo.

As much as they wanted to reach Bexar as soon as possible, they didn't push the horses beyond a slow canter. Despite the night of rest, the fillies were still weary because of the long run north to Houston, and foot sore from their grueling pace across the frozen prairie. They needed several days of rest to regain their peak condition and be able to run at top speed for any significant distance.

In the late afternoon, they stopped to water the horses in a brook less than five miles north of Bexar.

"We should be close enough to hear the Mexican

cannon from here, Hawk."

"The wind's out of the north. That might account for it," Hawk reasoned.

"Let's swing east, toward that long line of trees on the horizon. They'll give us some cover until we get closer to Bexar."

They reached the trees without incident, and using them as a shield, rode to within a mile of Bexar's northeastern outskirts.

"This is the old mill where General Austin held the main army before Old Ben Milam and the others hit Bexar. Just over the next hill, there's a deep arroyo that leads to the edge of town. I used it when I was doing courier duty during that battle," Hawk said.

They rode into the deep arroyo and followed it to the foot of Calle Acequia, where it ended. This was the place where Old Ben Milam and his force began their assault toward the Military Plaza. An ancient dilapidated barn was the one building in the area still standing. The others had been destroyed by Mexican cannon fire or persistent Texican crowbars and axes.

"Let's hide the horses in the barn," Dan suggested.

"In these white pantaloons and loose blouses we're wearing, we can pass for peons. The sun has burned the exposed parts of our bodies dark enough to get by. Just keep your sombrero pulled down. Your red hair is a dead give away."

Staying in the mass of rubble created by the Battle of Bexar, and aided by the fading light, Hawk and Daniel moved slowly up the length of Calle Acequia and then though the shadows around the edge of the Military Plaza. A short distance beyond the far side of the plaza, a large crowd was milling around. From there, one could see the Alamo. The crowd, coupled with an absence of cannon fire, was an ominous sign that the siege was over. They moved along the fringe of the crowd until they could see the old mission. A blood-red flag was flying over the battlement. They stopped to listen to the conversations of two elderly men.

"Did they kill everyone?" asked one.

"They spared the wife of one man, her daughter, and a slave. They burned all of the other bodies!"

"Burned them?" The man was incredulous.

"Yes! Santa Anna ordered a huge funeral pyre to be constructed, and the bodies were incinerated."

"That is a terrible fate for brave men. What would possess him to commit such an act?"

"I don't know, Juan! Instead of providing decent burials, or turning the bodies over to their relatives, Santa Anna had the corpses thrown into the fire like so many pieces of useless timber. Such an order cannot be justified, particularly by a man who professes to be a practicing Catholic."

Daniel and Hawk had known the Alamo would fall. Defeat was inevitable. They had steeled themselves for that. It was Santa Anna's desecration of the Texicans' bodies that filled them with rage and grief. How could any man, especially one who professed to be a classic warrior and Catholic gentleman perpetrate such a pagan act and exhibit such a complete lack of chivalry?

"Men who fight gallantly owe each other honor and respect in death," Daniel said softly. "Worthy enemies deserve to be treated with reverence, mercy, and justice. Anything less is a disgrace. The utter disdain of this wanton act is anathema to every courageous man who died here, be they our friends or the Mexican troops who opposed them. What Santa Anna did here is a denial of everything moral men hold dear."

"Santa Anna is a barbarian to be sure!" Hawk agreed. "Both sides believed in their cause and deserve to be acknowledged for their dedication to those causes."

"Hawk, you and I won't forget these events. No Texican will ever forget! We will all remember the Alamo, and make certain that Santa Anna and his minions are punished."

They drifted back through the crowd, retracted their steps to the barn where they mounted their horses, and followed the arroyo to the outskirts of Bexar.

"What's our next move?" Hawk asked as they emerged from the end of the arroyo.

"The only Texican fighting forces in this area are with Fannin. Let's ride toward Goliad and try to find one of his patrols."

They rode slowly for four days, dodging Lancer units and allowing the fillies to regain their strength, as they searched for other Texicans.

On March 11th, they encountered a Texican force of one hundred fifty men led by Captain Ward at the Refugio Mission. Early the next morning, they were attacked by a large party of Lancers, estimated by Ward as numbering eight hundred. A fierce battle raged for the next three days as the Texicans sought to defend the mission and heap as much punishment as possible on the Lancers who responded in kind. By nightfall of the 15th, thirty Texicans and about the same number of Lancers had been killed. Since the Lancers far outnumbered them, a one for one ratio was good for the Lancers and bad for the Texicans. Shortly before midnight, Captain Ward ordered his men to mount up and run for cover.

They rode about ten miles before they stopped to tend to the wounded. As dawn broke, they were once more attacked by the Lancers. Before they were able to break off and retreat, sixteen more Texicans were killed and thirty, mostly wounded, were captured.

For the next ten days, small bands of Texicans met and fought large Dragoon and Lancer units. At Kerr Creek, on the 17th, twenty-five Texicans skirmished with seven hundred fifty Mexicans. The next day, near Goliad, Captain Horton's fifty men fought a running battle with General Urrea's nine hundred. On the 20th, Colonel Fannin and his force of two hundred seventy-five were surrounded by over a thousand of Urrea's Lancers and forced to surrender. They were marched into Goliad.

On the 22nd, near Las Juntas, Captain Ward, Daniel, Hawk, and nearly a hundred of the original force, were surrounded by Urrea's over-powering strength and forced to surrender after Urrea promised them humane treatment as prisoners-of-war and their release at the end of hostilities. They were also marched into Goliad.

At Copano, on the 23rd, Urrea surrounded and captured eighty more Texicans and marched them into Goliad. This brought his prisoner total up to three hundred seventy-three.

The next day, General Urrea made an announcement.

"You are all prisoners-of-war. Therefore, you will

receive the same food rations and medical aid as my own soldiers. You have nothing to fear unless you break your parole and attempt to escape. If you try to climb the fence that surrounds you, you will be shot. Rest assured that this foolish war is all but over. Soon you will be released and allowed to return to your homes and your families. Until then, if you act courteously toward us, we will do the same to you."

The attitude in the compound where the prisoners were confined brightened perceptibly. They still had faint hope that Houston and some of the other Texan military leaders might pull off a miracle and defeat Santa Anna's armies; but even if they had to endure the hardships they had fought to rectify, at least they would be alive. Daniel was not convinced. He didn't trust Santa Anna. He shared his concern with Hawk.

"In the first meeting that Uncle Stephen and I had with Santa Anna, he made it abundantly clear that he would execute anyone who dared rebel against him. I still recall his words about his treatment of rebels. *I promise you the only creatures left alive will be dogs fighting over rebel bones among the charred remains of their once proud villages.'* That doesn't sound like amnesty to me. Urrea may want to treat us humanely, but I'm almost certain that Santa Anna will countermand his orders."

That afternoon, General Urrea sent a dispatch to Santa Anna, apprising him of the current situation, and the presence of nearly four hundred prisoners.

"… Almost all of the prisoners, many of them who have been in Tejas less than six months, surrendered because I guaranteed their personal safety, and granted them the full honors of war. I am well aware of your policy concerning insurgents, but I pledged my word to treat these men in an honorable fashion and I am bound to do so. I must with due respect refuse to execute these men while they are unarmed and under my protection."

On the evening of the 26th, he received Santa Anna's furious reply.

*"Do you intend to disobey the law that was passed last year after the American invasion of Tampico? It orders an **immediate execution** of all foreigners who invade our sacred land! Therefore, I admonish you to give immediate effect to that ordinance in respect to the foreigners who have had the audacity to come and insult the republic. I trust you will inform me when public vengeance has been satisfied by the punishment of these detestable delinquents. This is a direct order, General Urrea: **Execute the rebels!**"*

Early the next day, the Texicans and their Tejano allies were separated into three equally-sized groups. The first group was lined up and marched out of the compound by an overwhelming guard force of at least five hundred Mexicans. An hour later, the same Mexicans returned and marched a second section of prisoners away in a different direction. Daniel, along with Hawk, Captain Ward, and many other survivors from his command were left in the compound.

"Did you take a close look at those guards when they returned," Daniel asked Hawk. "Something was terribly wrong with a great many of them. Did you see their grim, sad, furtive expressions? An inability to look us in the eye? If they were merely going to take us to a new location, why did they march our men away in two different directions? I'm convinced that they acted as executioners this morning! If our friends are alive, where are they? No way Urrea is going to turn them loose, and there is no other place in Goliad where prisoners can be confined. No, Hawk, the other men are dead, and the rest of us soon will be. When they march us away, we must try to escape. Better to be shot down trying to survive than to submit to Santa Anna's treachery. Let's tell the rest of the men."

They circulated throughout the enclosure, warning the others. It was agreed they would make a break and run away the instant they heard Daniel's signal.

The guard force returned, assembled the rest of the prisoners, and marched them off in a third direction.

About a mile from the compound, the path they were following led through a narrow gap, bounded on one side by a steep cliff that fell away to a rushing, rock-strewn river, and on the opposite side by a wide field, behind which stood a big grove of thick trees.

As soon as the tail end of the column had filed into this gap, the guards were startled by the shrill howl of a hunting panther, an eerie, unearthly sound they had never heard before. In an instant, every prisoner broke from the ranks and raced away. Most of them dashed across the field toward the woods. A few, willing to risk painful death on the rocks below, hurled themselves over the cliff toward the danger-laden river fifty feet below.

Very few of the prisoners lived to reach the trees. Only a few of the swiftest runners were able to cross the open ground to safety before musket balls tore into their backs and toppled them to the earth. Those who chose the cliff disappeared from sight before the guards had time to react, but in most cases, sharp rocks ended the lives of the men who escaped the musket fire. Daniel, Captain Ward, and Hawk opted for the river. Captain Ward, jumping between them, died instantly when he careened into a large, moss-covered boulder. Quite near him, Daniel and Hawk, falling just beyond touching distance, were fortunate enough to miss the rocks and fall into open spaces in

the river. At that point, the water was deep enough to slow their descent before they reached the sandy river bottom. As they rose to the surface, Dan tugged Hawk's sleeve and guided him back toward a string of reeds that grew next to the rocky bluff.

Once they were hidden from the guards under the lip of the cliff, he whispered to Hawk just as a bevy of shots rang out.

"They're firing at the men who survived the fall and are trying to swim away. Let's out-fox them."

Dan broke off two reeds and handed one to Hawk.

"Lie on the bottom and breathe through this reed. Pick out a rock heavy enough to hold you down and hold it on your stomach. So many of us were killed jumping, the guards will quit after a cursory search. Once we're sure they're gone, we can sneak back to the compound."

Hawk followed Daniel to the river bottom, found a stone heavy enough to hold him in place, and spent the long afternoon hours breathing through a hollow reed that protruded scant inches above the surface.

During the period of submersion, Hawk wondered why Dan intended to return to the compound. He finally stopped pondering, secure in the knowledge that his friend had a reason for everything he did.

They surfaced when night closed over the river. Then, cloaked in the blue-black darkness, they found a path leading to the summit. Moving stealthily from one deep shadow to the next, they finally reached the outskirts of the compound where the horse herd was being held.

"We're going to steal our horses for the second time," Daniel announced, "but we won't get away with our silver saddles this time."

Daniel had trained Raven and Sovereign to answer two different whistles. One brought them at a gallop. The other was for situations exactly like the one they currently faced. Daniel emitted the whistle, and then waited. Several minutes passed without any noticeable movement in the horse herd beyond a normal milling about. Then, as if by magic, Raven, followed closely by Sovereign, emerged from the shadows. Since Dan and Hawk hadn't heard them coming, it was safe to assume that the herders hadn't either. They vaulted onto the fillies broad backs and walked them slowly out of the area. By midnight when they stopped, they were many miles away. In the morning, they would ride to find Houston.

Many men had died to buy General Houston the time he needed to raise and train an armed force to meet Santa Anna, Daniel thought, as he and Hawk curled up for the night on opposite sides of a small, but warm fire. Now it was time for Houston and the rest of them to make sure that none of the gallant

Texican heroes who had bought that precious time had died in vain.

Travis's challenge of *Victory or Death* had ended in death and victory. I was there when it all began. I was at the Alamo and Goliad. Now I'm going to be in on the finish, but where will that finish be, and how will it all end? Daniel wondered as he drifted off to sleep.

XX
SAN JACINTO

SABINE RIVER
APRIL 21, 1836

Daniel and Hawk rode into Houston's camp three days after the Goliad massacre. Additional survivors straggled in every day for the next week, until the thirty-first man arrived. He was destined to be the last. Santa Anna had murdered three-hundred forty-two prisoners-of-war who had been promised life and eventual liberty. Word of the travesty swept across the Texan prairies like wildfire. Not only the eight hundred furious men that Houston had gathered into an army vowed that their friends would be avenged, but every man, woman and child capable of reasoning, reviled the horror, and burned with a thirst for vengeance.

Houston knew he couldn't hope to win conventional battles with Santa Anna's overwhelming force, but the man who engineered the victory of Horseshoe Bend was a seasoned Indian fighter who realized that if he nipped at Santa Anna's heels for long enough, he eventually would be able to find a chink in his amour. When he did, he would take advantage of that

437

opportunity.

Houston and his volunteers rode south on the first day of April. As soon as they reached Santa Anna's perimeter, they began staging hit-and-run nuisance raids at every opportunity. The indignant Santa Anna, vowing to defeat these upstart Texicans once and for all, went in immediate pursuit of Houston's force as he retreated northeastward. Several minor skirmishes were fought by the opposing forces, but on each occasion, Houston withdrew before the main Mexican army could close with him. Santa Anna didn't lose any of these engagements, but he didn't win any either. For three weeks, the Mexican army crept a bit closer to the retreating Texicans each day. On the evening of April 20th, the Mexican army marched until dusk, before finally bivouacking for the night on swampy land between two rivulets at a place called San Jacinto.

A few minutes before dawn, Santa Anna decided to give his men a badly needed day of rest before continuing the chase the next morning. Fresh men and horses might close the gap on the 22nd and trap the Texans. Throughout the morning and early hours of the afternoon, sentries patrolling the camp's perimeter were cautioned to maintain vigilance for a possible Texan nuisance raid; but, by mid-afternoon, Santa Anna was convinced that Houston had cleared out of the area.

Houston had not retreated. He and his men lay concealed in a large grove of live oaks that grew on the edge of swamp, just west of Santa Anna's camp. If he attacked, the sun would be behind his men, and shining into the eyes of the Mexicans. But beyond that, Houston knew he needed a bit of luck if his outnumbered force was to carry the day. It was then that fate intervened.

As the afternoon wore on, Santa Anna became convinced that Houston would not dare to attack at such a late hour with a badly outnumbered force. He decided to dine earlier than usual, and then take a *siesta*. He consumed a heavy meal, followed by a soupcon of opium. His weariness, coupled with the food, the opium, and the warm stillness of the day, conspired to put him into a trace-like stupor. His staff officers also decided that a *siesta* would be a wonderful way to wile away an hour. The net result was that without proper supervision, sentries were not posted, picket lines were left unguarded, and every bugler joined the *siesta*.

Houston chose that moment to attack. Striking with awesome force, the Texicans smashed into the Mexican lines. No signals were sent to headquarters. No one in authority would have been there to accept them if they had been sent. In those first few minutes, the battle was won. Before the Mexicans could rally, the Texicans were rampaging through their lines, creating havoc and dealing death. When the panicky Mexican troops sought refuge in the swamps, the Texicans followed them into the waist-deep bayou water, then shot them in the back or dispatched them with their long, slashing knives.

To avoid certain death, many Mexicans threw their hands in the air and shouted. "Me no Alamo! Me no Goliad!" But the slaughter continued.

Houston, more humane than Santa Anna, shouted a plea not to kill any Mexicans that could be taken prisoner. When Houston rode by, a Texican officer whose brother had been murdered at Goliad, shouted his response.

"We know how to take prisoners, don't we boys? Take them with the butt of your rifle! Remember the Alamo and Goliad, and knock 'em in the head."

The entire melee lasted only eighteen minutes and when it was over, six hundred Mexicans were dead and five-hundred others were prisoners. Only three Texicans were killed, and seven others would later die from their wounds.

In the heat of the battle, Santa Anna recovered enough to awaken and dash out of his tent. Seeing that all was lost, he abandoned his men and fled into the swamp, where he hid throughout the night. The following morning, Daniel, Hawk, and three others, discovered a man, covered with mud, sitting under a small tree.

"There's one that got away," Daniel observed.

"Let's round him up and put him with the others," Hawk said, moving forward.

"On your feet," Hawk ordered as they approached the slumped figure. As the man struggled to his feet, Daniel recognized a face through the plastered mud that had haunted his dreams.

"Hawk, this muddy fugitive is Presidente Antonio Miguel Lopez de Santa Anna! Presidente, you don't look much like the Napoleon of the West today! Despite your tawdry appearance, I'm sure General Sam will be glad to see you."

Houston was glad to see Santa Anna. He knew that General Vincente Filisola, with seven thousand men, was camped along the Brazos River, much too close for comfort. There were some other Mexican forces in other areas. None of them had been affected by Santa Anna's loss at San Jacinto. Texas was now a republic, though a very fragile republic which could not withstand protracted warfare. Houston kept Santa Anna in chains for fifty-two days while he suffered the indignity of the negligence that had resulted in his inglorious defeat. At the end of that time, Santa

Anna regained his conniving willfulness and made a deal with Houston. He signed a cease fire agreement that immobilized the remaining Mexican forces, and persuaded Houston to release him. In return for his freedom, he would act as the good will ambassador between Mexico and the fledgling Texas Republic.

Santa Anna did not return to Mexico City. He went directly to New Orleans, where he charmed a Mexican Consul out of enough money to pay for a luxurious journey to Washington. He became the sensation of the moment, presenting Mexico's case to President Andy Jackson and members of the Senate. The weeks Santa Anna spent there gave Sam Houston and the other leaders of the new-born republic the time and the space they needed to consolidate their precarious position.

Houston asked Daniel and Hawk to join his staff on the day he took office as first President of the Texas Republic. Hawk agreed, but Daniel decided to work for his Uncle Stephen when he took up his office as the Texan Secretary of State.

The day he reported to the Secretary of State's Washington-on-the-Brazos office, Daniel realized that his uncle could not live much longer. He was correct. Stephen Austin succumbed to tuberculosis before the end of 1836. This short lived, but exciting and eventful experience, made Daniel cognizant of the rewards and difficulties of the Secretary of State's office.

After Stephen Austin's death, Daniel spent several years on Sam Houston's staff with Ken Hawkins. During those years, Houston groomed both of them for public service positions in which he felt they would excel. Hawk eventually became United States Senator Kenneth Hawkins, and Daniel served Texas as her Secretary of State, and finally, as her Governor.

Their political careers ended about the same time, and the Lone Star leaders organized a gala celebration in honor of these two men who had accomplished so much. Announced well in advance, the gala brought national and international dignitaries, as well as the friends and families of both men to the state capitol in Austin on a soft spring day in April, 1884. The procession of handsome carriages carrying the families' members and the past and present dignitaries, stretched along the parade route for half a mile or more. As he and Hawk entered the carriage that would complete the procession, an open phaeton, Daniel wondered how many carriages had been required to transport Monica and their nine grown children, as well as their sixty plus grandchildren and great grandchildren.

Their liveried driver swung the sleek phaeton into

position, and moments later Hawk and Daniel began waving a bit self-consciously to the cheering throng that lined their route.

"It wasn't like this when we met, Daniel," Hawk smiled.

"No," Daniel grinned back. "We didn't have any friends around us on that night."

"We've both enjoyed a lifetime of blessings since then."

"I thought about that very thing this morning. I remembered my twenty-second birthday in Bexar, as Uncle Stephen and I prepared to leave for his meeting with Santa Anna—and that fierce blizzard along the way that nearly killed every traveler in the wagon train. I thought of Captain Almonte—Monica and her grandfather—getting thrown into prison and escaping with Monica's help—and being lucky enough to be close by when the Mendozas and their bandits brought you into their camp."

"I was nearly done in," Hawk recalled. "I couldn't have survived for much longer, but I don't believe in luck enough to believe you 'just happened to be there.' I remember the pair of us, dashing off across the prairie on Sovereign and Raven, and thinking how wonderful it was to be alive and free."

"If we hadn't found that high mesa in the nick of time, Hawk, when the war party jumped us, we wouldn't have been alive for very long."

"No," Hawk agreed. "The Lord sure was taking care of us. We've had mostly good days, but we've had hard times, too. I still find it difficult to believe that you solved the Miranda enigmas, Daniel. That truly was remarkable! Remember how thrilled everyone was when we walked down the hidden ramp and actually entered the mine? Slaving like beavers all winter to harvest the silver seemed like a lark. Then suddenly losing it all, and losing so many of our good friends as well, broke our hearts."

"Yes, Hawk, those were bad days. But I remember the moment that Raven tripped. She was the most sure-footed horse I ever rode. For her to stumble at exactly the right spot to reveal the skull Miranda used as his major clue can't be written off as luck. That was obviously divine intervention. Why we lost the silver, or why our friends died, only God can answer that."

"Daniel, there will never be a day in this world when I will forget all of the things that we've been through, and the great friends we've had."

"We've certainly known our share of great men, Hawk. Uncle Stephen, Sam Houston, Buck Travis, Old Ben Milam, Davy Crockett, Jim Bowie, and all the men at the Alamo. Perhaps Jim Bowie, despite his hard life, his weaknesses, and terrible sorrow, was the greatest of all."

They fell silent, each lost in his own memories.

Daniel's thoughts once again drifted back over the past fifty years to the morning he and Uncle Stephen began the journey to Mexico City. He recalled his eagerness and trepidation.

Young and inexperienced as he was, he had come to Texas seeking adventure and wondering if he might run into more trouble than he could handle. He had enjoyed far more excitement and adventure than ten ordinary men, and had run into a lot more trouble than he ever could have imagined. Yet somehow, he had always found a way to win and survive; but there had been many mighty close and dangerous calls. He and Hawk had enjoyed wonderful careers, and moral, happy, productive lives that they could recall with justifiable pride. They had been lifelong friends and close allies in both peace and war.

His daydream was so real that for a fleeting instant, Daniel wondered where the years had gone. Could that first meeting with Hawk in the bandit camp really have occurred fifty years ago? Memories whisked him back in time, and he visualized Raven and Sovereign thundering over a sun-bleached prairie, carrying them out of harm's way, so long, so very long ago.

The driver stopped at the main entrance, climbed down, and opened the door for his renowned passengers. As they entered the building, Hawk and

Daniel exchanged an amused grin that only special friends can share. They were still smiling as they entered the State House Rotunda and acknowledged the huge crowd's tumultuous applause.

Bruce T. Clark

EPILOGUE
FULL CIRCLE

AUSTIN MILITARY COLLEGE
AUSTIN, TEXAS
MARCH 6, 1936

The Austin College Military Ball, commemorating the one hundredth anniversary of the Alamo, was less than an hour away. Cadet Captain Alonzo Almonte finished dressing and looked into the mirror in his top floor dormitory room. Alonzo was quite pleased with the reflection that gazed back at him. He was tall, slim, and extremely good-looking. Last summer, he had seen the movie *Captain Blood,* starring Errol Flynn. Flynn's pencil mustache gave him a swashbuckling look that Alonzo admired. Since senior cadets were permitted to grow facial hair, he decided to emulate the dashing film star. The mustache achieved the desired effect. It actually made him look like Errol Flynn. Now, clad in a dark blue uniform with gold epaulettes and sash, his swashbuckling quality was quite apparent.

Actually, Alonzo was a modest young man who stood near the top of his senior class. He was following in the wake of many relatives who had served as military officers. He'd been named for his great grandfather's brother, the brave Lancer captain who had died at the Alamo. His father, Estaban, often recounted the captain's valorous deeds in battle and his great friendship with Jim Bowie. At special times, his father would unlock his safe, and display the knife that had played such an important part in Bowie's life. Since Alonzo was the eldest son, on his wedding day, his father would entrust the knife to him, until he, in turn, passed it on to his eldest son. Alonzo always felt a terrible sadness during moments that he held Bowie's knife in his hands. Sadness that so many brave men had died and sorrow that Jim Bowie had left no descendents who could share in his memory or his legacy.

Alonzo willed away his reverie, donned his blue kepi, and checked the cap's rakish angle in the mirror. The cadets were escorting girls from Hathaway Academy to the Military Ball this year. Each cadet had drawn a number which identified one of the young ladies. They were scheduled to arrive at the grand ballroom about 8:00 P.M. Alonzo wondered if his partner would be attractive. Oh, well, he decided, I probably won't see her again once this evening is over anyway.

All the cadets were waiting to welcome the girls as they alighted from the Academy bus. Ranking cadets headed the reception line. Alonzo, a senior

449

captain, was seventh in line. As his partner emerged and came toward him, he blinked in astonishment. Blond, fair, and blue-eyed, she was easily the most dazzling girl Alonzo had ever seen. He wondered if she possibly could be as charming and delightful as she appeared. She took his arm and he escorted her into the ballroom.

"Catherine, are you a native Texan?"

"No. I was born and raised in the Louisiana bayou country. I come from a long line of dark-skinned Cajuns. My mother says I'm a throwback to my great-grandfather, James. He was blond-haired and blue-eyed. I was named in honor of James' mother, my great, great-grandmother. Her name was also Catherine Villars.

Jim Bowie's great, great-granddaughter looked into the eyes of the handsome cadet, and gave him a dazzling smile.

An Old Promise

I have always been fascinated by an author's reason behind his writing a particular novel. I've also discovered that many other readers share my curiosity. For "cat-curious" readers, herein lies the genesis of *The Blood~Red Flag.*

In the foreword of his novel, *Texas,* James A. Michener, for many years the dean of American storytellers, observed that if we eliminate publications about California, there have been more books written about Texas than all of the other states combined. He added that books about Texas outnumber those about California by a whopping margin of six to one. A fair question is Why? Fair answers are glamour and mystery.

Born in 1935, I was celebrating my sixth birthday the day Japanese planes bombed Pearl Harbor. For the next forty-four months, Americans lived under black war clouds. Fathers, brothers, uncles, and neighbors went off to fight aggression in regions that, before December 7th, were nothing but obscure places with funny names on world maps.

Kids of that World War II era were drawn into the conflict in very personal ways, mainly because of relatives serving overseas and because of the nightly war news on the radio which at the war's beginning was pretty grim. We all became familiar with ration books that we needed to buy scarce foods and goods, and Victory Stamps that students across America bought every Friday at their schools for a dime or a quarter. We started and

451

maintained our own Victory Gardens, and helped gather newspapers and old tin cans in "scrap drives" designed to "help the war effort." We were submerged in the war drama for six days each week—Monday through Friday in school, and in church on Sundays, praying for victory—but every Saturday, we could "escape."

Saturday afternoon movies, double features, were a way of life for youngsters who grew up in the war years. Admission was a dime, and for a quarter, if you had a quarter, you could buy enough stale popcorn to guarantee a three-day bellyache. Movie cowboy stars were bigger than life in those days for all of us rootin', tootin', cap-gun shootin', ring-tailed buckaroo saddle pals of Roy Rogers, Gene Autry, Hopalong Cassidy, and John Wayne. Each week, a new sagebrush hero galloped across the silver screen and provided us with an afternoon of guileless glitter and gleam, as well as the determination to be straight-shooting, clean-living, winners just like them.

Of course, every cowboy star was a Texan. The fact that the big four of Rogers, Autry, Wayne and Cassidy, were born in Ohio, Oklahoma, Iowa, and New York City, really didn't matter. They convinced us that the guys who wore white hats always won, as we sat glued to our theater seats, sometimes by discarded chewing gum, but mostly by visions of the Lone Star state's vast prairies—deepening twilight, the rich, blue-black velvet of darkness descending on chuck wagons, a glow of flickering flames as saddle-weary cowboys shivered in the cold and moved as close to the dying embers of their banding fires as they dared. Living legends, lulled to sleep by their lowing

452

cattle, too tired to stir as a lonely coyote's mournful howl rang across the stillness in a magical world of mesquite, tumbleweed, and adventure called Texas.

I learned to love the Old West on those long ago Saturday afternoons and, for a few hours, I forgot the war. One special Saturday, I decided to give something back. *The Blood~Red Flag* is the fulfillment of that promise. Hopefully, this tale of heroes: Bowie, Austin, Travis, Crockett, Houston and Milam, will convince others to learn more about history and inspire them to give something back. Knowledge of America's past and its heroes not only teaches us about our great history, it also makes us much more optimistic about our future.

Bruce T. Clark
Front Royal, VA
August 25, 2004

453

Bruce T. Clark

ABOUT THE AUTHOR

Who's Who Historian, Bruce T. Clark, has had a sixty-year love affair with America's past. Since his return from military service in 1962, Mr. Clark has been a teacher, speechwriter, political consultant, and radio talk show host, as well as a frequent lecturer for academic and political organizations. In 1994, due to poor circulation, his leg had to be amputated. During his recovery he began writing his first historical novel as a form of therapy. The result of that effort was *The Custer Legacy*, published in 1997 by Four Winds Publishing. It was selected as one of the ten best historical novels of the year by the Western Heritage Society, and the Catholic novel of the year by the Catholic Woman's Guild. *The Castro Conspiracy* was published in 2003. *The Blood~Flag* is his third historical novel.

Mr. Clark and his wife, Dr. Mary Kay Clark, founder and Director of Seton Home Study School, were married in 1961. Proud parents of seven sons and grandparents of thirty, they reside in Virginia's historically rich Shenandoah Valley.

CPSIA information can be obtained
at www.ICGtesting.com
Printed in the USA
BVHW080330030921
615817BV00001B/42

9 781420 810707